Debt and Disorder

About the Book and Author

One of the most important and controversial challenges facing the international financial and trading system is the need for developing countries to meet their high and rapidly growing external debt obligations and foreign exchange requirements. Developing countries have suffered major shocks in the form of global recession, high real interest rates, weakened terms of trade, and rising protectionism against their exports. The International Monetary Fund, the World Bank, Western central banks, and private financial institutions are seeking to avoid a collapse of the international financial system, and developing countries are seeking to grow through increased trade and access to external financing. Yet the fragility of current international trade and monetary systems seriously threatens the achievement of both sets of objectives. Professor Loxley integrates the structural adjustment experience of Third World countries with the policies, practices, and relationships of external financial agents in his discussion of options for reforming policy and of the limitations inherent in implementing these reforms.

John Loxley is professor and head of the Department of Economics at the University of Manitoba, Canada. He has worked for many years in Tanzania as an adviser to officials of the nationalized banking system and was the country's first director of the Institute of Finance Management.

Published in Cooperation with
the North-South Institute, Ottawa

Debt and Disorder

External Financing for Development

John Loxley

Westview Press / Boulder and London

Westview Special Studies in Social, Political, and Economic Development

This Westview softcover edition was manufactured on our own premises using equipment and methods that allow us to keep even specialized books in stock. It is printed on acid-free paper and bound in softcovers that carry the highest rating of the National Association of State Textbook Administrators, in consultation with the Association of American Publishers and the Book Manufacturers' Institute.

Published in 1986 in the United States of America by Westview Press, Inc.; Frederick A. Praeger, Publisher; 5500 Central Avenue, Boulder, Colorado 80301

Library of Congress Cataloging-in-Publication Data
Loxley, John.
Debt and disorder.
(Westview special studies in social, political, and economic development)
Bibliography: p.
Includes index.
1. Debts, External—Developing countries.
2. Developing countries—Economic policy. I. Title.
II. Series.
HJ8899.L68 1986 336.3'435'091724 86-4097
ISBN 0-8133-7218-6

Composition for this book was created by conversion of the author's computer tapes or word-processor disks.
This book was produced without formal editing by the publisher.

Printed and bound in the United States of America

The paper used in this publication meets the requirements of the American National Standard for Permanence of Paper for Printed Library Materials Z39.48-1984.

10 9 8 7 6 5 4 3 2 1

This book is dedicated, with love and gratitude,
to Elizabeth Loxley and the late John Loxley.

CONTENTS

TABLES

FOREWORD

One of the most important and controversial challenges facing the international financial and trading system in recent years has been the need for developing countries to meet their high and rapidly growing external debt burden and foreign exchange requirements. Developing countries have suffered major negative external shocks in the form of global recession, high real interest rates, weakened terms of trade and rising protectionism against their exports in industrialized country markets. The extreme pressures of adjustment and the increased policy conditionality attached to external sources of finance have raised important theoretical and policy questions concerning the impact on economic performance and internal distribution of income.

Professor Loxley has responded to the proliferation of Third World structural adjustment problems with an important attempt to integrate the adjustment experience of many countries and the policies, practices and relationships among the external financial agents involved. The issues are of urgent importance from both the analytical and policy viewpoints, and this study makes a substantial contribution itself and should also help stimulate other much needed work in the area, by both scholars and policy advisers.

Recognizing the need for more comprehensive treatment of these vital policy issues, the North-South Institute helped organize and advise on this study and is appreciative of the financial support of the Swedish International Development Authority.

Bernard Wood
Director, North-South Institute

ACKNOWLEDGMENTS

The draft of this book was written while I was a Visiting Fellow of the North-South Institute, Ottawa, in 1982/83, although I was physically located at the Institute of Policy Analysis, University of Toronto, during that period. I wish to thank the Swedish International Development Agency (SIDA) for their financial support, which made the research possible, and Ernst Michanek of the Swedish Foreign Ministry, who was instrumental in arranging SIDA sponsorship. Richard Bird kindly provided me with accommodation at the Institute of Policy Analysis while Lorelle Triollo provided secretarial assistance at that stage. I wish to thank the University of Manitoba for allowing me to proceed on leave in that year.

I wish to express my gratitude for the constant but critical support of Gerry Helleiner of the University of Toronto/North-South Institute. Gerry provided encouragement and assistance throughout this project and took the time and trouble to read drafts and provide comments, ideas, and suggestions for improvements and further reading. Above all, he managed to stimulate and maintain my enthusiasm for the project even while disagreeing fundamentally with parts of the analysis. Without his friendship and assistance it is unlikely that the book would ever have been completed.

I wish also to thank the North-South Institute, and specifically its director, Bernard Wood, for sponsoring this study. Critical comments and helpful suggestions were received from several NSI staff and in particular Roger Young, Margaret Biggs and Réal Lavergne. Bruce Campbell cooperated closely with me throughout the writing of the book and prepared several drafts of Chapter 3. In addition he assisted by collecting data and information for other chapters and by providing commentary and suggestions for each chapter. His enthusiasm, humour and belief in the usefulness of the approach being taken were invaluable in seeing the project through to completion. For their part in seeing the book through to publication, my thanks go to Maxwell Brem, NSI's senior editor, and to Patricia Udokang.

The help and advice of Roy Culpeper, Tom Naylor, Reg Green, Brian Van Arkadie, Donna Brown, Stephen Gelb and Aurelie Mogan is also acknowledged, as is the first rate secretarial support provided by Carol Plumridge. To my colleagues in C.S.S.C. I acknowledge my debt of gratitude for their friendship and support, the price of which, unfortunately, was a considerable delay in completing the project!

To Salim and Camille I can only say that I hope the end product compensates for the many months of enforced absence and neglect, and I thank them for their understanding and cooperation.

John Loxley

1

THE NATURE AND ORIGINS OF ECONOMIC INSTABILITY IN THE THIRD WORLD

Since the late 1960s the countries of the Third World have, as a group, experienced severe economic instability and increasing economic difficulties. In the early 1980s these problems came to a head in the form of what is now popularly known as the debt crisis, in which a number of Third World countries which had borrowed large amounts of money from Western banks were unable to meet their debt payments. At the same time many more, essentially poorer, Third World countries were experiencing economic crises of a rather different sort which though not as dramatic or as threatening to the interests of the industrialized capitalist world as the debt crisis, posed equally complex questions of policy for the countries involved and for the world at large. While the symptoms of both types of crisis (and this word is used advisedly to describe the acute state of economic disorder which characterizes these economies and the attendant political problems to which they give rise) are not difficult to describe, there is little agreement on their causes and more importantly, on possible solutions. In this chapter, we shall examine these symptoms and assess the contribution of global disorder to the problems of the Third World. In the process we shall also indicate some important ways in which trends which are perceptible in the global economy might act to constrain the prospects for stability and growth in the Third World in the immediate future.

The Symptoms of Third World Economic Crisis

The Overall Picture

Over the past decade, Third World countries as a group, excluding major oil exporting countries, have experienced a marked slowdown in their real rates of growth relative to those in the previous five years (Table 1.1). The decline has been steady since 1978 with the result that in each year between 1981 and 1983, real growth rates per head of the population were, in fact, negative.[1] Since 1978 inflation rates have, on the other hand, risen steadily so that by 1983 the mean rate was over four times as high as the average for 1968–72, and much higher than elsewhere in the world.

Table 1.1

Third World Countries Excluding Major Oil Producers: Selected Economic Indicators, 1968–1983

	Average 1968–72	1973	1974	1975	1976	1977	1978	1979	1980	1981	1982	1983
Real GNP Growth (%)[a]	6.0	6.1	5.4	3.3	6.0	5.7	6.4	5.1	5.0	2.8	1.5	1.6
Current Account												
Balance of Payment ($ billion)		−11.3	−37.0	−46.3	−32.6	−28.9	−41.3	−61.0	−89.0	−107.7	−86.8	−56.4
Export Volume (% change)	8.6	9.3	−0.1	−0.3	11.3	4.9	8.7	9.6	9.0	6.3	0.8	5.3
Export Unit Value (% change)	2.8	31.8	38.2	−0.2	6.8	14.0	5.5	17.6	16.0	−1.0	−5.0	−2.3
Import Volume (% change)	7.7	11.8	7.6	−4.1	4.5	7.2	8.5	10.3	4.7	2.6	−7.7	−0.6
Import Unit Value (% change)	2.9	25.1	46.8	9.0	0.8	7.7	9.6	18.0	23.6	3.0	−2.3	−3.3
Terms of Trade	−0.1	5.3	−5.9	−8.5	5.9	5.9	−3.7	−0.3	−6.2	−3.9	−2.7	1.1
Inflation Rate[a]	9.1	21.9	28.5	27.6	27.3	26.5	23.4	28.8	36.5	36.5	38.3	44.1

[a]Also excludes China.

Source: International Monetary Fund, *World Economic Outlook* (Washington, D.C.: IMF, 1983 and 1984).

When major oil exporters are excluded, the countries of the Third World experienced a dramatic rise in their deficits on the balance of payments current account, from $11 billion in 1973 to between $90 and $108 billion in 1980–82. In relative terms, as a percentage of their total export earnings, these deficits rose from between 10 percent (mean) and 16 percent (median) in 1973 to between 19 percent and 41 percent respectively in 1982.[2] The decline in the total current account deficits since 1981 is indicative of the growing problems countries faced in financing those deficits and was caused largely by an absolute reduction in spending on imports. This followed three years in which the rate of growth of real imports, while positive, had declined steadily. For countries heavily dependent on imports of capital goods, intermediate goods and, often, of such key commodities as food, the large fall in import volume in 1982/83 signified that for many countries their domestic economic difficulties were coming to a head.

Table 1.1 shows that Third World countries as a whole experienced significant deterioration in their terms of trade (the prices of their exports divided by the prices at which they buy imports) in the years 1974/75 and in all years since 1977 except 1983. These adverse shifts in relative prices were caused largely by persistent increases in import prices. They were offset in some years by Third World countries selling a greater volume of export goods, but in 1974/75 export volume growth was itself negative, and while it has been positive since that time, the growth rate has declined steadily since 1979. By 1982 it was barely positive. Recovery in 1983 was quite strong but moderated by a fall in export prices for the third straight year in a row.

For the period as a whole, import volume growth exceeded export volume growth and, given the overall deterioration in the terms of trade, the result was the large and, up to 1981, growing current account deficits. Maintenance of these deficits was possible only because the Third World had access to external sources of finance. There can be no doubt that this factor contributed significantly to the relatively high rates of growth of the Third World in the 1970s. It is equally clear that increasing balance of payments problems since the late 1970s have played an important role in the slowing down of growth rates.

The Picture Disaggregated

Growth Rates. So far we have examined aggregate figures of all underdeveloped countries excluding major oil exporters and China. These are, however, of very limited use as they hide some major differences in the experiences of different groups of countries. Disaggregating the data is necessary but unfortunately, the country groupings on which published data are based are less than satisfactory.[3] Nevertheless, notwithstanding the shortcomings of the data, it can be seen from Table 1.2, that the better-off middle-income countries which are 'net oil exporters' and 'major exporters of manufactures' grew much faster than other groups in the 1970s. The

Table 1.2

Real Growth Rates of Third World Countries Excluding Major Oil Producers and China, 1968–1983
(in percentages)

	Average 1968–72	1973	1974	1975	1976	1977	1978	1979	1980	1981	1982	1983
Average	6.0	6.1	5.4	3.3	6.0	5.2	5.4	4.6	4.3	2.4	1.5[a]	1.6[a]
Net Oil Exporters	7.0	8.3	6.5	6.2	6.7	3.5	6.2	7.2	7.3	6.4	0.8	−1.5
Major Exporters of Manufactures	8.0	9.5	6.5	1.3	6.7	5.6	4.9	6.4	4.5	−0.2	0.2	−0.1
Low-Income Countries	3.4	2.0	3.0	5.4	4.4	5.2	5.5	−0.1	3.2	4.4	3.0	2.6[b]
Other Net Oil Importers	5.4	4.1	5.5	2.7	5.9	5.4	5.5	3.4	3.0	3.1	0.5	1.1

[a]Includes China
[b]Excludes India and China
Source: International Monetary Fund, *World Economic Outlook* (Washington, D.C.: IMF, 1983 and 1984).

latter group, however, experienced sharp set backs in 1975 and, especially, 1981/82.

The growth in manufacturing exports from Third World countries to industrialized countries, and to a lesser extent to major oil producers and to other Third World countries, represents one of the most significant structural developments in the world economy since World War II. Manufacturing exports now account for over 40 percent of total non-fuel exports of these countries compared with 20 percent in 1965, and now supply 13 percent of the imports of manufactures by industrialized capitalist countries compared with only 7 percent in 1973.[4] Yet only a handful of Asian and Western Hemisphere countries are involved in this development, eight of them accounting for over three-quarters of the export growth between 1970 and 1976.[5] Multinational corporations played a significant role in the industrialization of these countries as they sought to offset declining profit rates in industrialized countries by exporting capital to countries where labour is cheaper and corporate taxes and controls generally lower;[6] their role in the growth of exports from these countries was not, however, as great as that of locally owned corporations.[7]

The major exporters of manufactures enjoyed relatively high rates of growth in the 1970s, capturing a growing share of the market in industrialized capitalist countries. They are, however, particularly vulnerable to demand restraint and to protectionist measures in these markets. These factors combined to reduce export growth to almost zero in the 1975 recession and to 6.5 percent in the 1982 recession,[8] cutting growth rates of real income drastically in the latter year and plunging a number of countries into serious economic and financial crises. This raises fundamental questions about the extent to which this outward-oriented model of growth is, in fact, sustainable and of whether or not it is generalizable to the rest of the underdeveloped world; questions to which we shall return later in the study.

Low-income countries were also the slowest growing on balance but even their record was better than that of the industrialized capitalist countries (see Table 1.2). Perversely, their real growth accelerated in 1980 and 1981 and, although it slowed down in 1982, was then the highest of any group. This is explained by high growth rates in the agricultural sectors of some larger Asian countries; the growth performance of smaller countries, and especially African countries, more dependent on trade with industrialized capitalist countries, has been less satisfactory.

Current Account Deficits. All country groups have experienced persistent current account deficits since 1973. For poorer-income group countries, in 1983 these deficits were caused largely by adverse trade balances but for both the net oil exporters and the major exporters of manufactures, negative flows on account of services and transfers were the main element (see Table 1.3).

The deficits of other net oil importers were largest in absolute terms but those of the low-income countries were much more important in relative

Table 1.3

Trade and Balance of Payments Indicators by Country Group, 1983 ($ billion)

	Net Oil Exporters	Major Exporters of Manufactures	Low-Income Countries	Other Net Oil Importers
Merchandise				
Exports	57.0	160.7	14.2	68.1
Imports	49.2	164.1	25.8	87.7
Trade Balance	7.8	– 3.5	– 11.6	– 19.7
Net Services and Private Transfers	– 14.7	– 13.7	1.8	– 4.6
Current Account Balance	– 6.9	– 17.1	– 9.8	– 24.3
Current Account Balance as % of Exports (including services)				
Mean	– 8.8	– 8.0	– 45.2[a]	– 25.1
Median	– 18.6	– 5.3	– 73.9[a]	– 30.3
Trade Indicators 1973 = 100				
Import Volumes	156.0	140.9	106.5	111.2
Import Prices	268.4	249.4	298.1	300.9
Export Volumes	168.7	181.8	130.2	126.1
Export Prices	323.5	220.2	187.8	224.4
Terms of Trade	120.6	87.7	62.6	70.6
Purchasing Power of Exports	198.1	158.6	81.7	89.0

[a]Estimate

Source: Derived from International Monetary Fund, *World Economic Outlook* (Washington, D.C.: IMF, 1984).

terms, being the equivalent of between almost a half and three-quarters of the total exports of goods and services of these countries. The deficits of other net oil importers were equal to between a quarter and a third of their total exports.

Table 1.3 throws some light on the origin of these large relative deficits. Low-income countries and other net oil importers suffered the greatest increase in import prices and the lowest increase in export prices over the period. Between 1977 and 1982 the terms of trade of low-income countries deteriorated by about a third; those of other net oil importers by about a quarter. Growth in export volume was also poor, being about 30 percent between 1973 and 1982 compared with over 80 percent for the major exporters of manufactures and almost 70 percent for net oil exporters.

These trends combined to reduce the purchasing power of exports (the value of exports weighted by import prices) over this period so that, in spite of large deficits, the low-income countries were not able to expand the real volume of their imports much above their 1973 level. The performance of other net oil importers in this respect was only moderately better.

Both the major exporters of manufactures and the net oil exporters enjoyed a strong increase in the purchasing power of exports and a steady expansion in the volume of imports. Both achieved marked expansion in export volume, strong enough in the case of the exporters of manufactures to offset deteriorating terms of trade. Net oil exporters were alone among underdeveloped countries in experiencing an improvement in the terms of trade over this period.

In 1982 all country groups experienced a decline in export earnings, a deterioration in their terms of trade and cut backs in import volumes. With the collapse of oil prices, net oil exporters were particularly badly affected, their terms of trade deteriorating by 16 percent in 1983.[9]

Current account balances of all country groups improved in 1983, largely on account of import contraction but, additionally, because of some recovery in export volume growth.

Financing Deficits. To finance the steady growth in current account deficits and a modest increase in foreign reserves in the seventies, Third World countries had to raise over $600 billion (see Table 1.4). This they did largely by borrowing overseas, just under half coming from private banks. In the process, indebtedness to foreign banks rose tenfold and is now over half of all their outstanding long-term foreign debt.[10]

But only a relatively small number of middle-income countries have access to private debt. These are in general the same countries that received direct foreign investment and are essentially major exporters of manufactures and net oil exporters. Nine such countries account for over two-thirds of all private foreign debt owed by underdeveloped countries.[11] Since 1973 private long- and short-term debt has gradually overtaken official debt and transfers in importance for all but the low-income countries.

Low-income countries barely have any access to private overseas borrowing. Instead, they rely heavily on loans and grants from governments and international agencies, 70 percent of their overseas capital coming from these sources in the 1970s. Since 1973 their dependence on official loans has increased significantly, raising the ratio of their outstanding foreign debt to exports to the highest in the underdeveloped world (see Table 1.5). Their debt-servicing ratios are, however, the lowest and, unlike those of other country groups, declined over the period. This is because official loans are generally obtained on concessional terms and because the share of concessional borrowing in their total has been increasing.

Many of those countries drawing on the private debt market encountered serious difficulties in the early 1980s. Poor export markets and adverse terms of trade drove reserve levels down to the equivalent of barely two months' imports and forced countries to borrow record amounts to cover their trade deficits. At the same time, the deteriorating world situation made it difficult for countries to service past debt. This was particularly so after contractionary monetary policies in the industrialized capitalist countries drove interest rates to unprecedentedly high levels. Annual debt and interest payments averaged $100 billion p.a. in 1981/82[12] and debt-servicing ratios (annual interest and amortization payments as a percentage of total exports) reached dangerously high levels. Increasingly, countries began to borrow more simply to meet payments on outstanding debts. Thus in 1981 all but $18 billion of the $62 billion borrowed went immediately to offset debt-servicing obligations,[13] making the term 'debt trap' seem ominously more appropriate now than when it was first coined in the mid-1970s.[14]

Inevitably, a number of countries have been unable to meet commitments and have had to negotiate debt-rescheduling agreements with their creditors. The growth in reschedulings will be examined in later chapters; at this point it should merely be noted that in 1981/82 "almost as many developing countries . . . had to reschedule loans . . . as in the previous twenty-five years."[15] Throughout 1982 and 1983 many feared that a collapse of the world banking system was imminent, with such notable personages as Johannes Witteveen, Chairman of the Group of Thirty and a former managing director of the IMF, speaking of the likelihood of a "crisis of confidence in the international banking system [which] could turn the worldwide recession into a depression."[16]

In the event, collapse was forestalled in those years by a series of emergency measures designed to prevent large debtor countries from defaulting on their loans. As will be shown later, these measures involved banks, the IMF, the Bank for International Settlements and the governments of lending countries in massive bail-out exercises which accompanied debt reschedulings. Whatever the longer-term implications of these interventions, the immediate effect has been that banks are now much more cautious in lending to Third World countries as a whole; hence a repeat in the 1980s of the massive growth in bank financing of Third World current account deficits that took place in the 1970s is out of the question. Those countries which were large borrowers in the last decade can expect to encounter tighter credit markets in the next. They will, therefore, have to adjust their

Table 1.4

Finance of Current Account Deficits of Third World Countries Excluding Major Oil Producers, 1973–1983 ($ billion)

	Cumulated 1973–1983	%
Current Account Deficits	598	—
Net Accumulation of Reserves	80	—
Overall Financing Required	678	—
Financed by:		
Overseas Borrowing:		
Banks	299	44
Other Private	26	4
Official	156	23
Net Direct Investment	85	13
Transfers to Governments	109	16
Borrowing from IMF	30	4
SDR Allocations, Valuation Adjustments, Gold Monetization	9	1
Payment Arrears	12	2
Other (including errors & omissions)	−48	−7
Total	**678**	**100**

Source: Derived from International Monetary Fund, *Annual Reports* (Washington, D.C.: IMF, various years).

Table 1.5

Reserve Ratios and External Debt Ratios of Third World Countries Excluding Major Oil Producers, 1973–1983

	Reserves as % of Imports		Debts as % of Imports		Annual Debt Service as % of Exports	
	1973	**1983**	**1973**	**1983**	**1973**	**1983**
Net Oil Exporters	27.5	18.7	154.7	198.3	29.0	31.0
Major Exporters of Manufactures	35.3	15.5	91.7	122.3	14.5	19.4
Low-Income Countries	23.3	15.4	227.9	262.9[a]	14.6	11.4[a]
Other Net Oil Importers	30.4	16.2	96.9	170.6	12.7	24.0

[a]Estimate

Source: International Monetary Fund, *World Economic Outlook* (Washington, D.C.: IMF, 1983 and 1984).

economies to temper the growth in deficits which they have financed, hitherto, by borrowing.

Never having enjoyed such ease of access to international credit, the low-income countries face different problems in meeting their deficits. They are much more concerned with the flow of official development assistance (ODA) which grew much less rapidly between 1978 and 1982 (by 200 percent) than their deficits (280 percent) or private lending (628 percent).

The share of low-income countries in ODA, at 37 percent, was no higher in the early 1980s than in 1971. The most recent projections suggest that the growth in ODA to the mid-1990s will be less than 3.0 percent p.a. in real terms, while the share of the low-income countries will remain unchanged. On this scenario, "ODA as currently planned falls far short of the needs of the developing countries, especially of the low-income countries, if world poverty is to be seriously tackled."[17] One can expect, therefore, that unless there are substantial improvements in their terms of trade and/or export sales, the low-income countries will continue to be faced with the problem of import growth compression, and growing problems with payments arrears, which have been with them for decades already.

Inflation, Fiscal Deficits and Real Exchange Rates. The experience of inflation both between and within country groups has been so varied that generalization is difficult. For all groups there was, however, a surge of price increases in 1974 reflecting oil price increases. For the major exporters of manufactures (and especially South American countries) which have by far the highest rate of inflation, this upsurge continued for three years, while the recovery in low-income (especially Asian) countries, which have the lowest, was achieved within one (see Table 1.6).

The second large oil price increase of 1979–80 hit all the non-oil exporters immediately. The low-income countries were affected the worst in relative terms, their rates more than doubling, but even then their absolute rates of inflation were still the lowest.

Inflation rates in all country groups are higher than their 1960 levels by factors of between 2 and 18, and well in excess of those in industrialized capitalist countries. In many countries which attempt to practise price control, actual inflation rates exceed official ones as goods shortages have given rise to extensive unofficial market activities for which, of course, data are not available.

Trends in the growth rates of money supply and fiscal deficits for Third World countries as a whole are similar to those for inflation. The growth of money and quasi-money (M2) has risen from an average (mean) of 32 percent in 1974–75, to 36 percent in 1976–79, to 58 percent in 1983. Fiscal deficits as a percentage of Gross Domestic Product have moved from 3 percent to 4 percent to 4.6 percent over the same period.[18] Data from country groups are incomplete but it is known that the low-income countries have been experiencing even higher relative fiscal deficits of 4.0 percent, 5.5 percent and 6.0 percent of GDP in these years. Their money supply growth rates have, however, declined from 19–20 percent p.a. in 1976–79

Table 1.6

Changes in Consumer Prices in Third World Countries Excluding Major Oil Producers, 1968–1983
(in percentages)

	1968–72	1973	1974	1975	1976	1977	1978	1979	1980	1981	1982	1983
Net Oil Exporters	4.1	11.1	20.6	14.6	14.9	22.8	17.7	17.7	24.2	24.3	44.0	74.2
Major Exporters of Manufactures	14.1	21.3	24.9	40.1	55.7	40.6	37.4	44.9	54.1	62.1	62.9	86.5
Low-Income Countries	6.5	21.9	29.7	13.4	– 0.2	10.7	6.8	11.3	15.9	18.2	13.6	11.1[a]
Other Net Oil Importers	8.4	30.4	38.8	27.3	18.8	19.6	18.6	23.9	31.5	19.6	16.3	16.0

[a]Estimate

Source: International Monetary Fund, *Annual Report* (Washington, D.C.: IMF, 1983 and 1984).

to 15–16 percent p.a. in 1980–81, raising from some quarters the criticism that this could only have been achieved at the cost of 'crowding out' the private sector.[19]

It is apparent that the country group with the highest rates of inflation, and money supply growth—the major exporters of manufactures—also enjoyed the highest growth rate during this period. This is explained by their willingness to use exchange rate policy to maintain international competitiveness. Thus between 1973 and 1982 the real effective exchange rate[20] hardly changed at all for this group while the nominal rate fell by three-quarters. Real rates declined substantially in 1983, however, as countries aggressively pursued stabilization policies.[21]

At the other extreme, the real effective exchange rates of low-income countries (excluding China and India) appreciated significantly, by 17 percent after 1973;[22] those of the African region appreciated by over 40 percent.[23] In part this reflects higher rates of domestic inflation relative to those of trading partners; for some countries it was also partly the outcome of their currencies being tied in part, or in whole, to the U.S. dollar which appreciated strongly relative to other currencies after 1979.[24]

Taking all Third World countries together, effective exchange rates are much more volatile than those of the rest of the world. This volatility has increased markedly since 1973 as world currency markets have also become more unstable, and is generally considered to be detrimental to trade stability and expansion.[25]

External Shocks and the Crisis of the Third World

A strong case can be made that many of the problems facing Third World countries at this time have their origins in structural changes in the world economy, and especially in the capitalist world economy, since the end of the 1960s. These changes are essentially threefold. First of all, the 'engine of growth' of the industrialized economies has been slowing down quite noticeably since that time and has also become increasingly erratic. Secondly, competitive rivalry between industrialized capitalist economies has increased significantly in recent years. This has been stimulated by their slower and more unstable growth rates and in turn has contributed to them. It has given rise to restrictive policies which have adversely affected the Third World. Within this general context, the third structural change, that of massive increases in world oil prices by 400 percent in 1973/74 and 165 percent between 1979 and 1981, dealt a particularly harsh blow to oil importing Third World countries. Together, these three factors and the policy responses to them by corporations and governments in the industrialized countries, have been responsible for exposing Third World countries to a series of external shocks that have, in turn, played a key role in generating the domestic economic problems examined above.

Table 1.7 summarizes some of the major dimensions of the economic problems facing the major capitalist countries and highlights both the

Table 1.7

Industrialized Capitalist Countries: Selected Economic Indicators, 1963–1982

	Average 1963–72	1973	1974	1975	1976	1977	1978	1979	1980	1981	1982	1983
Real GNP Growth (%)	4.7	6.1	0.5	– 0.6	5.0	4.0	4.1	3.4	1.3	1.2	– 0.3	2.3
Inflation Rates (%)	3.9	7.7	13.1	11.1	8.3	8.4	7.2	9.0	11.8	9.9	7.4	4.8
Unemployment[a] ($ million)	7.1[b]			14.0						21.0		28.5
Unemployment Rates[a] (seven largest countries)	3.2	3.4	3.8	5.5	5.4	5.4	5.2	5.0	5.7	6.4	8.1	8.3
Volume of Imports (% change)	9.0	11.5	1.4	– 8.1	13.3	4.5	5.1	8.5	– 1.5	– 2.4	– 0.5	4.1

[a]Organization for Economic Cooperation and Development, *Main Economic Indicators* (Paris: OECD, 1970–1983). Nineteen Countries.
[b]1970
Source: International Monetary Fund, *World Economic Outlook* (Washington, D.C.: IMF, 1983 and 1984).

instability of income, prices, unemployment and trade *and* the recessions of 1975 and 1980–82. Rates of growth have declined significantly since the sixties and were negative in the two recessions. Inflation rates have generally been at least double the average of the 1960s and in 1980 rose to three times that level. There has been a pronounced slowing down in the growth rates of international trade since 1979 (Table 1.8) as the recession led to cut backs in import demand by the industrialized world (Table 1.7).

The sensitivity of Third World economies to recession in industrialized capitalist countries is widely recognized. According to the IMF, "every reduction of 1 percentage point in the growth of the industrial countries for a one year period typically reduces the exports of the non-oil developing countries by about 1½% or more than $2 billion."[26] Yet this sensitivity varies from country group to country group. The two middle-income groups, 'major exporters of manufactures' and other 'net oil importers', seem to be the most sensitive because of the greater importance of manufactured exports to their economies.[27] The least developed countries are also adversely affected but relatively less so because their exports are a much smaller percentage of GNP (which in itself partly reflects longer-run problems of low export growth) and because domestic agriculture tends to be relatively more important in GDP than in middle-income countries. Deterioration in the terms of trade, caused in part by the increased rates of inflation in industrialized capitalist countries, combined with uneven bargaining power between those countries and weaker Third World trading partners, appears to have been a more serious problem for the least developed countries since 1973 than export volume fluctuations.[28]

A key factor in the terms of trade deterioration of most Third World countries and in explaining the increased tendency to recession and economic crisis in the industrialized world was, of course, the oil price explosion of the 1970s. It is to be emphasized, however, that this served to exacerbate tendencies toward slowdown, inflation and disorder in the world economy which were already apparent; while adding to these in a massive way, it did *not* create them and, in part, must be interpreted as a reaction to them.[29]

The oil price increase of 1973/74 had a dramatic effect on the balance of payments positions of both the industrialized capitalist nations and the non-oil developing countries (Table 1.8) and led immediately to a recessionary contraction in world trade. World adjustment was, however, quite rapid; the industralized countries as a group quickly restored their balance of payments position and world trade expanded at a respectable rate between 1976 and 1979. The balance of payments deficits of the non-oil Third World, however, rose dramatically. In part this was a direct result of the oil price increase, these countries being relatively slow to adjust to the new price levels. It was also the result of a steady increase in the prices of goods purchased from the industrialized capitalist nations. More importantly for the current debt crisis, the growth in these deficits reflected the recycling of oil surpluses through the international banking system to the handful

Table 1.8

World Trade Growth and the Balance-of-Payments, 1973–1982

	Average 1963–72	1973	1974	1975	1976	1977	1978	1979	1980	1981	1982	1983
Volume of World Trade (% change)	8.5	12.0	4.5	−3.5	11.0	5.0	5.5	6.5	2.0	0.5	−2.5	2.0
$ Value of World Trade (% change)	3.0	23.5	40.0	9.5	1.5	8.5	10.0	18.5	20.0	−1.0	−4.0	−4.5
Balance of Payments on Current Account ($ billion)												
Industrialized Capitalist Countries		20.3	−10.8	19.8	0.5	−2.2	32.7	−5.5	−40.4	1.9	−1.4	−1.2
Major Oil Exporters		6.7	68.3	35.4	40.3	29.4	5.7	62.5	111.0	53.4	−12.0	−16.2
Non-Oil Developing Countries		−11.3	−37.3	−46.3	−32.6	−28.9	−41.3	−61.0	−89.0	−107.7	−86.8	−56.4

Source: International Monetary Fund, *World Economic Outlook* (Washington, D.C.: IMF, 1983 and 1984).

of middle-income countries that were to become major borrowers. This permitted them to finance much higher levels of imports than would otherwise have been possible; it also speeded up world adjustment to the oil crisis, offsetting much of the recessionary impact of the huge resource transfers involved in the price increase.

By 1978 the oil surpluses had all but disappeared, absorbed largely by higher import expenditures by oil producers, mirrored in the large surpluses of industrialized capitalist economies (Table 1.8). The terms of trade also moved sharply against oil producers in that year. This was followed by disruption in the supplies of Iranian oil due to the civil war in that country. The response was another large increase in the price of oil, a restoration of the oil surplus at the expense of other country groups, a reinforcement of global tendencies to recession as world trade contracted, and another round of loan recycling to the large debtor countries of the Third World. Meanwhile, the global recession and the oil price increase exposed those Third World countries that did not have access to bank debt, and were not oil producers, to acute foreign exchange constraints.

Underlying these developments in the last decade and contributing independently to global instability has been the increased rivalry and competitiveness among the industrialized capitalist nations. In particular, the post–World War II economic dominance of the United States is now being challenged by Japan and West Germany. The collapse of the Bretton Woods monetary arrangements in 1971 and 1973, involving the replacement of fixed exchange rates and the convertibility of the dollar into gold by a system of more or less freely fluctuating exchange rates, permitted the U.S. to devalue its currency in an effort to retrieve lost competitiveness with its trading rivals.[30] The outcome has been a world monetary system in which exchange rates are highly volatile, fluctuating sensitively to differential conditions between countries, fuelling world inflation and destabilizing commodity markets.[31]

Fluctuations in exchange rates have been the result largely of industrialized capitalist countries being affected unequally by and/or responding differently to the economic problems under discussion. Throughout the 1970s Japan and West Germany maintained higher real growth rates and lower rates of inflation than other countries; but even West Germany experienced negative growth in 1981 and 1982, while growth rates in Japan slowed down markedly in those years. At the other extreme Italy, France and the United Kingdom had extremely high inflation rates over the last decade. In the case of the United Kingdom, inflation rates were more than halved between 1980 and 1982 but at the cost of a doubling of the unemployment rate.[32]

This differential experience within a general environment of economic difficulties has given rise not only to exchange rate and interest rate volatility in response to capital flows and attempts to regulate them, but also to a new wave of protectionism as each country seeks to overcome the national crisis at the expense of the others. The degree of protectionism seems to have increased markedly in the latter part of the 1970s. It has taken the form mainly of bilateral non-tariff restrictions on a limited range of specific goods some of which, like shoes and clothing, are important to underdeveloped country exports. Other goods involved, such as steel and automobiles, are more crucial to trade between the industrialized capitalist countries themselves but also affect countries like Brazil. Many fear that such protection may become even more generalized, nullifying the beneficial effects of earlier generalized tariff reductions,[33] and slowing the pace of global recovery with particularly serious implications for Third World countries pursuing export-oriented growth strategies.

Explaining Economic Instability in Industrialized Capitalist Countries

There is more agreement on the symptoms of economic malaise in the industrialized capitalist world than there is on its root causes. Some see the oil shocks as being so huge as to overshadow any other possible causes of the recession. One variant of this approach adopts a Keynesian interpretation, arguing that oil surpluses raised savings propensities and therefore reduced aggregate demand. Another is more neo-classical in content maintaining that oil price increases caused serious distortion in relative prices and hence led to structural problems, adjustment to which takes time. Yet a third variant argues that the oil price increase occurred at a time when world liquidity was growing too slowly and, while bank recycling avoided a generalized Keynesian underconsumption problem in the world economy, several European capitalist countries (as well as numerous but less influential poorer countries) had no option but to contract imports. The problem is seen to be, therefore, one of *financing* deficits which affects some countries more than others.[34]

The fact that slowdown and increased rivalry characterized the world system even before the oil shocks, has led others to seek alternative explanations. One of these is that the industrialized capitalist countries are in the trough of a long cycle which could persist for some time.[35] Many of the expansionary influences at work in the immediate aftermath of the Second World War—the reconstruction of Europe, the backlog of demand for consumer durables, the 'third technological revolution,' and the U.S. wars in Korea and Indo-China—have long been exhausted and the underlying tendencies of the system to falling rates of profit and depression have asserted themselves. Inflation is seen as the outcome both of attempts to maintain demand through credit creation and of social struggles around income shares, struggles which intensified as growth faltered. Oil price increases simply reinforced these tendencies by further squeezing profits, by reducing demand and by stimulating yet greater price increases.[36]

The essence of this interpretation is that capitalism as an economic system is *inherently* unstable because, in the pursuit of profit which motivates the system, there is a constant need to replace labour by machinery and to expand production. Self-expansion of the system will last only as long as profits and profitability grow and secondly, as long as profits are reinvested. At the peak of a cycle, profit performance weakens as labour militancy grows and expansionary opportunities dwindle. The result is a contraction of investment spending and of demand generally, and a slide into recession/depression, causing capital values to be written down and labour militancy to be weakened by unemployment. In consequence, profit rates are restored as the prelude to an upturn. The long cycle is superimposed on more frequent short cycles and describes the general direction of these over a long period. Trade and capital flows transmit these fluctuations throughout the world system, their volume being crucial to the 'realization' of profits.

Adherents to this viewpoint would, in addition, argue that economic management of industrialized capitalist countries has also become much more difficult with the growth in the activities of transnational corporations. The ability of these corporations to transfer capital, production capacity and jobs across national boundaries plays an important role in the major changes which took place in international liquidity and the structure of international production and trade in the post–Second World War period. Thus the erosion of confidence in the dollar in the early 1970s had much to do with the international investment activities of the U.S.-based transnational corporations (within, of course, the 'expansionary' context of the Vietnam War) which resulted in the creation of the Eurodollar market, the massive increase in U.S. liabilities overseas relative to gold reserves and, ultimately, the devaluation of the dollar and the freeing up of the gold price.[37] A crucial element in this process was the building up of industrial capacity in offshore production centres, primarily in a limited number of underdeveloped countries, by TNCs in pursuit of larger profits than could be obtained domestically. This had the effect of undermining the U.S. balance of payments surplus and, therefore, of confidence in the dollar, as local production overseas replaced U.S. exports[38] and, to a lesser degree, also led to increased imports.[39] This industrial expansion was financed not only by direct investment flows by industrial TNCs, but also by credits from transnational banks, and both types of flow were unregulated by governments. On this view the inadequacy of state policy, exercised within a national framework, to deal with the increasing internationalization of production, trade and financial transactions, is a major cause of instability in the global economy.

Against this 'systemic' view of capitalism are to be counterposed theories which argue that the failures are essentially ones of domestic policy which are, in fact, considered avoidable. Keynesian theorists would argue that appropriate state intervention can compensate for inherent instability in the system, with special emphasis being placed on fiscal policy, while 'monetarist' theories see excessive state intervention as a major cause of crisis.[40] Monetarists would argue that inflation is the product of the state allowing money supply to grow too rapidly, in part to finance in Keynesian fashion, its own deficits. They also view minimum wage laws, unemployment and welfare relief, direct state ownership, trade union powers and restrictions as 'structural bottlenecks' which, along with increasing monopolization of the private sector, prevent the market mechanism from functioning as it should. One result of this is that the 'cleansing' and profit restoration functions of recession/depression do not operate as smoothly now as they did pre–World War II so that adjustment to, and hence recovery from, economic downturns now take longer. Monetarist solutions are consistent with this diagnosis and involve tighter control over money supply growth, sharp cut backs in the size of the government sector and of state deficits, and 'supply side' initiatives designed to restore the workings of the market or, more narrowly perceived, the rate of profit.

It was this monetarist view of the causes of the crisis that gained political prominence in the late 1970s as governments in a number of capitalist countries found it increasingly difficult to manage their economies in the Keynesian manner that had become popular after World War II. In particular, monetarism seemed to offer a solution to 'stagflation' which emerged as a major problem in the period under review. The Reagan government in the U.S.A. and the Thatcher government in Britain were simply the first of a number of governments elected on this conservative platform. The effects of their tighter monetary policies quickly spread throughout the world economy as sharp contractions in the growth of money supply raised interest rates to record levels (Table 1.9).

The real growth of money supply was virtually nil in 1980 while real interest rates turned from negative to highly positive after 1979. Third World countries which had greatly expanded their borrowing in 1979 were suddenly facing interest rates of 17.5 percent or more on their foreign loans. In turn, the tight money policies greatly contracted demand in the markets for their exports as income growth rates in the industrialized countries fell and unemployment rose to levels not seen since the 1930s.

It will be shown below that these same monetarist policies created a less hospitable environment for bilateral aid flows and also propelled multilateral institutions in the direction of conservative lending policies toward the Third World. As argued earlier, these policy shifts mean that flows of official development assistance to Third World countries will be constrained to rates of growth unlikely to exceed the real growth rates of income of major donors. At the same time, and this will be a major theme in what follows, the new conservatism seems to be generating an unprecedented degree of donor intervention in the determination of the domestic economic policies of aid recipients.

Tight monetary policies and high interest rates in the United States also led to a strong appreciation of the dollar by attracting foreign capital. This in turn caused dollar prices in commodity markets to fall relative to the prices of industrial goods, again with negative implications for developing countries, including oil producers, whose surpluses had disappeared completely by the end of 1982 (Table 1.8). The restoration of the pre-eminence of the dollar, which is perhaps an end in itself of Reaganite policies, has also generated record U.S. current account deficits, strengthening the drift

Table 1.9

Average Money Supply Growth and Interest Rates for Seven Largest Industrialized Capitalist Economies, 1976–1983

	1976	1977	1978	1979	1980	1981	1982	1983
Change in Stock of Money (%) = **Broad Definition**								
Nominal	12.9	11.8	10.9	9.9	9.8	9.8	9.5	9.0
Real	5.5	4.6	3.0	2.0	0.3	1.5	3.5	5.2
Short-Term Interest Rates								
Nominal	6.9	6.4	6.8	9.2	11.7	13.3	10.9	9.2
Real	− 0.3	− 0.6	− 0.3	1.2	2.4	4.2	4.0	2.9

Source: International Monetary Fund, *World Economic Outlook* (Washington, D.C.: IMF, 1983), pp. 226-227; Ibid., 1984, pp. 118 and 120.

toward protectionism as U.S. companies find it increasingly difficult to compete with imports.

U.S. foreign policy and especially a return to a more aggressive military posture, has, however, complicated the economic policy of the Reagan administration. Notwithstanding cut backs in discretionary social service expenditures, a pronounced increase in military spending, on both nuclear weapons and on costly interventions in Grenada, Lebanon, and Central America, unavoidable contractual social expenditure increases and the high costs of government debt have, ironically, led to an escalating U.S. budget deficit. While this unplanned 'Keynesian' initiative undoubtedly assisted a tentative recovery of the U.S. economy in 1983/84, it also prevented interest rates from falling in line with domestic inflation by crowding out private borrowers from credit markets. The result of this blend of tight monetary, lax fiscal policy is that real rates remain high, causing management problems for European countries which also have to maintain high interest rates to quell capital outflow, dampening their private sector recovery. These economies continue to experience relatively low rates of growth and very high rates of unemployment are predicted into the foreseeable future. The high value of the dollar continues also to depress commodity prices relative to those of industrial goods.

Future world growth rates will depend, crucially, on the ability of the U.S. government to curb its budget deficit. This will involve, however, either raising taxes or sharply cutting back public expenditures. Tax increases, and further wage restraint or social service cut backs would undoubtedly generate social protest and hence are unlikely until at least after the impending U.S. presidential elections. Cut backs in defence spending would require an abrupt about-face in U.S. foreign policy which is not anticipated.[41]

In short, whatever one's view of the origins of the global crisis, there are serious questions about the likely strength and duration of a recovery spearheaded by the U.S. economy. Policy prescriptions for Third World countries to deal with their economic crises must recognise these uncertainties and their likely implications for flows of trade, aid and debt in the immediate future.

Notes

[1] World Bank, *Annual Report* (Washington, D.C.: World Bank, 1983), p. 27. In 1981 and 1982 overall real per capita GDP growth was −0.1%. Per capita income growth was clearly negative in 1983. See International Monetary Fund, *World Economic Outlook* (Washington, D.C.: IMF, 1984), p. 70.

[2] IMF, *World Economic Outlook*, 1983, p. 191.

[3] The country classifications are those used by the IMF and are as follows:

Net Oil Exporters: Bahrain, Bolivia, Peoples' Republic of the Congo, Ecuador, Egypt, Gabon, Malaysia, Mexico, Peru, Syria, Trinidad and Tobago, Tunisia. The criteria used are that while their exports of oil exceed their imports, they do *not* produce at least 100 million barrels a year and/ or account for at least 1 percent of world oil production and hence are *not* regarded as *major* oil exporters.

Major Oil Exporters: covers 12 oil producing countries.

Major Exporters of Manufactures: Argentina, Brazil, Greece, Hong Kong, Israel, Korea, Portugal, Singapore, South Africa, Yugoslavia.

Low-Income Countries: 43 countries whose per capita GDP, as estimated by the World Bank, did not exceed the equivalent of $350 in 1978.

Other Net Oil Importers: Defined as middle-income countries that in general export mainly primary commodities. This includes 32 countries, data for which are published in the IBRD world indicator tables. There are also 21 small countries which qualify for inclusion in this category, data for which are *not* published in the IBRD world indicator tables. It is not clear how the IMF treats these countries.

To some degree these categories are quite arbitrary. Thus, India, a major exporter of manufactures, is categorized as a 'low-income country'. All 'socialist' countries are excluded except China which, despite being a net oil exporter, is categorized as low-income. We have chosen to exclude China on the grounds that its structure and political economy are quite different from those of other underdeveloped countries and that it is, in any case, excluded from much of the published data. For 1983, however, it is not possible to obtain published data excluding *only* China. Where possible, therefore, estimates have been used.

Some major exporters of manufactures (e.g., Thailand, the Philippines and Chile, are classified as 'other net oil importers.'

Any categorization based on quantitative economic measures is likely to be questionable at the margin. More fundamentally, such measures hide the disparities and similarities in the social structures of these societies which is a much more important shortcoming from the point of view of political economy. We do not, however, have data categorized in this way and hence have chosen to use the IMF data, with all its imperfections.

[4] World Bank, *World Development Report 1982* (New York: Oxford University Press, 1982), p. 12.

[5] *North-South: A Programme for Survival*, Report of the Independent Commission on International Development Issues under the Chairmanship of Willy Brandt (London: Pan Books, 1980), p. 174.

[6] Ibid.

[7] Deepak Nayyar has estimated that the share of TNCs in manufactured exports of Third World countries was not much greater than 15% in 1974. See his "Transnational Corporations and Manufactured Exports from Poor Countries" *The Economic Journal* 88 (March 1978), pp. 59–84.

[8] IMF, *World Economic Outlook*, 1983, p. 182. For a discussion of the scope and impact of protectionist policies in industrialized capitalist countries, see IBRD, *Adjustment Policies and Problems in Developed Countries*, Staff Working Paper No. 349 (Washington, D.C.: IBRD, 1979), pp. 116–159; and Commonwealth Secretariat, *Protectionism—Threat to International Order—The Impact on Developing Countries*, Report by a group of experts (London: Commonwealth Secretariat, 1982), Chapters 1 to 3; and *North-South: A Programme for Survival*, Chapter 11.

[9] See IMF, *World Economic Outlook*, 1984, pp. 181–182.

[10] Ibid., 1983, p. 200.

[11] World Bank, *Annual Report*, 1982, pp. 25–26.

[12] IMF, *World Economic Outlook*, 1983, p. 204.

[13] Ibid., 1982, p. 25.

[14] See Cheryl Payer, *The Debt Trap—The International Monetary Fund and the Third World* (New York: Monthly Review Press, 1974).

[15] World Bank, *Annual Report*, 1983, p. 34.

[16] *The Globe and Mail* (Toronto), October 6, 1982.

[17] World Bank, *World Development Report, 1983* (New York: Oxford University Press, 1983), p. 33.

[18] IMF, *World Economic Outlook*, 1984, pp. 50–52.

[19] Ibid.

[20] Real effective exchange rates are nominal exchange rates weighted by the relative importance of different currencies in the economy of the country concerned (effective exchange rates) and then weighted further by the rates of inflation in these countries relative to that in the country in question. See Chapter 2 for more details.

[21] IMF, *World Economic Outlook*, 1983, p. 133, and 1984, p. 53. See Chapter 2 for a discussion of exchange rate policy and stabilization.

[22] Ibid. These figures apply to 1982 data. Comparable figures are not available for 1983 but it is clear from the 1984 reference that real exchange rates continued to appreciate strongly for these country groups.

[23] Ibid., 1982, pp. 120–126.

[24] In 1980 no less than 40 Third World countries pegged their currencies to the dollar. Several others gave the dollar an important weight in baskets of currencies to which the local currency was pegged. See IMF, *Annual Report* (Washington, D.C.: IMF, 1980), p. 53.

[25] See UNCTAD, *Trade and Development Report* (New York: United Nations, 1981), p. 76, which reports that "the average monthly variability of effective exchange rates rose for a group of developed market-economy countries from 1.1 percent in the period January 1967 to March 1973 to 1.7 percent in the period April 1973 to December 1978, and for another group consisting almost entirely of developing countries from 1.7 percent to 2.4 percent in the same period."

[26] IMF, *World Economic Outlook*, 1980, p. 8.

[27] Morris Goldstein, and Mohsin S. Khan, *Effects of Slowdown in Industrial Countries or Growth in Non-Oil Developing Countries*, Occasional Paper No. 12 (Washington, D.C.: IMF, August 1982).

[28] Ibid.

[29] See, for instance, Ronald L. McKinnon, *An International Standard for Monetary Stabilisation* (Washington, D.C.: Institute for International Economics, 1984), p. 56; and Harry Magdoff, "The U.S. Dollar, Petrodollars and U.S. Imperialism", *Monthly Review* (January 1979).

[30] Riccardo Parboni, *The Dollar and Its Rivals* (London: Verso, 1981), Chapter 2. The dollar devaluation was also a reflection in the loss of confidence in the dollar as a financial asset as a result of the increasing economic and political problems in the U.S. in the late 1960s, early 1970s, problems closely connected to the slowdown in U.S. growth and to the impending defeat in Vietnam. See Herbert G. Grubel, *International Economics* (Homewood, Illinois: Irwin, 1981), Chapter 25.

[31] For a clear exposition of the link between floating exchange rates and inflation in the 1970s, see McKinnon, *Monetary Stabilisation*, Chapter 4. For a 'left' interpretation of these developments, see Ernest Mandel, *The Second Slump* (London: New Left Books, 1979), Chapter 3.

[32] See IMF, *World Economic Outlook*, 1983, Appendix B, Tables 1, 5, 6 and 7 for details. For an analysis which puts 'uneven development' at the heart of the crisis, see E. A. Brett, *International Money and Capitalist Crisis: The Anatomy of Global Disintegration* (London: Heinemann, 1983).

[33] See references in footnote 8 above.

[34] See Parboni, *The Dollar*, pp. 101–108, for an elaboration of these various theories.

[35] The notion of 'long waves' or 'long cycles' was first developed by Kondratief but has recently been incorporated into the economic analysis of contemporary economic crises by Ernest Mandel. See his *Late Capitalism* (London: Verso, 1978).

[36] See Mandel, *The Second Slump*, Chapters 1, 2, and 3.

[37] Ibid., Chapter 3.

[38] See Magdoff, "U.S. Imperialism", p. 12. He emphasizes the fact that this investment had negative effects on the U.S. balance of payments mainly by reducing U.S. exports to Third World countries, rather than by increasing U.S. imports. This view is supported in part by Nayyar who argues that the main motivation for transnational investment in industry in Third World countries was to secure a share of the local market. See Nayyar, "Transnational Corporations and Manufactured Exports".

[39] See G. K. Helleiner and R. Lavergne, "Intra-Firm Trade and Industrial Exports to the United States", *Oxford Bulletin of Economics and Statistics*, Vol. 41 (November 1979). This paper demonstrates that U.S. imports of manufactured goods from developing countries through TNCs was important for certain high technology products such as machinery and from certain countries such as Mexico, Philippines, and Hong Kong which welcome TNC investment. Intra-firm trade in the import of manufactures from LDCs by the U.S. accounted for 37% of the total of such LDC imports in 1977. This seems to represent a sharp increase in the figures reported by Nayyar for 1974, though the data are not directly comparable. See Nayyar, "Transnational Corporations and Manufactured Exports".

[40] For a concise review and comparison of Keynesian, monetarist and Marxian theories of crisis, see Bob Chernomas, "Keynesian, Monetarist and Post-Keynesian Policy—A Marxist Analysis", *Studies in Political Econonomy*, No. 10 (Winter 1983).

[41] For an elaboration of this theme, see John Loxley, "Saving the World Economy", *Monthly Review* (September 1984), pp. 22–34.

2

DOMESTIC POLICIES OF STABILIZATION AND ADJUSTMENT

On Finance and Adjustment

Third World countries have but two ways in which they can attempt to deal with external shocks of the magnitude of those outlined in Chapter 1. The more fortunate ones can hope to *finance* resulting balance of payments deficits by obtaining loans or grants from abroad. This is the preferred option since it avoids or postpones the alternative of *adjusting* their economies to eradicate deficits. The major alternative sources of financing available to Third World countries form the subject matter of Chapters 3 to 6. Our contention in these chapters will be that the majority of countries will find it more difficult to finance deficits in future than they did in the 1970s. This suggests that they will need to rely more heavily on appropriate domestic policy measures to minimize or offset the disruptive influence of external shocks.

Except in the limiting case, however, 'financing' and 'adjustment' are not to be regarded as substitutes. They generally go hand in hand.[1] A given mix is a matter of national policy, but policy is shaped by the amount and nature of adjustment required and by the amount and terms of external finance to which governments have access. A central theme of this work is that the most important sources of external finance available to Third World countries are, increasingly, requiring that particular types of adjustment policies be implemented as a *condition* for making available their financing.

In order to properly situate the whole question of this type of 'conditionality' attached to sources of finance, it is important to review the literature on 'stabilization' and 'structural adjustment' to ascertain both its theoretical and its policy foundations. In doing so, it will be necessary to question the extent to which this literature has been shaped by stabilization and adjustment experiences of the 1960s and 1970s—experiences which may be less relevant in the current context of global disorder and of anticipated slowdowns in the growth rates and financing capabilities of the industrialized capitalist world.

On Stabilization Versus Structural Adjustment

Before proceeding further it might be useful to clarify the terms 'stabilization' and 'structural adjustment' which tend to be used interchangeably in the literature.

Stabilization describes the process of restoring balance between supply and demand in the economy, whether it be for foreign exchange or for goods and services. Traditionally, 'stabilization' implied short-run policy-induced changes in the balance of payments, the rate of inflation, etc. with the principal emphasis being placed on domestic demand management and only a subordinate role being given to supply stimulation. Latterly, stabilization efforts considered successful in conventional literature have been associated with far-reaching changes in the 'trade regimes' of Third World countries. These changes have taken the form of substantial shifts in the structure of investment and production and in the orientation, outward versus inward, of the economy. Often, the balance between state control and the use of market incentives has shifted significantly. The policy tools employed encompass and go beyond those of 'stabilization' with the relative emphasis having moved away from demand management toward supply stimulation. Thus, the term 'structural adjustment' simply makes more explicit the fact that contemporary stabilization programs frequently imply substantial changes in the direction of the economy, in its sectoral priorities and in its institutional make up. If any difference remains in the use of these two terms it lies, therefore, not so much in objectives as in the range of tools, the relative emphasis being given to different policy variables and in the time horizon over which policies are expected to take effect. In what follows, however, we shall bow to what is becoming convention and use the terms interchangeably. It should be emphasized, however, that this blurring of the distinction between them is a conjunctural phenomenon reflecting the depth of global disorder at this time; at other times, in other situations, the two terms could have quite different meanings and stabilization programs could embrace objectives which are different from, and possibly even contradictory to, those of structural adjustment programs. This will become apparent when alternative approaches are discussed below.

Policy Instruments of Stabilization and Structural Adjustment

The wide variety of policies available to governments to deal with instability can be categorized under four broad headings: (i) demand restraint policies using monetary or fiscal instruments; (ii) exchange rate and other major relative price adjustments; (iii) direct controls; and (iv) liberalization measures. The first seeks to improve external balance both by reducing total expenditures and therefore, those on imported goods, and by freeing up goods for export by restraining domestic spending. Curbing demand also serves to reduce inflationary pressures which, in turn, may further strengthen the balance of payments by making local goods more competitive with those from abroad. The second and the fourth policy measures aim primarily at 'getting prices right' which means, essentially, allowing market forces more influence in determining price levels and relative prices. The objective here is to stimulate production through price incentives and to 'switch' the composition of output and demand in such a way as to boost exports and investment and reduce imports and consumption. More generally, the aim is to increase the production of tradable as opposed to non-tradable goods. In the short-run this can be achieved *either* by altering administered prices, such as the exchange rate, producer prices or consumer prices, *or* by replacing administered prices by market-determined ones. Some would advocate making these adjustments by 'liberalizing' the economy; that is, by dismantling government institutions or control procedures designed to administer resource allocation. This latter approach generally takes longer to implement and in extreme forms may involve the denationalization of public sector enterprises. 'Getting prices right' need not, of course, always imply institutional reform of this type. The third measure, direct controls, is an alternative to (ii) and (iv) in which the state deliberately intervenes to curb the influence of the market by allocating resources administratively and/or by controlling price levels.

In practice the precise blend of policy instruments will vary greatly from program to program depending on the nature and severity of the economic difficulties being faced, the structure of the economy concerned, and the time path over which adjustment is felt to be necessary and possible. The ideological orientation and the degree of political stability enjoyed by the government will also help shape the type of program adopted. In addition, the prevailing *theoretical* interpretations of the causes of instability which, in reality, cannot be entirely separated from *ideological* considerations, will play a crucial role in the design of stabilization programs.

The Influence of Monetarist Thinking on Contemporary Stabilization Prescriptions

At the theoretical and ideological level, one particular interpretation of the nature and causes of instability, that of the monetarists, has been more influential than others in conventional approaches to stabilization in recent years.[2] 'Monetarists' believe that balance of payments problems and problems of inflation have their causation in monetary factors.[3] They see the balance of payments as a purely monetary phenomenon and deficits as the result of governments permitting an excess supply of domestic credit relative to the demand for money. Inflation is also viewed as the product of too rapid an expansion of money supply which, in situations of fixed exchange rates, puts further pressure on the balance of payments by reducing the incentive to export and by increasing the relative attractiveness of imports. Where interest rates are also controlled by government, as is common in developing countries, inflation can reduce them to negative levels in real terms. This further weakens the balance of payments by encouraging capital outflow or discouraging capital inflow. Such interest rate levels also discourage local savings.

Monetarists argue, therefore, that in small open economies the authorities can, in the long-term, independently determine only one of the following policy variables: the domestic credit supply, the price level, the exchange rate and the level of interest rates.[4] Having chosen one, the other three must adjust accordingly under pressure from domestic and foreign supply and demand. They hold that with complete integration into the world economy, trade and payments flows will bring domestic prices and interest rates in foreign currency terms into equality with those prevailing internationally. In the long-run, therefore, balance of payments deficits will be self-correcting. Attempts by governments to resist supply or demand pressures by trying to regulate more than one of the above policy variables can only lead to disequilibrium in real or financial markets.

The monetarist approach to stabilization is, therefore, premised on the view that most underdeveloped countries attempt to *over determine* the system giving rise to internal and external imbalances.[5] Inappropriate government policies are thus considered to be a prime cause of instability and also the main reason why economies fail to adjust smoothly when instability is externally induced. This emphasis on the failure of domestic policy lies at the heart of monetarist analysis; it is also a theme which permeates the literature on stabilization.

While monetarism is not the sole theoretical influence on that literature, it is a major one and this inevitably finds reflection in conventional policy prescriptions. These almost always include strict control over domestic credit creation and, therefore, over the money supply, as a key element in demand management. Reducing government budget deficits is considered central to credit restraint and therefore to demand control in most conventional programs. A typical fiscal package would involve reducing government spending by ending the price-distorting subsidization of basic commodities, such as food or transportation, and the bailing-out of unprofitable public sector corporations. It would entail cutting back recurrent government spending and possibly also state investment expenditures. Revenue might be raised by levying user fees on goods or services supplied by the state such as health, education or water supply, and taxes might also be increased but in ways that minimize disruption to market-determined relative prices and incentives.

'Getting prices right' in orthodox stabilization packages usually entails allowing international prices to play a greater role in the determination of local prices. Policy measures to achieve this would include the reduction or abolition of taxes on exports and those on imports competing with goods produced by well-established domestic industries. It might also include the introduction or expansion of export subsidies. Adjustment in the exchange rate, a devaluation or depreciation, is also often prescribed to bring domestic prices more into line with those faced in international markets. This usually involves bringing the real effective exchange rate back down to some previous year's level where it was considered to be in some sense, in 'equilibrium'. If the rate has been allowed to appreciate significantly from this level then large adjustments may be necessary. By raising the price of foreign exchange to more accurately reflect its scarcity a devaluation would, it is argued, restore the incentive to export and, simultaneously, encourage efficient import substitution.[6]

In a similar fashion, interest rates would be allowed to rise to levels more appropriate to the scarcity of capital and, in the extreme, might become positive in real terms, that is, reach levels in excess of the rate of inflation. The expectation is that this would discourage consumption, promote local savings and help attract capital from abroad. It should also encourage the more efficient use of capital in the form of bank credit, etc.

Freeing up the exchange rate and interest rate and the reduction or abolition of price distorting subsidies or taxes are but part of a broader bias in orthodox stabilization packages against 'direct controls' generally and in favour of 'liberalization'. This emphasis is often extended to the dismantling of controls over foreign exchange allocation, imports, domestic prices and the abolition of minimum wage regulations. Each of these controls, it is argued, represents state interference in the market mechanism causing distortions in relative prices and, therefore, in resource allocation and in incentives. Such controls merely stimulate the growth of parallel or unofficial markets putting pressure on the government budget by reducing tax revenues from official transactions and by raising expenditures on policing, etc. In extreme cases, liberalization might also take the form of replacing state marketing agencies or other nationalized entities by the private sector or of 'privatizing' services hitherto delivered by the government.[7] The rationale for this might be the presumed greater efficiency of the private sector or simply an attempt to create a more hospitable 'climate' for local and foreign private capital. In this connection, it is worth emphasizing that the one form of control that tends to be advocated by the orthodoxy, is that of a ceiling on wage increases.

The immediate impact of this type of policy package is quite often very deflationary. Any improvement in the balance of payments in the short-run is likely to be the result of a fall in import demand due to reductions in the level or growth rate of local 'incomes' induced by credit restraint, and, as we shall see, by devaluation. More positive, supply-induced improvements will take longer as expenditure switching and export promotion are, by definition, structural adjustments which cannot be effected overnight. Proponents argue, however, that these short-run costs, amounting to one or two percentage points of GNP for a year or 18 months, are inevitable. The longer-term benefits, it is argued, can be as high as two or three additional points of GNP growth and, over time therefore, should easily offset these short-run costs.[8] Where longer-run benefits do accrue, they derive from improved export performance and greater accessibility to international capital that this sometimes brings with it, from increased output for domestic use and from improved savings performance. The philosophy underlying orthodox stabilization programs is, therefore, one of 'short-run pain for long-run gain.'

The Relevance and Effectiveness of Orthodox Stabilization Prescriptions

There are a number of grounds for questioning the appropriateness of the typical stabilization package described above. To begin with, some of the underlying theoretical assumptions, and especially the monetarist ones, can be challenged. The adoption of alternative, more structuralist, assumptions would suggest a need for somewhat different approaches to policy management. In addition, important questions can be raised about the relevance of orthodox prescriptions in the context of widespread instability among Third World countries, an instability resulting more from global disorder than from internal policy failures. These issues will be dealt with in this section. Other, equally crucial questions about the model of growth implied in these prescriptions and about the distributional and political consequences of switching to this model will be dealt with later in this chapter.

The gist of the structuralist critique of monetarism is that both domestic and external imbalances have their origins in deeply rooted structural characteristics of Third World countries; rapid domestic credit creation is a reflection of those imbalances and permits their continued existence but does not explain their origin.[9] Both inflation and balance of payments deficits can be rectified by domestic credit restraint but because of structural rigidities, this restraint would have to be very severe and protracted to be effective. The social costs of rectifying instability in this way are, therefore, likely to be very high and, unless the underlying structural causes are addressed, imbalances are likely to recur. The structural characteristics of Third World countries also reduce the efficacy of price signals in both the stimulation and the switching of production.

For a variety of structural reasons, demand restraint can be expected to function less smoothly as an inflationary device than monetarists predict. In many Third World countries prices are set monopolistically and thus have a certain rigidity independent of the level of demand. Interest costs on credit tend also to be a significant item in price determination so that credit restraint policies might exert cost push inflationary pressures by raising interest rates.[10] Where inflation is directly linked to foreign exchange shortages, as in many low-income countries, demand restraint can only help if it improves the balance of payments, and, as we shall see, for structural reasons it may have this effect only slowly if at all. Where inflation is more directly linked to acute social struggles over income shares and/or to structural bottlenecks in food supplies, as is thought to be the case in some middle-income Latin American countries, demand restraint alone will be of limited use in reducing inflation in the long-term.[11]

In addition, though, there are good reasons to suppose that in many instances the typical stabilization package as a whole might increase inflationary pressures rather than reduce them. High interest rate policies can, as we have seen, directly affect prices; in some situations they can also do so indirectly by encouraging an inflow of capital which if not stabilized, can lead to monetary expansion. The immediate effects of certain liberalization measures, such as the lifting of price controls (but not, of course, of ending minimum wage controls) will also be inflationary as will attempts to rectify budget deficits which take the form of abolishing subsidies or raising fees or taxes. Devaluation will also exert upward pressures on prices by raising the domestic currency price of both exports and imports. Some of these pressures may, however, be absorbed by reductions in premia (rents) earned previously by those with privileged access to foreign exchange. To the extent that local currency prices of exports are raised as a result of devaluation, and this is a matter of policy, increases in the prices of competing commodities, such as foodstuffs, can be expected to follow. Historically, the evidence is that within a two-year period of an exchange rate adjustment, the inflation rate has increased by an amount in excess of the initial rate of depreciation,[12] so that the real effective exchange rate is, ironically, even higher after devaluation than before it. Some writers maintain that this is due partly to inflationary expectations of essentially oligopolistic firms which lead them to overcompensate for devaluation, 'overshooting' what would otherwise be the price level if expectations were rational and foresight perfect.[13]

In summary, one could say that the inflationary consequences of the orthodox package would be greater the smaller the inflow of foreign finance accompanying it, the less responsive is output to price signals, and the more acute is social conflict over income shares. The reverse argument also holds true.

The impact of demand restraint on the level of activity and employment is usually less ambiguous, being generally negative. Devaluation may also reinforce this contractionary influence although there is no single explanation for this. Some argue that if there is an initial large current account deficit, a devaluation would immediately absorb more purchasing power through the import price increases than it would generate through increases in the local currency prices of exports. The resulting contraction of demand would be stronger the less responsive are exports and imports to price changes.[14] Other explanations focus on the tendency of price 'overshooting' and the failure of wages to keep up with this, leading to reduction in workers' living standards.[15] Devaluation may also reduce domestic demand by increasing the local currency cost of foreign debt servicing and, theoretically, by raising government recurrent revenues by more than it expands government recurrent spending. Government spending restraint would simply reinforce this fiscal impact. Increased interest rates may choke off investment in both fixed capital and inventories while the 'real balance effect' of money supply not keeping pace with inflation would also lead to a contraction in domestic spending.[16] Whatever the precise cause, which will vary from situation to situation, the outcome is that stabilization packages sometimes have an immediate stagflationary impact on Third World economies.

There also are sound structuralist reasons for doubting the contribution demand restraint might make to improving the balance of payments of certain Third World countries. Often the substitutability of traded for non-traded goods is very low, meaning that many imports do not compete with goods produced locally and that many exports are not consumed locally to any degree. Restraining domestic demand may not, therefore, reduce import demand significantly, nor free up for export goods consumed domestically.[17]

Structural factors may also reduce the contribution to supply stimulation of measures taken to 'correct' prices. Thus, food output may not respond to increased consumer and producer prices if land is held by semi-feudal 'Latifundia' rather than by profit or income maximizing farmers. Likewise, the structural characteristics of many Third World countries limit the potential effectiveness of exchange rate adjustment in improving the balance of trade.

'Elasticity pessimists' argue that the theoretical conditions necessary for a devaluation to lead to improvement in the balance of trade in foreign exchange terms—the so-called Marshall-Lerner conditions—are not met by Third World countries. These conditions stipulate that where both export and import supplies are elastic, the sum of the price elasticity of demand for exports and the price elasticity of demand for imports must be greater than one.[18] This pessimism appears to conflict with the findings of a number of empirical studies which reveal that, during the period studied, the elasticities of underdeveloped countries were such as to satisfy the Marshall-Lerner conditions;[19] that, in practice, devaluation *did* tend to raise the price of traded relative to non-traded goods (a requirement for expenditure switching),[20] and that, generally, devaluation tended also to improve export performance.[21]

The findings in each of these studies are, however, very much influenced by the presence in the sample of countries with a significant industrial capacity and with established export markets in manufactured goods.[22] For such countries, a devaluation can have an immediate impact on foreign currency prices in the markets for their manufactured goods (i.e., suppliers are *not* price takers). Also, manufactured goods previously consumed in the home market can readily be shifted into export markets (i.e., export supply is elastic). For these reasons, devaluation is likely to have a greater stimulating effect on export earnings in these countries than in others. The assumption of elasticity pessimism may, therefore, be an inappropriate assumption for those countries which have a highly developed manufacturing sector, but might have more relevance for low-income primary exporting countries. For the latter, which face given world prices for both exports and imports, the Marshall-Lerner condition simply requires that the sum of the elasticity of supply of exports and the elasticity of demand for imports, exceed zero.[23] Elasticity pessimists would argue that there may be structural reasons why this condition might not be so easily met. Exports may respond only slowly, if at all, to price incentives. Primary exports are generally not consumed locally so little expenditure switching is possible.[24] It may take several years before investment in tree crops or mineral extraction capacity produces increases in output. If consumption goods or capital goods are in short supply, as is often the case in the poorest countries where import constraints are severe and inventories at a minimum, then an increase in producer prices may have no impact at all on production: instead, it might simply fuel inflation. At the same time an increase in the domestic price of imports might not reduce foreign currency expenditures on imports if excess demand for imports is large or if non-price factors are important in determining import demand. This, in situations where actual imports are only a half to two-thirds of import demand, where government is a major importer or where foreign aid and/or emergency food supplies figure prominently in total imports, raising the domestic price of imports through a devaluation might have little impact on the total foreign currency demand for imports. Where imports are licensed the huge rents earned by those fortunate enough to obtain a licence reduce the sensitivity of import demand to devaluation.[25] Thus, while for this type of an economy, a devaluation cannot cause a deterioration in the trade balance, it may not lead to much of an improvement. At the same time devaluation should be quite disruptive in terms of generating or exacerbating domestic inflation.

Structuralists would also argue that raising interest rates to positive real levels is unlikely to raise real savings in Third World countries. The distribution of income, the state of the government's recurrent budget, and the reinvestment (or remittance abroad) of profits, are considered to be prime determinants of savings and each is considered to be relatively insensitive to interest rates (except for government savings which are negatively related to interest rates). While there is evidence that positive rates increase savings held in financial form, sometimes this simply means a movement from an informal financial market to a more formal one and *not* an increase in real savings. This is what appears to have happened in the much quoted case of Korea.[26] Recent empirical work, however, casts doubt on the view that "the interest elasticity of savings is significantly positive and easy to detect in developing countries."[27] It should also be added that even proponents of market-determined rates do not claim any strong association between increased financial savings and improved growth performance.[28]

The more developed the financial system and the more closely it is integrated with foreign financial systems, the more important will interest rate policy be to stabilization programs. Positive real interest rate policies have been successful in some Latin American countries in attracting foreign credits. They have also had the effect in some countries of increasing the concentration of ownership of companies. This is the result of asset values in the productive sector being written down to permit returns to rise to match those on financial assets, a development which has permitted larger companies (local and foreign) with access to relatively cheaper foreign credits to buy up stock cheaply.[29]

A further reservation about the wisdom of applying orthodox stabilization programs to the numerous Third World countries in crisis at this time is one that focuses on the international origins of the crisis. If the causes of crisis are accepted to be depressed markets and adverse terms of trade for Third World products, high interest rates and declining real flows of capital to Third World countries, then it is questionable whether this *general* problem can be adequately addressed by orthodox solutions applied to *individual* Third World nations.[30] Generalized demand restraint to the degree currently being demanded of major debtors, for instance (see Chapter 4), cannot be said to be contributing positively to global recovery. Also where export markets are stagnant or where protectionism is a growing threat, the reliance of numerous Third World countries on devaluation as a stabilization tool may not be helpful, even where there has been no evidence of elasticity pessimism assumptions being correct in the past.[31] This is because, given the global origins of the problem, exchange rate adjustment as a generalized prescription may lead only to competitive devaluations and not to expansion in the total market for Third World products. The net effect may, therefore, be simply to worsen problems of domestic inflation without relieving balance of payments difficulties. The surge of inflation in many middle-income countries since 1979 is undoubtedly, in part, the result of exchange rate policies designed to preserve or expand export levels in the face of a depressed world market.

Thus, a strong argument can be made that the widespread application of orthodox stabilization programs to Third World countries since 1979 has been ill-advised, committing two closely related errors of prescription. The first is essentially based on a fallacy of composition; namely, that policies which might make sense to a single country might make no sense at all if a number of underdeveloped countries are pursuing them simultaneously. The second error is that of projecting into the present factors that were crucial in overcoming past instability (i.e., a buoyant export market), but which no longer have the potential they once had because of the global crisis now being experienced.

We shall examine in the last section of this chapter the type of policy advice that might flow from these critiques and reservations. Before doing this, however, it is necessary to examine the possible structural, distributional and political implications of implementing orthodox stabilization packages.

The Structural Implications of Orthodox Stabilization Prescriptions

The perceived failures of domestic policy that orthodox stabilization and structural adjustment packages seek to redress often take the form of a commitment to a development strategy which is weighted too heavily in the direction of 'import substitution' in the manufacturing sector to the neglect of other sectors of the economy. The narrowness of the domestic market for many of the goods produced under this strategy leads to small-scale production and excess capacity. As a result, industry is often inefficient and uncompetitive and survives only through high levels of tariff protection and/or controls over competing imports.[32] Protection permits the emergence of a class of people, domestic or foreign-based, earning profits from this sector and of a small but relatively well paid urban working class. The narrow interests of these groups, and of the urban sector generally tend to have a disproportionate influence on the policy interventions of the state and on institutional developments. In effect, therefore, the import substitution strategy evolves into a whole new 'regime of accumulation'[33] with its own peculiar economic, political and social dimensions.

It is argued that an import substitution regime often introduces a number of biases into the economy. Relative prices tend to move to the disadvantage of the non-manufacturing sector as farmers and others face higher prices for manufactured goods that are now produced, more expensively, locally and as agricultural prices are kept low by price controls on foodstuffs sold in urban areas and by an overvalued exchange rate. The allocation of foreign exchange, domestic savings and skilled personnel, tends also to be skewed toward the urban sector. These biases combine to reduce incentives to produce outside this sector. Poor growth performance results, putting pressures on revenues to the state budget and, in turn, giving rise to inflationary pressures as the state pursues deficit financing to compensate for revenue shortfalls. In the context of state controls over nominal consumer prices, interest rates and exchange rates, these pressures lead to even greater distortions in relative prices putting further negative pressure on production, savings and the balance of payments. Internal and external instability are, therefore, closely linked attributes of the state-sponsored import substitution strategy which is considered to have only limited growth potential.[34]

Domestic policy 'failures' of the type outlined need not, of course, always be accompanied by an explicitly pronounced import substitution industrialization (ISI) strategy, but their effect will be, nevertheless, to impart an 'inward-looking' bias to the economy with all the implications for external and internal balance associated with the ISI model.

Orthodox approaches to stabilization explicitly advocate abandonment of inward-looking strategies and the adoption of more outward-oriented and especially export-oriented strategies of growth. The theoretical rationale for this is that these strategies offer better growth prospects, are more efficient and also more resilient to external shocks.[35] Breaking out of the confines of production for the small domestic market is held to offer more potential for longer-run growth as well as the possibilities of reaping economies of scale. The pressure of international competition would also minimize cost and profit levels and guarantee greater efficiency. Trading in the international market might expose countries to larger initial external shocks in the context of global instability but, it is argued, producers would draw on their competitive experience to adjust product lines, quality and inputs to meet these shocks more quickly and smoothly than their ISI counterparts who tend to be heavily dependent on imported inputs *and* slow to adapt to changing circumstances. Dismantling the inward-looking ISI regime would bring domestic prices into line with world prices and might therefore promote import substitution industries of a more efficient type. Underlying the orthodox approach there is, therefore, a belief that exports have been discriminated against and that import substitution has been inefficient. A shift in the incentive structure is, therefore, recommended to rectify both these perceived deficiencies in policy.

Empirical studies of adjustment experiences in the 1960s and 1970s, several of them under the direction of Bela Belassa, a consultant to the

World Bank, are invoked to provide support for the alleged theoretical superiority of externally oriented strategies.[36] For instance, Belassa has argued that during the 1974–78 period, countries pursuing outward-oriented strategies enjoyed higher growth rates, higher domestic savings rates, lower external debt and debt-servicing ratios and lower incremental capital-output ratios, than countries pursuing inward-looking strategies. These findings were held to apply to less developed countries as well as newly industrialized countries.[37]

Using a slightly different methodology, Jaspersen has reached similar conclusions for the 1974–77 period, arguing that "those countries which accelerated diversification of the productive structure and adopted policies aimed at integrating their economies more closely with the world economy were generally able to adjust to the new petroleum prices and the slowdown in world trade with the least disruption of their growth and pursuit of broader development objectives."[38]

Both studies conclude that successful adjustment toward an outward-oriented strategy requires a combination of policy measures acting simultaneously on demand restraint, growth stimulation and the switching of production toward investment, tradable goods and, especially, exports. The economic policies of Chile and Uruguay during this period are applauded by both authors as models to be followed by other Third World countries. Each of these countries provides a textbook example—albeit an extreme one—of what an 'orthodox' or 'typical' stabilization program would look like—with devaluation, abolition of price controls, reduction of tariffs, establishment of real positive interest rates, the reduction of budget deficits and public consumption, and widespread liberalization of financial and other markets. In the words of Ronald Mckinnon, "Chile . . . remains the purest example of a comprehensive economic liberalisation in the Third World."[39] Other countries held up as successes are Taiwan, Korea and Singapore. Each has vigorously pursued export-oriented growth strategies.

The study by the World Bank of adjustment experiences in 22 oil importing developing countries during the most recent global recession appears to confirm the benefits of outward-looking policies.[40] This found that "countries with strong export growth had GDP growth of 3.8 per cent a year, compared with 2.8 per cent a year where export growth was average and 1.3 per cent a year where it was weak." The study also concluded that "those countries pursuing active trade policies (including elements of both export promotion and efficient import substitution) grew faster . . . than those which relied mainly on import restrictions." These findings are supported by other studies which show a close association between export growth rates and GDP growth rates over the medium- and long-term.[41]

Orthodox Prescriptions and Political Repression

There would appear to be both theoretical and empirical support, therefore, for the strategic thrusts of orthodox stabilization programs. From the discussion earlier, however, it should be clear that moving from an inward-looking to an outward-looking strategy is not simply a matter of manipulating policy instruments in a narrowly perceived technical sense. Rather, in the extreme, it implies the replacement of one 'regime of accumulation' by an entirely different one, suggesting quite radical shifts in income and wealth, in institutional structure and practice and, inevitably, in political power. To effect these shifts and, more especially, to maintain them over any length of time, requires their legitimation politically and socially. As Thorp and Whitehead have argued, this aspect of stabilization and structural adjustment is largely ignored in orthodox programs which tend to be overly preoccupied with reducing disequilibria and promoting the outward-oriented strategy of growth in narrow economistic terms.[42] Yet a number of the countries considered to have successfully introduced outward-oriented structural adjustment programs since the late 1960s were clearly not able to legitimate these programs by mobilizing popular political support for them; instead, they imposed and maintained them by resorting to extreme political repression, often through military dictatorships. That proponents of outward-oriented growth can hold up Pinochet's Chile as a model to be followed by other Third World countries and can do so without even a passing reference to the widespread murder, torture and other forms of gross violation of human rights on which that regime and its economic policies were founded,[43] is a sad reflection of the ideological nature of much of the literature on structural adjustment.

There is no single or simple explanation for the association between political repression and market-oriented economic policies observable in Latin America, South-East Asia and elsewhere. Sheahan argues that in Latin America repression was seen "falsely but understandably" as being necessary to deal with structural distortions in the economy which had arisen over a number of years and which had been exacerbated by ISI strategies.[44] Improving the efficiency of these economies and raising growth performance would, inevitably, reduce urban wages and concentrate income and wealth even further in the hands of small capitalist and landowning classes. Thus "the straightforward economics of the situation . . . greatly increased the likelihood that emphasis on efficiency criteria would foster repression."[45] Diaz Alejandro, on the other hand, sees repression as a reaction to "unhinged macro-conditions" caused by "chaotic populism"; that is, that the misguided economic policies of populist governments caused short-term chaos which made it possible for military 'coup d'Etats'.[46] This interpretation need not, of course be inconsistent with Sheahan's longer-term perspective on the issue. Indeed, it could be argued that a structuralist perspective is required to understand why populist (or left wing) governments come to power in the first instance. Diaz Alejandro's explanation would certainly not be adequate to describe the intense domestic social cleavages that characterized Chile under the Allende government, nor the external intervention that assisted the military take-over there, but it may have more relevance in Argentina during this period.[47] What is obviously called for is a case-by-case analysis of specific country experiences.

Whatever the precise reason was for the coming to power of authoritarian regimes in these countries, their subsequent monetarist-inspired stabilization programs could clearly not have been implemented without repression as their impact was to drastically cut the real wages of urban workers. In Chile (1973–78), Argentina (1976–78), Uruguay (1974–78) and Brazil (1964–67) real wages fell by between 30 and 40 percent while unemployment rose significantly.[48] Political opposition was contained only by harsh repression of workers' movements and by curtailing the democratic freedoms of society at large. Such repression is also characteristic of several non-Latin American countries which have achieved varying degrees of success in pursuing outward-oriented growth strategies; for example, South Africa and the Philippines (with grossly inequitable income distribution) and South Korea and Taiwan (with relatively equitable income distribution). Most such countries also enjoyed access to foreign bank lending in the 1970s which undoubtedly assisted their shift in trade regime.

The recent past provides evidence, therefore, of a close association between 'successful' stabilization programs, the adoption of outward-oriented strategies, the inflow of private credit and the existence of authoritarian regimes.

Many economists are very uncomfortable with this association, denying (correctly) the *necessity* of the link either between successful stabilization policies and repression[49] *or* between authoritarian regimes and outward-oriented strategies.[50] Likewise, the banks seek to deny any connection between the perceived creditworthiness of their clients and the harsh political climate that prevails in many borrowing countries.[51] Yet, while not being a necessity, this close association is an indisputable historical fact that should prompt those advocating orthodox adjustment strategies to pause for reflection. Without repression, it is unlikely that the distributional implications of demand restraint and of correcting the 'bias' in relative prices—the keys to most adjustment programs—could have been contained politically. Creating a suitable investment climate hinged on preventing labour from successfully resisting real wage cuts and on dismantling the economic institutions erected by previous 'structuralist' governments (populist or otherwise). Without repression, therefore, it is unlikely that many of the countries in question could have pursued an outward-oriented strategy and its foreign finance with quite the vigor they did in the 1970s: at the very least, adjustment would have proceeded much more slowly and uncertainly. Where the model of growth has not been legitimated by concensus, it has a very tenuous domestic political base, one which began to crumble quite perceptibly in such countries as Brazil, Chile, Argentina, the Philippines and even South Africa in the early 1980s as export growth was arrested by the collapse of world markets. Some writers have maintained, however, that even without the global economic crisis, the authoritarian model would inevitably encounter political crisis as significant cross sections of society, including elements of the property-owning classes, would tire of the constant repressive environment.[52] The collapse of authoritarianism would undoubtedly have implications for the long-term viability of the outward-oriented strategy as pursued to date, if this unleashed the social tensions previously repressed militarily.

A Closer Look at Outward-Oriented Growth Strategies

In assessing the wisdom of a generalized commitment by Third World countries to an outward-oriented growth strategy, some further observations both on the experiences of the recent past and on the theoretical formulations of this strategy seem to be in order.

To begin with, the single most important lesson of the 1970s is that export pessimism of the structuralist school, 'dependista' or otherwise, proved to be unfounded for the Third World as a whole. Export volume growth rates of non-oil developing countries averaged 8.4 percent p.a. during 1968–72 and 6.7 percent p.a. during 1973–80.[53] It is this favourable historical record that provides the main rationale for contemporary policy prescriptions. Secondly, historical experience would seem to indicate that political repression was neither *necessary* for *all* countries pursuing this model (e.g., Barbados, Trinidad and Tobago, Hong Kong) nor *sufficient* in itself (e.g., Haiti, Poland and the Philippines).

Advocates of this strategy feel, therefore, that it can be justified on solid theoretical and empirical grounds and that it can be applied independently of the nature of the political system.

In theoretical terms, however, the case for such a strategy is not as unambiguous as its proponents claim.[54] Exposure to the world market is no guarantee of avoiding inefficiency which can be caused by numerous factors—poor management, poor quality product, excessive scale, labour alienation, etc. Also, excessive protection possibly giving rise to negative value added can, theoretically, occur equally in export industries through high subsidies as it can in import substitution industries through high tariffs. Also, shifting relative prices toward export industries through devaluation and removal of tariffs could, theoretically, raise the profits of inefficient export industries while reducing those of efficient import substitution industries. There is also a potential conflict between the need for large-scale production to compete effectively in the world market and the need for competition and freedom of entry locally. Such qualifications should serve to caution against an uncritical acceptance of arguments for the theoretical superiority of the outward- versus the inward-oriented strategy.

The empirical evidence in support of outward-oriented strategies likewise needs careful qualification. Export success in the 1970s was, as argued in Chapter 1, virtually synonymous with exporting either oil or manufactured goods. But adjustment through raising manufactured exports presupposes an already developed manufacturing sector. The superior export performance of the handful of newly industrialized countries was, therefore, "related to their already more advanced economic structure and flexibility, their generally greater credit worthiness, and their greater access to external capital."[55]

Other, less developed countries and especially the poorer ones, did not share in this export-led growth, largely because their economic structures were not sufficiently developed. While Belassa's findings appear to contradict this conclusion, a conclusion supported by several other empirical studies,[56] this is so only because of the definition he employs of 'less developed countries'. In this category he includes Thailand, Morocco, Egypt, the Philippines, Zambia and Tunisia[57]—all of which are considered by the World Bank to be middle-income countries and all of which have well-established manufacturing and/or oil producing sectors.

Virtually without exception countries which are now major exporters of manufactured goods went through a period of varying duration, in which they pursued inward-looking import substitution strategies with high tariff rates and strong import controls.[58] The danger in applying across-the-board prescriptions for export-oriented growth and in using blunt macro-instruments such as tariff abolition or devaluation for this purpose, lies in the possibility of destroying local industry before it is strong enough to compete internationally.

The historical record contradicts orthodox prescriptions in other ways too. It is simply not the case that successful export promotion was the product of liberalization in the sense of unbridled, private enterprise. Countries such as Taiwan, Korea, Singapore, South Africa, Brazil and Mexico were propelled into exports largely through massive state intervention in product, finance and labour markets. Furthermore, there has been no uniformity in the degree of openness of these economies as the amount and nature of state intervention has varied considerably. Also, within individual countries, there has been no uniformity of openness in the three key areas of trade, foreign investment and foreign credits; state policy has at different times given different weights to openness in each of these areas.[59]

The empirical evaluation of the outward-oriented growth model has also focused very narrowly on its efficacy in either raising growth rates or in closing external imbalances. As implied earlier, other quite valid criteria such as distributional equity and/or political legitimacy are more often than not ignored. Yet there are strong grounds for believing that the urban impact of such a strategy is often regressive.[60] Whether or not this is so of the impact on the overall economy depends very much on the structure of production and of social relations in the rural areas. If production there is shifted toward exports and is in the hands of independent peasant producers, the impact could well be progressive; but if ownership is dominated by large landowners, corporate or otherwise, or if distribution of peasant produce is handled by inefficient state marketing agencies, and/or if the elasticity of supply is very low, then the overall outcome may not be progressive.[61] Certainly, one of the structural effects of such a strategy could be expected to be a withdrawal of resources from meeting basic needs of people directly. Resources would be shifted away from private and public consumption toward investment, and the pattern of investment would be altered away from the satisfaction of domestic needs toward satisfying foreign demand. Unfortunately, empirical studies throw little light on these issues as those export-success countries considered to have pursued equitable distributional policies (e.g., Taiwan) did so for unique historical reasons unconnected with the strategy itself.[62]

One aspect of successful stabilization in the least developed countries in the 1970s which has received insufficient attention in the literature (perhaps because, while being consistent with efficient import substitution emphases it might be seen by some to contradict the export orientation prescription), was the expansion of food production.[63] Countries such as Bangladesh and India were able to restore domestic balance and improve foreign balance by pursuing improved food strategies. Whether or not this contributed to greater equity depended very much on national and local conditions with regard to food entitlement, including ownership structure.[64] Although greater land concentration often accompanied increases in output, the negative impact of this was offset to some extent by lower food prices and increased employment.[65] Were expanded food production strategies to be given priority in adjustment programs in Africa, where most low-income countries are located and where over 20 countries are currently experiencing acute food crises, landowning systems are such that success in terms of growth would probably also imply success in terms of equity *and* basic needs. The contribution of improvements in total food production to the successful adjustment experiences in the 1970s of some *middle-income* Asian countries (e.g., Thailand and Korea), seems also not to have been given the attention it deserves in the literature on structural adjustment.

Can the Outward-Oriented Growth Model Be Generalized and/or Sustained?

While not all those countries considered successful in pursuing outward-oriented strategies in the 1970s can be characterized as having authoritarian regimes, it is still questionable whether their success could be generalized as a viable long-run model of growth, even if it were felt to be a desirable model on equity grounds. First of all a number of them have unique resource bases (e.g., oil); others have historically received large amounts of foreign capital for strategic or unique commercial reasons (e.g., Israel and Singapore), while some have labour supply situations that are quite different from those prevailing in many other Third World countries (e.g., Hong Kong). The superior adjustment performance of several South-East Asian countries might also owe a great deal to their proximity to Japan which has a record of much stronger growth and more rapid adjustment to the global crisis than other industrialized countries.

Above all, the very success of those MEMs to date may imply that the markets in industrialized capitalist countries are, from the point of view of the medium/long-term, close to saturation point. This is not easy to establish since 'saturation' is not a static concept. It cannot really be divorced from the level of activity, and the consequent shifts in the protectionist environment, in the markets of industrialized capitalist countries. A recent study has, nevertheless, argued that the East Asian experience cannot be replicated without very high levels of OECD market penetration being achieved.[66] If all LDCs were to achieve the same export intensity as Hong Kong, Korea, Singapore and Taiwan, then exports of manufactures from LDCs would have to rise from 16.7 percent of OECD manufactured goods imports in 1976 to 60.6 percent, with a much higher percentage in sectors already strongly supplied by LDC exports. Even on less ambitious assumptions on which only seven NICs replicate the intensity of the above few countries, LDC exports would have to increase dramatically their relative importance in OECD consumption of manufactured goods. The conclusion reached is that strong protectionist responses would be generated, and terms of trade would move violently against these products, well before these levels were reached. The study points out, however, and this is extremely relevant for our analysis, that there may still be considerable scope for individual countries to improve their long-run export performance before these responses are encountered.

The ability of countries which are already pursuing outward strategies to continue doing so at a reasonable rate of growth, and the ability of others to successfully emulate them, depends crucially on anticipated levels of activity in OECD countries, on their levels of protection, on interest rates and on the flow of capital to Third World countries. Projecting these variables with any degree of accuracy is an almost impossible task at the best of times; in the midst of current global instability it may even border on foolishness. Nevertheless, the IMF has estimated what would happen to the growth of Third World export volumes on the basis of certain assumptions about OECD economy performance and the results are of some interest for the topic at hand.[67] The assumptions are that (i) OECD countries grow at 3.25 percent p.a. between 1984 and 1990; (ii) inflation in the U.S.A. remains at 4 percent p.a.; (iii) petroleum prices remain constant in real terms between 1985 and 1990; (iv) interest rates fall steadily from 1985; (v) the terms of trade of non-oil developing countries remain unaltered; (vi) there is no increase in protection against Third World exports; (vii) private lending rises by 7 percent p.a.; between 1986–90; (viii) official development assistance remains constant at its 1984 level; (ix) direct foreign investment rises at 9.5 percent p.a.; and (x) real exchange rates among major currencies are unchanged. If these assumptions are met *and* Third World countries "pursue financial policies aimed at the restoration of domestic and external stability"[68] (i.e., orthodox stabilization programs) then export volume growth rates and GDP growth rates will be as in Table 2.1.

It can be seen that export volume growth rates are anticipated to be much lower in the next six years than they were in the previous twelve for all non-oil developing countries as a group. The export growth performance of net oil exporters and MEMs will be markedly inferior and, consequently, GDP growth rates will be well below the levels of the 1970s. The poorer Third World country groups are, however, anticipated to experience a pronounced improvement in export volume growth rates and

Table 2.1

IMF Medium-Term Projections (% growth p.a.)

	Actual Averages 1968–72	1973–80	Projected Averages 1985–87	1988–90
All Non-oil Developing Countries				
Export Volume	8.4	6.7	5.4	5.3
Real GDP	6.0	5.1	4.6	4.6
Net Oil Exporters				
Export Volume	4.1	4.9	2.6	3.0
Real GDP	7.0	6.6	4.5	4.5
Major Exporters of Manufactures				
Export Volume	12.0	10.0	6.9	6.5
Real GDP	8.0	5.6	4.3	4.3
Low-Income Countries				
Export Volume	2.8	0.9	4.7	4.0
Real GDP	3.4	3.9	3.5	3.5
Other Net Oil Importers				
Export Volume	7.7	3.9	5.2	4.8
Real GDP	5.7	4.6	3.9	4.1

Source: International Monetary Fund, *World Economic Outlook* (Washington, D.C.: IMF, 1984), p. 220.

especially the low-income countries. Nevertheless, GDP growth rates for these groups will be significantly below those experienced in 1973–80.

If these projections prove to be inaccurate the likelihood is that this will be because they err on the side of optimism. Within three months of their publication, interest rates had begun to rise in the U.S.A., the Iraq-Iran war had begun to disrupt oil shipments from the Persian Gulf and there were clear signs of the U.S. recovery faltering. Above all, the assumption that all Third World countries will vigorously pursue 'correct' adjustment strategies is a very heroic one indeed, but it would appear to be particularly crucial to the favourable results obtained for poorer Third World countries.

After allowing for this overoptimism, the above projections would appear to support those who argue[69]

(i) that the very rapid growth rates of Third World manufacturing exports in the 1970s are unlikely to be repeated in the coming decade;

(ii) that established exporters of manufactures can be expected not only to retain past market shares but also to improve on them at a respectable, albeit slower, rate thereby registering healthy increases in real GDP per capita;

(iii) that the prospects for less well established and would-be exporters of manufactures are more ambiguous and one should certainly not expect to see many, if any at all, breaking into the 'major exporters of manufactures' group;

(iv) that low-income countries are constrained in their export capability due to economic structure. Nevertheless, there would still appear to be *selective* opportunities for expanding manufacturing exports; these would be greater for Asian countries, whose production structure is more diversified, than for low-income African countries.

Alternative Policy Prescriptions

The dominance of orthodox policy prescriptions can be explained by the clarity (simplicity?) of their theoretical foundations and by their coherence as a body of advice. Above all, they enjoy ideological and political support at this time from major governments and from the international institutions whose policies are shaped largely by those governments. By comparison, the 'critique of the orthodoxy' lacks a coherent theoretical base and, more importantly, offers no widely accepted package of policy alternatives. Nevertheless, it is possible to piece together the kind of policy advice that seems to flow, logically, from the critique of the orthodox package discussed earlier. Many of the elements of that advice enjoy political support among a number of Third World countries dissatisfied with orthodox prescriptions and are also gaining popularity in the left/liberal literature on stabilization and alternative models of development.[70] It is, however, a basic tenet of the philosophy underlying this alternative approach that the concrete economic, social and political realities of specific country situations will determine what is possible and desirable by way of stabilization. For this reason the alternative does not emerge as a 'blueprint' for action in quite the way the orthodox approach tends to be offered by its proponents. Rather, it is better seen as a series of guidelines stemming from the critique of orthodoxy which would need to be applied flexibly as warranted by circumstances.

The impetus behind this attempt to outline a possible alternative approach lies in a belief that all too frequently the critique of the orthodoxy is an entirely negative exercise which is not very helpful to countries experiencing economic crises. Also, in focusing on the short-comings of orthodox solutions to crises, there is often a tendency to down-play failings in domestic policy on the part of Third World governments and their contribution to those crises. True, external shocks have clearly been a major factor contributing to instability in the recent period and the fact of global disorder should rightly be stressed by Third World governments in their legitimate political demands for global reform and for increased (and more appropriate) emergency external assistance. This broader environment will, as we have seen, place real constraints on what domestic policy initiatives might achieve. But in few Third World countries can government economic policy not be said to have played a part in exacerbating the current economic difficulties and most Third World governments have no option but to attempt to deal with the crisis by adjusting their economies since foreign financing is, in any case, not available in sufficient quantities for them to avoid adjustment even if they wished to do so. Excessive unproductive spending by governments on bureaucracy, defence, luxury consumption items or poor investment projects is a fact of life in many Third World countries. Policies which discriminate against the rural sector or against export products to the point where the growth of production and the surplus are discouraged and investment and imports constrained are unquestionably common. These and other examples of policy failings *are* within the purview of Third World governments and their rectification must be an objective of adjustment policies—orthodox or otherwise. In this respect most adjustment programs will contain a number of common elements. The objective of this section is, however, to focus on how an alternative approach might differ from the orthodoxy, notwithstanding these common elements.

A brief summary of what an alternative stabilization approach might look like would be as follows. The policy package would be tailored to the specific structural characteristics of the economy in question. It would rely more on selective policy instruments designed to influence behaviour in particular sectors or industries than on blunt instruments designed to have an economy-wide impact. It would favour gradual shifts in policy over 'shock treatment.' It would be more sensitive to distributional implications and especially to the importance of preserving and/or extending the provision of basic needs, goods and services. Above all it would seek to establish broad political support for adjustment efforts thereby maintaining, or even strengthening, democratic institutions. Such a package would undoubtedly imply less reliance on unfettered market forces and greater use of selective direct controls (including exchange controls, import controls, some price control and a general incomes policy) than would orthodox packages. It would avoid a blanket commitment to an outward-oriented economy. It would put national economic integration and the meeting of basic needs to the forefront of economic strategy. In consequence of the emphasis on more gradual and more equitable adjustment, an alternative program would almost certainly require a different blend of finance and adjustment than the orthodox approach.

To elaborate, this alternative package is premised on the belief that the export-oriented model of growth cannot be a panacea for the Third World as a whole. On optimistic assumptions about global recovery and stability, this model should continue to afford steady growth opportunities for those countries already committed to it although, as we shall see, not necessarily at a rate that avoids a major debt crisis. For other countries as a group, this orientation will not be easily achieved and neither does it hold out the prospect of the types of growth rates experienced by the MEMs in the past. Economic policies should be tailored to these differing market realities and for most Third World countries this would suggest the use of selective, sector by sector, if not product by product, adjustment policies to take advantage of specific, clearly identified, export opportunities. The use of blunt, macro-, export-oriented policy approaches that presuppose limitless export possibilities at prevailing prices and which assume, moreover, that domestic adjustment can proceed quickly and smoothly, may succeed only in causing further economic and political upheaval. Likewise, an across-the-board, sudden, liberalization of imports may wreak irreversible havoc on local industry.

The choice of policy instruments for stablization should be determined, therefore, by the structural nature of the economy in question. In general, the balance of payments is likely to be more responsive to orthodox demand restraint and price adjustment measures (i) the greater is the substitutability of traded for non-traded goods; (ii) the fewer have been controls over imports; (iii) the greater has been the experience of the country in penetrating new export markets; and (iv) the more are financial markets integrated with those abroad. This suggests that the orthodox package is likely to be particularly suspect in low-income countries which have little flexibility structurally, relatively tight import budgets, little experience of export diversification and little access to foreign capital markets.

Even where structural characteristics are such that the balance of payments responds positively, this might be achieved at a high cost in terms of increased domestic disequilibrium. Thus it appears that orthodox measures designed to correct external imbalances are often likely to raise, rather than lower, inflation rates.[71] This is especially so in middle-income countries where urban classes and class conflict are more developed and where social/structural obstacles to increasing food production are often, seemingly, more intractable than elsewhere. This would reinforce the suggestion that policy instruments be used very selectively. It would also imply that 'shock treatment' in the form of large devaluations, sudden decontrolling of prices or abolition of subsidies is generally to be avoided if political legitimacy for the program as a whole is to be retained and authoritarian state intervention to be avoided.

The exchange rate issue is a particularly controversial one in both theory and practice. Critics of the orthodoxy argue that large, sudden, devaluations (greatly favoured by the IMF) often leave real effective exchange rates unchanged by generating large domestic price increases.[72] The evidence for this is drawn from the experience of countries which export manufactures which could be expected to have the 'right' elasticities for a devaluation to improve external competitiveness and to raise domestic supply. The case against sudden large devaluations could be expected to be even stronger in countries where export supply and import demand elasticities are lower. There is, therefore, an increasingly held view that, where needed, adjustments should preferably take the form of small relatively frequent changes in nominal exchange rates.[73]

It might be thought that the logical extreme of this argument would be to advocate the adoption of freely floating rates by underdeveloped countries once an 'equilibrium' level has been achieved. Some monetarists favour this arrangement.[74] Its appeal lies in reducing the need for foreign reserves and in taking the exchange rate out of the realm of policy management. These are not very persuasive arguments. As shown in Chapter 1 (Table 1.5) reserve holdings are in practice usually very low, perhaps no higher than would be needed for working balances under a floating exchange rate system. Rigidities in commodity markets and the narrowness of financial markets could possibly give rise to huge fluctuations in rates which might not be dampened by private arbitrage and which might mean considerable departure in short-term rates from the level felt to be desirable for long-term structural change in the economy.[75]

An intermediate position might be that of the crawling peg, as adopted by a number of Latin American countries.[76] This protects local currency returns to exporters by periodic preannounced depreciations tied to the domestic inflation rate. Unfortunately in a number of countries it has also given rise to large destabilizing capital account movements as large corporations sought to take advantage of international differentials in interest rates. The result has been that countries adopting the crawling peg have often been less successful in maintaining export competitiveness than those adopting small, gradual exchange rate changes.[77] The evidence is, however, ambiguous and the crawling peg might still be worthwhile considering by those countries which do not attract foreign capital in this way or by those maintaining exchange controls on capital movements.

It has been assumed so far that countries adopt only a single exchange rate. There is, however, a theoretical case to be made for multiple exchange rates. An exchange rate policy could be devised that concentrates price incentives on those commodities with the highest elasticities and to obtain the greatest shift in expenditures from the non-traded to the traded goods sector.[78] The case against the multiple exchange rates that would ensue is a practical one. It would be difficult to administer the system on a commodity-by-commodity basis and even where differentials are based on much broader transactions groupings (e.g., in Streeten's dual exchange rate proposal)[79] there is the possibility of abuse. Multiple exchange rate practices are also not permitted under Section 3 of Article VIII of the Articles of Agreement of the International Monetary Fund. Theoretically, it is possible to achieve the same results via export subsidies and import tariffs and in reality, many countries adopt this approach, an approach much favoured by critics of the orthodoxy, but one which raises management problems similar to those associated with multiple exchange rates.

It is to be stressed that most critics of conventional packages do not deny the need for general exchange rate adjustment in situations where, for reasons of domestic inflation, "the cost of production of a country's staple exports . . . had got seriously out of line with world prices expressed in terms of local currency at the prevailing rate of exchange."[80] Even in this situation however, a devaluation will be useful (i.e., the new real rate will be sustained) only if the income redistribution it implies is acceptable politically, so that speed and timing of adjustments are still relevant considerations. In all other situations (e.g., where inflation or balance of payments problems are globally induced and where income redistribution through inflation is resisted) generalized exchange rate changes are of questionable usefulness.

Caution in allowing world prices to influence domestic prices is but part of a broader concern that critics of the orthodoxy share over the desirability of allowing market forces to shape stabilization efforts. Structuralists hold that market prices are a poor guide to efficient resource allocation or to optimal investment in a context in which social costs and benefits deviate from private ones—which is especially likely when far-reaching structural change is taking place in the economy. At the same time, market-oriented decisions are often unacceptable on distributional grounds. These situations provide a powerful rationale for the widespread use of direct controls and for different types of state intervention in many Third World countries. As John Williamson has argued, Latin American experience suggests that prices are so "profoundly important . . . that markets cannot in general be trusted to set them."[81]

Socialists who believe that underdevelopment is rooted in the existing structures of production and distribution that manifest themselves as 'market forces' place particular emphasis on direct intervention. It is for this reason that physical planning replaced the market in the key sectors of the economy in the early stages of the transformation of those countries now described as 'communist.' Only after the initial structural transformation was completed, did some of these countries allow market forces to play an important role, and even then, unrestrained market forces are not allowed to influence a number of key sectors and many major decisions.[82] This is often inadequately appreciated by those justifying market-oriented stabilization programs for underdeveloped countries with socialist aspirations.[83]

A number of critics are concerned that, by emphasizing an outward-oriented strategy and a premature and excessive reliance on market forces, including world prices, orthodox stabilization programs would undermine efforts at national economic integration and frustrate attempts to meet the basic needs of people. Some socialists like Thomas would argue that, at best, an export strategy should be the outgrowth of a strategy of converging local demands with local needs (through income redistribution) and local needs with the local resource base.[84] Exports would then be residual once local needs have been met rather than the prime object of economic strategy. Such a 'convergence' strategy has much in common with, but is less autarkic than, the autocentred growth proposal of Samir Amin which involves socialist Third World countries delinking from the world economy to build up mass consumption and investment goods sectors.[85] Rather than withdrawing altogether from the international division of labour, countries pursuing a convergence strategy would gradually alter the terms on which they participate in it.

Not all countries pursuing strategies of national economic integration and aiming at providing minimal consumption requirements need be socialist. Thus the Lagos Plan of Action commits African signatories to these policies.[86] The objective in all cases is, however, the same; it is to strive to build up an internally propelled economy in which global instability has minimal, if any, negative impact on the ability of the nation to meet the basic needs of its citizens. In most Third World countries, this type of economic transformation would inevitably require the importation of machinery and capital goods in order to create a future domestic capability to produce these very items. Thus, ironically, it would initially generate enhanced demands for foreign exchange.[87] Not all of these demands are likely to be met by foreign borrowing or foreign aid and hence it would be necessary for some time to promote exports. Since an across-the-board commitment to outward-oriented growth would be directly in conflict with this strategy and since delinking obviously provides no answers to the question of securing necessary capital goods and technology, the case for selectively expanding exports seems valid even when the strategic thrust is an inward-looking one. This might involve selective incentives to specific sectors or commodities in the form of price increases, subsidies, preferential access to scarce consumption or investment goods, etc.

Unlike orthodox approaches, the alternative would, therefore, put the preservation of basic needs very much to the fore and would have a heavy emphasis on increasing food production. The distributional impact of stabilization would be clearly evaluated and the burden of adjustment shared throughout society in such a way as to safeguard minimal consumption standards. Government programs geared to the relatively poor in such areas as health, education, water supply and food subsidies would be protected as far as possible. Supply stimulation measures would receive priority and would be aimed first and foremost at increasing food supplies in order to guarantee food security for all. In more radical strategies of transformation, such as the 'convergence' or 'autocentred' strategy, the emphasis might be more on non-price incentives such as land redistribution and 'moral' suasion in the form of mass political campaigns. Where price incentives are used, it might be necessary to provide a protective cushion for the urban and rural poor through budget subsidization of the major staple or through minimum wage adjustment. In these ways, distributional considerations can be built into stabilization programs much more explicitly than they tend to be at this time.

There are, of course, limits to the extent to which the urban and rural poor can be shielded altogether from the costs of adjustment, given their relative importance in many Third World countries. If imbalances are large, the best that might be achievable even with a government committed to basic needs, and even on optimistic assumptions about supply response, might be a sharing of the burden of adjustment among different income groups.

It follows, therefore, that some degree of demand restraint on large sections of society may often need to be a feature even of alternative programs. Unfortunately, there is a long and sad history of Third World governments attempting to pursue utterly incompatible policies with regard to income distribution, growth and pricing with the result that unsustainable pressures are created both domestically and in terms of external balance. Populist and left-leaning governments have, historically, been particularly prone to such macro-economic distortions, being committed to policies which attempted to significantly redistribute income.[88] The resulting imbalances have probably been as much the product of resistance to these policies from powerful vested interests as they have of simple 'mismanagement', although it is the latter explanation which tends to find expression in the literature on stabilization.[89] Whatever their causation, however, imbalances need addressing and demand restraint will often be an essential element in the balancing process. What is at question, therefore, is not so much *the need* for demand restraint as the *degree, timing* and *distributional impact* of that restraint. On these issues, the critique of the orthodoxy would tend to lead to quite different prescriptions from what has become the norm.[90]

If adjustment is to proceed without 'shock treatment' in an equitable manner that aims specifically to preserve minimal consumption levels for the poor, and if adjustment policies are not to detract from efforts at national economic integration, then local savings deficiences and balance of payments deficits might take longer to rectify than they would under orthodox programs. For this reason, the need for external finance would be greater under this approach than under the orthodox one. It is not surprising, therefore, that critics of the orthodox approach to stabilization tend, in general, also to be stronger advocates of international monetary and financial reforms which would greatly increase the flow of financial resources to the Third World than do those subscribing to the orthodoxy.[91] Most Third World countries, and the poorest in particular, have little flexibility at this time; their pursuit of alternative stabilization approaches of the type sketched out will be almost impossible without both a redirection of current foreign financial flows and, more importantly, without a significant increase in those flows.[92] This should not be interpreted as a plea for an increase in the long-term dependence of Third World countries on foreign aid. On the contrary, as will be shown in Chapter 6, a strong case can be made that aid dependence by many countries is already excessive and has, in some instances, contributed to their current economic difficulties. Others would argue that aid dependence has also severely overburdened the institutional infrastructure of Third World governments, thereby undermining their capacity to govern.[93] In the medium-long-term, therefore, many countries would benefit by scaling down aid dependence. This is not likely to happen because of the vested political interests in aid in both recipient and donor countries. In the short-run, however, donors could play a key role in assisting Third World recovery by reducing project aid in favour of increased balance of payments or import support, since further project assistance at this juncture would simply *add* to balance of payments and domestic inflationary pressures rather than ameliorate them. In the chapters that follow, the major sources of external finance will be examined and assessed from the point of view of the contribution they might reasonably be expected to make to financing the stabilization programs of Third World countries;

particular emphasis will be laid on the compatibility of the 'conditionality' attached to them with the type of alternative approaches to stabilization suggested in this chapter.

Notes

[1] For a useful discussion of the relationship between finance and adjustment as well as the different approaches to adjustment, see Tony Killick, and Mary Sutton, "Disequilibria, Financing and Adjustment in Developing Countries" in *Adjustment and Financing in the Developing World—The Role of the International Monetary Fund*, ed. Tony Killick (Washington, D.C.: International Monetary Fund, 1982), pp. 48–72.

[2] Killick and Sutton distinguish between 'conventional' programs and 'new orthodox' programs—the former focusing on short-run stabilization while the latter adds a longer-term 'liberalization' element. In what follows the term 'orthodox' or 'conventional' will be used to mean the same as Killick and Sutton's 'new orthodox' since this approach has now become the convention. Ibid.

[3] See, for instance, Andrew Crockett, *International Money: Issues and Analysis* (London: Nelson, 1980), pp. 52–55.

[4] Michael G. Porter, "International Financial Integration: Long Run Policy Implications" in *Money and Finance in Economic Growth and Development*, ed. Edward S. Shaw (New York: Marcel Dekker, 1976), p. 283.

[5] Ibid., p. 282.

[6] For an elaboration of the role of exchange rate adjustment in orthodox programs, see William R. Cline, "Economic Stabilisation in Developing Countries: Theory and Stylized Facts" in *IMF Conditionality*, ed. John Williamson (Washington, D.C.: Institute for International Economics, 1983), pp. 176–181.

[7] Alejandro Foxley, "Stabilisation Policies and Their Effects on Employment and Income Distribution: A Latin American Perspective" in *Economic Stabilisation in Developing Countries*, ed. William R. Cline and Sidney Weintraub (Washington, D.C.: The Brookings Institute, 1981), pp. 196–198.

[8] Anne O. Krueger, "Interactions between Inflation and Trade Regime Objectives in Stabilisation Programs" in Cline and Weintraub, *Economic Stabilisation*, p. 111.

[9] See Foxley, "Stabilisation Policies and Their Effects" for a modern structuralist interpretation of instability in Latin America. For a general review of the monetarist-structuralist debate, see David Colman and Frederick Nixson, *Economics of Change in Less Developed Countries* (Oxford: Phillip Allan, 1979), pp. 271–286.

[10] S. van Wijnbergen, "Stagflationary Effects of Monetary Stabilisation Policies: A Quantitative Analysis of South Korea", *Journal of Development Economics*, Vol. 10, No. 2 (April 1982).

[11] Colman and Nixson, *Economics of Change*.

[12] See Anne O. Krueger, *Foreign Trade Regimes and Economic Development: Liberalisation Attempts and Consequences* (New York: Ballinger for the National Bureau of Economic Research, 1978), pp. 82–83.

[13] Foxley, "Stabilisation Policies and Their Effects", pp. 206–210.

[14] M. Bruno, *Stabilisation and Stagflation in a Semi-Industrialised Economy* (Jerusalem: Hebrew University of Jerusalem, December 1977) quoted in Foxley, "Stabilisation Policies and Their Effects", p. 217. As Foxley correctly points out, the weakness in this explanation is that it overlooks the fact that trade deficits must

somehow be financed and that a devaluation will also alter the value of these financial flows.

[15] Foxley, "Stabilisation Policies and Their Effects".

[16] The contractionary effects of devaluation are dealt with at length, from a structuralist perspective in Lance Taylor, *Structuralist Macroeconomics: Applicable Models for the Third World* (New York: Basic Books, 1983).

[17] Andrew D. Crockett, "Stabilisation Policies in Developing Countries: Some Policy Considerations", *IMF Staff Papers*, Vol. 28, No. 1 (March 1981), pp. 54–79.

[18] See, John Williamson, *The Open Economy and the World Economy* (New York: Basic Books, 1983), p. 153.

[19] M. S. Khan, "Import and Export Demand in Developing Countries", *IMF Staff Papers* (November 1974).

[20] R. M. Cooper, "Currency Devaluation in Developing Countries" in *Government and Economic Development*, ed. G. Rains (New Haven: Yale University Press, 1971); and M. Connolly and D. Taylor, "Adjustment to Devaluation with Money and Non-Traded Goods", *Journal of International Economics* (June 1976).

[21] Cooper, "Currency Devaluation"; and A. Bhagwat and Y. Onitsuka,"Export Import Responses to Devaluation Experience in the Non-Industrial Countries in the 1960's", *IMF Staff Papers* (July 1974).

[22] In Khan's study, all but one of the 15 countries studied had manufacturing sectors which, as early as 1960, contributed between 12 and 20% of GDP. See World Bank, *World Development Report*, 1982 (New York: Oxford University Press, 1982), Table 3.

Bhagwat and Onitsuka themselves conclude that "non-traditional exports [were] an important element in the export performance of many countries." All but 4 of the 15 countries they studied had manufacturing sectors which contributed more than 12% of GDP in 1960.

Cooper's study includes 11 of the 15 countries included in Khan's study but is even more biased in its findings because it also includes Canada, Spain and Iceland, classified by the IMF as "industrialized" and Korea and Israel, both of which are classified as "major exporters of manufactures."

[23] See Williamson, *The Open Economy*, p. 152.

[24] Ibid.; and Crockett, "Stabilisation Policies in Developing Countries".

[25] These and similar reservations about the usefulness of a general devaluation are elaborated upon in Nicholas Kaldor, "Devaluation and Adjustment in Developing Countries", *Finance and Development*, Vol. 20, No. 2 (June 1983), pp. 35–37.

[26] Wijnbergen, "Stagflationary Effects of Monetary Stabilisation Policies", p. 167.

[27] Alberto Giovannini, "The Interest Elasticity of Savings in Developing Countries: The Existing Evidence", *World Development*, Vol. 11, No. 7 (1983), p. 603.

[28] Anthony Lanyi and Saracoglu Riisdii, "The Importance of Interest Rates in Developing Countries", *Finance and Development*, Vol. 20, No. 2 (June 1983), pp. 20–23.

[29] Foxley, "Stabilisation Policies and Their Effects", pp. 210–215.

[30] Sidney Dell, "The International Environment for Adjustment in Developing Countries", *World Development*, Vol. 8, No. 11 (November 1980), pp. 833–842.

[31] Sidney Dell, et al., *Structural Adjustment Policies*, Report to the Group of Twenty-Four (Geneva: UNDP/UNCTAD, June 1981), p. 11.

[32] Krueger, "Interactions between Inflation and Trade Regime Objectives", pp. 87–91.

[33] This term is drawn from Michel Aglietta, *A Theory of Capitalist Regulation—The U.S. Experience* (New York: New Left Books, 1979).

[34] Bela Belassa has been an outspoken critic of ISI strategies. See, for instance, his "Structural Adjustment Policies in Developing Economies", *World Development*, Vol. 10, No. 1 (1982), pp. 23–38.

[35] Ibid.

[36] Ibid. See also, B. Belassa, Andre Barsony, and Anne Richards, *The Balance of Payments Effects of External Shocks and of Policy Responses to these shocks in Non-Opec Countries* (Paris: OECD Development Centre, 1981).

[37] Belassa, "Structural Adjustment Policies".

[38] Frederick Z. Jaspersen, "Adjustment Experience and Growth Prospects of the Semi-Industrial Economies", *World Bank Staff Working Paper*, No. 477 (August 1981), p. 20.

[39] Ronald McKinnon, comments on Carlos F. Diaz Alejandro's "Southern Cone Stablisation Plans!" in Cline and Weintraub, *Economic Stabilisation*, p. 146.

[40] A summary of the results of this study, from which the following quotations are drawn, is to be found in World Bank, *World Development Report*, 1984 (Discussion Proof, p. 2, 21).

[41] See, for instance, Michael Michaely, "Exports and Growth: An Empirical Investigation", *Journal of Development Economics*, Vol. 4, No. 1 (March 1977), p. 49–54; and his "Exports and Growth: A Reply", *Journal of Development Economics*, Vol. 6, No. 1 (March 1979), pp. 141–143.

[42] Rosemary Thorp and Lawrence Whitehead, eds., *Inflation and Stabilisation in Latin America* (London: Nelson, 1980), pp. 52–55.

[43] Belassa, "Structural Adjustment Policies"; and McKinnon, see footnote 39 above. Many other proponents of the orthodoxy would, of course, share the view that Chile is an extreme and unfortunate case.

For three penetrating analyses of the weak theoretical base of the Chilean experience of stabilization policies, see Joseph Ramos, "The Economics of Hyper-stagflation—Stabilisation in Post 1973 Chile", *Journal of Development Economics*, Vol. 7(1980), pp. 467–488; Ricardo Ffrench-Davis, "The Monetarist Experiment in Chile: A Critical Survey", *World Development*, Vol. 11, No. 11 (1983), pp. 905–926; and Alejandro Foxley, *Latin American Experiments in Neo-Conservative Economics* (Berkeley: University of California Press, 1983).

[44] John Sheahan, "Market Oriented Economic Policies and Political Repression in Latin America", *Economic Development and Cultural Change*, Vol. 28, No. 2 (January 1980), pp. 267–291.

[45] Ibid., p. 291.

[46] Carlos F. Diaz Alejandro, "Open Economy Closed Polity" (Economic Growth Centre, Yale University, Discussion Paper 390, December 1981, Mimeo.), p. 40.

[47] Foxley, *Experiments in Neo-Conservative Economics*, pp. 195–196.

[48] Ibid., pp. 196–205.

[49] See comments by Arnold C. Harberger on Foxley in Cline and Weintraub, *Economic Stabilisation*, p. 229.

[50] E.g., Carlos F. Diaz Alejandro, "Southern Cone Stabilisation Plans" in Cline and Weintraub, *Economic Stabilisation*, p. 133.

[51] See, for instance, the statement by the Chairman of the Bank of Montreal concerning loans to South Africa in *The Globe and Mail* (Toronto), February 27, 1978.

[52] Adolfo Canitrot, "Discipline as the Central Objective of Economic Policy: An Essay on the Economic Programs of the Argentine Government since 1976", *World Development*, Vol. 8 (1980).

[53] IMF, *World Economic Outlook* (Washington, D.C.: IMF, 1984), p. 220.

[54] What follows draws heavily on Paul Streeten's "A Cool Look at Outward-Looking Strategies for Development", *The World Economy*, Vol. 5, No. 2 (September 1982), pp. 159–169.

[55] Jaspersen, "Adjustment Experience and Growth Prospects", p. 21.

[56] E.g., Michaely, "Exports and Growth"; Peter S. Heller and Richard C. Porter, "Exports and Growth: An Empirical Re-Investigation", *Journal of Development Economics*, Vol. 5, No. 2 (June 1978); and G. K. Helleiner,"Outward Orientation, Import Instability and African Economic Growth, An Empirical Investigation" (Toronto: University of Toronto, April 1984, mimeo.).

[57] Belassa, "Structural Adjustment Policies", pp. 24–25.

[58] James H. Caporaso, "Industrialisation in the Periphery: The Evolving Global Division of Labour" in *World System Structure*, eds. W. L. Hollisi and J. N. Rosenau (London: Sage, 1981), p. 168. Hong Kong seems to have been an exception in this respect.

[59] For an elaboration of these points see Manfred Bienefeld,"Efficiency, Expertise, NIC's and the Accelerated Development Report", *IDS Bulletin*, Vol. 14, No. 1 (January 1983), pp. 18–23; and R. H. Green, "Things Fall Apart: the World Economy in the 1980's", *Third World Quarterly*, Vol. 15, No. 1 (January 1983), p. 85.

[60] Foxley, "Stabilisation Policies and Their Effects".

[61] For a review of the literature on the distributional impact of stabilization programs, see Cline, "Economic Stabilisation in Developing Countries", pp. 191–195.

[62] The relative success of growth with equity programs in Taiwan has much to do with land redistribution in that country. See Wayne E. Nafziger, *The Economics of Developing Countries* (California: Wadsworth, 1984), Chapter 5. This in turn, is probably best explained by the pressure of example from the People's Republic of China.

[63] For instance, Krueger mentions increased food production as being of possible importance for stabilization but only in the context of a "chance" occurrence of a good harvest (see Krueger, "Interactions between Inflation and Trade Regime Objectives", pp. 103–104). She does not follow this through to its logical conclusion and argue that enhanced food production might be a desirable key element in adjustment policies for many Third World countries, and that donors might usefully focus their attention on aid to food production for both stabilization *and* equity reasons (pp. 113–114).

[64] The notion of entitlement is central to A. K. Sen's analysis of famine and food insecurity. See his *Poverty and Famines: an essay on entitlement and deprivation* (Oxford: Clarendon Press, 1981).

[65] The judgement of many authors is that the net effect on income distribution of applying the 'Green Revolution' in non-socialist economies has nevertheless still been negative. See Nafziger, *The Economics of Developing Countries*, p. 116; and Kathleen Gough, "Green Revolution in South India and North Vietnam", *Monthly Review*, Vol. 29, No. 8 (January 1978).

[66] W. R. Cline, "Can the East Asian Model of Development be Generalised?", *World Development*, Vol. 10, No. 2 (1982), pp. 81–89.

[67] IMF, *World Economic Outlook*, 1984, pp. 67–72, 157–162, 218–222.

[68] Ibid., p. 158.

[69] Green has reached similar conclusions while Diaz Alejandro remains optimistic about the *selective* trade prospects of Third World countries. See Green, "Things Fall Apart"; Diaz Alejandro, "Open Economy-Closed Polity", p. 44.

[70] The Arusha Initiative, which was endorsed by a number of prominent academics and officials from, or concerned with, the Third World, contains a number of policy recommendations similar to those which follow. See *Development Dialogue*, no. 2 (1980). The author was involved in drawing up a stabilization program for Tanzania during 1981/82 which embodied many of the approaches described here viz: adjustment with equity and growth; a gradualist, selective approach to the choice of policy instruments, etc. See *Structural Adjustment Programme for Tanzania* (Dar es Salaam: Ministry of Planning and Economic Affairs, June 1982) for the official, revised, version of this program. Competent but generally critical summaries of structuralist approaches to stabilization are to be found in Killick and Sutton, "Disequilibria, Financing and Adjustment", pp. 64–66; and in Cline, "Economic Stabilisation in Developing Countries", pp. 182–186. Thorp and Whitehead present a more sympathetic but still critical review of structuralist approaches (see Thorp and Whitehead, *Inflation and Stabilisation in Latin America.*).

[71] Donal J. Donovan, "Macroeconomic Performance and Adjustment under fund Supported Programs: The Experience of the Seventies", *IMF Staff Papers*, Vol. 29, No. 2 (June 1982).

[72] Romeo M. Bautist, "Exchange Rate Variations and Export Competitiveness in Less Developed Countries Under Generalised Floating", *Journal of Development Studies*, Vol. 18, No. 3 (1982).

[73] Ibid. See also the Brandt Commission, 1983 *Common Crisis* (London: Pan, 1983), pp. 63–64. Arguments in favour of such an approach by Tanzania are outlined in R. H. Green, "Political-Economic Adjustment and IMF Conditionality: Tanzania 1974–81" in Williamson, *IMF Conditionality*, p. 366.

[74] There was some IMF pressure on Tanzania to adopt a freely floating exchange rate in 1981/82. See John Loxley, "Tanzania: Origins of a Financial Crisis" in *Banking on Poverty*, ed. Jill Torrie (Toronto: Between the Lines, 1983), p. 206; but this is not a position commonly associated with the IMF.

[75] Crockett, *International Money*, pp. 108–110.

[76] See John Williamson, *The Crawling Peg* (New Jersey: Princeton University, Essays in International Finance, No. 50, 1965).

[77] Bautist, "Echange Rate Variations and Export Competitiveness", p. 372.

[78] D. Schydlowsky, "Alternative Approaches to Short Term Economic Management" in Killick, *Adjustment and Financing in the Developing World*, pp. 105–135.

[79] Paul Streeten, "The Developing Countries in a World of Flexible Exchange Rates", *International Currency Review* (January–February 1971).

[80] Kaldor, "Devaluation and Adjustment", p. 36.

[81] John Williamson, "A Comparison of Macro-economic Strategies in South America", *Development Policy Review*, Vol. 1 (1983), p. 33.

[82] This is argued, persuasively, in C. Y. Thomas, *Dependence and Transformation—The Economics of The Transition to Socialism* (New York: Monthly Review Press, 1974), pp. 232–242. It finds support in a useful summary of the experiences of China, Hungary, Romania and Yugoslavia—all of which have in recent years introduced 'reform models' to one degree or another—in Peter B. Knight, *Economic Reform in Socialist Countries* (World Bank Staff Working paper, No. 579, 1983).

[83] For example, John Williamson in his "The Lending Policies of the International Monetary Fund" in Williamson, *IMF Conditionality*, p. 653, fails to address this historical point.

[84] Thomas, *Dependence and Transformation.*

[85] Samir Amin, "Accumulation and Development: A Theoretical Model", *Review of African Political Economy*, No. 1 (1974).

[86] See *Lagos Plan of Action For the Economic Development of Africa 1980–2000* (Geneva: International Institute for Labour Studies, 1981). For a commentary on this and alternative strategies for Africa see Timothy N. Shaw, "The African Crisis: Alternative Development Strategies for the Continent", *Alternatives*, Vol. 9, No. 1 (Summer 1983). Riccardo Parboni also sees outward-oriented growth strategies as a threat to policies of national independence and non-alignment. See his *The Dollar and Its Rivals* (London: Verso, 1981), pp. 188–192.

[87] For an excellent discussion of the interelationship between long-term strategies of national integration and short-term management of economic crisis, see R. H. Green, "African Economies in the Mid-1980's" in Jerker Carlsson, *Recession in Africa* (Uppsala: Scandinavian Institute of African Studies, 1983), pp. 173–203.

[88] See Thorp and Whitehead, *Inflation and Stabilisation in Latin America*, p. 17; Foxley, "Stabilisation Policies and Their Effects", pp. 192–196, Killick and Sutton, "Disequilibria, Financing and Adjustment", p. 65.

[89] Examples are to be found in Williamson, "The Lending Policies of the IMF", p. 653; Killick and Sutton, "Disequilibria, Financing and Adjustment", p. 65; and, in an extreme form in Dudley Seers, "The Tendency to Financial Irresponsibility of Socialist Governments and its Political Consequences", *IDS Sussex Discussion Paper 161* (June 1981). This paper is the preface to Stephany Griffith Jones', *The Role of Finance in the Transition to Socialism* (Allanheld: Osmun & Co., 1981), which adopts a much more subtle approach to the problem, giving due weight to the political environment in which policy failures occurred.

[90] It is amazing that the unique features of the Tanzanian Structural Adjustment Program in this respect were completely lost on at least one, relatively orthodox, observer, Stanley Please. In *The Hobbled Giant: Essays on the World Bank*, he concluded that the differences between SAP and World Bank (he should have added IMF) advice "are dwarfed by their commonalities". See Stanley Please, *The Hobbled Giant: Essays on the World Bank* (Boulder: Westview Press, 1984), p. 94. Cheryl Payer has, more astutely, noted that SAP had a "radically different" class orientation from orthodox adjustment programs. See her "Tanzania and the World Bank", *Third World Quarterly*, Vol. 5, No. 4 (October 1983), p. 801.

[91]This is *not* to imply that those subscribing to the orthodoxy (e.g., the IMF and the World Bank) do not also see a need for more concessional assistance. See Chapters 4, 5 and 7.

[92] Skepticism over the likelihood of expanded concessionary flows leads some observers to conclude that most countries pursuing stabilization have no option but to apply shock treatment. See Joan M. Nelson, "The Politics of Stabilisation" in *Adjustment Crisis in the Third World*, eds. Richard E. Feinberg and Valeriana Kallab (Washington, D.C.: Overseas Development Council, 1984), pp. 99–118.

[93] See Elliott R. Morss, "Institutional Destruction Resulting from Donor and Project Proliferation in Sub-Saharan African Countries", *World Development*, Vol. 12, No. 4 (1984), pp. 465–470.

3

TRANSNATIONAL BANK FINANCE AND STRUCTURAL ADJUSTMENT IN THIRD WORLD COUNTRIES

Introduction

The current Third World financial and economic crisis appears most outstandingly in the form of a mountain of unserviceable debt. The majority of this debt, and an even greater portion of debt-service payments, is owed to a small group of private transnational banks by a small group of Third World countries. Sixty industrial country banks lending to 20 Third World countries roughly circumscribe the universe we are dealing with here.[1]

The objective of this chapter will be to examine the growth in debt over the past decade and the form and meaning, both to debtors and creditors, of the term 'debt crisis'. To properly explain the vulnerability of the international banking system to this crisis it will be necessary to examine the evolution and workings of the Eurocurrency market, including the inter-bank mark, and the lending strategies of the banks. On the other side of the coin, the attractiveness and shortcomings of a debt-led growth strategy to borrowing countries, and the relationship between bank finance and the adjustment process, will also be discussed. The chapter will then outline the steps which have been taken by various national and international actors to ward off a banking crisis and will end with a review of how the debt burden of the Third World might evolve to 1990 according to IMF projections.

The Growth of Third World Debt and the Debt Crisis

The decade of the 1970s witnessed a veritable explosion of lending to Third World countries. Total debt outstanding rose from $130 billion in 1973 to over $800 billion by 1984 (Table 3.1), a compound growth rate of 18 percent p.a. The most rapid growth took place in debt advanced by the private sector and, within that category, in loans by financial institutions which grew by 30 percent p.a. over the period. Data on debt are notoriously

---

This chapter was written by John Loxley and Bruce Campbell.

Table 3.1

The Growth of Third World Debt ($ billion)

	1973	1977	1978	1979	1980	1981	1982	1983	1984[a]
Total	**130**	**329**	**398**	**472**	**560**	**647**	**725**	**768**	**812**
Short-Term Debt	18	52	64	76	107	128	148	126	97
Long-Term Debt	112	278	335	396	453	518	577	641	715
Long-Term Official Creditors	51	111	131	149	169	186	205	230	254
Long-Term Private Creditors	61	168	204	248	284	332	371	412	460
(of which financial institutions)	17	79	107	138	140	186	212	250	296
Debt as % of Exports	115	125	132	119	109	120	142	151	145
Debt as % of GDP	22	25	26	25	25	28	33	37	38

[a]Estimate

Source: International Monetary Fund, *World Economic Outlook* (Washington, D.C.: IMF, 1984; 1983 for 1973 figures).

Table 3.2

Gross External Debt and Bank Debt of Major Third World Borrowers ($ billion)

	Gross External Debt 1982	Bank Debt 1982
Argentina	38.0	25.3
Mexico	80.1	64.4
Ecuador	6.6	4.7
Brazil	85.5	55.3
Chile	17.2	11.8
Venezuela	29.5	27.2
Colombia	10.3	5.5
Philippines	16.6	11.4
Peru	11.5	5.2
Turkey	22.8	4.0
S. Korea	36.0	20.0
Thailand	11.0	4.8
Egypt	19.2	5.4
Yugoslavia	18.5	10.0
Algeria	16.3	7.7
Indonesia	25.4	8.2
Taiwan	9.3	6.4
Nigeria	9.3	6.7
Malaysia	10.4	5.3
Morocco	10.3	3.7
Total	**488.8**	**293.0**

Source: Morgan Guaranty Trust Company of New York, *World Financial Markets* (February 1983), p. 5.

unreliable but some claim that when short-term debt is included, bank debt now accounts for between 55 and 60 percent of Third Word debt;[2] data from the Bank for International Settlements, however, put the figure at $350 billion or just under 50 percent of the total in 1982.[3]

About 80 percent of the bank debt and two-thirds of debt of all types owed by the Third World has been borrowed by no more than 20 countries; of these, the *nine* largest borrowers account for 66 percent of bank debt and almost 50 percent of total debt owed by the Third World (see Table 3.2).

Taking the 1973–84 period as a whole, the growth of debt owed by Third World countries outstripped that of their exports and GDP. The sharp rise in the debt burden on these measures since 1980 (Table 3.1) clearly indicates the onset of the debt crisis. This crisis took the form of an inability on the part of several borrowers (large and small) to meet their debt-servicing commitments or annual interest and amortization payments. Such payments more than doubled between 1978 and 1982, to $124 billion (Table 3.3), some $30 billion in excess of the total current account deficits

Table 3.3

Debt-Service Payments by Third World Countries

	1973	1977	1978	1979	1980	1981	1982	1983	1984
Total ($ billion)	**18**	**40**	**55**	**71**	**88**	**114**	**124**	**115**	**123**
Interest	7	15	21	32	47	64	72	67	75
Amortization of Long-Term Debt	11	25	33	40	41	50	52	47	48
Debt Service Ratio (% of exports)	16	15	18	18	17	21	24	23	22
of which, Interest Payments Ratio	6	6	7	8	9	12	14	13	13

Source: International Monetary Fund, *World Economic Outlook* (Washington, D.C.: IMF, 1984; 1983 for 1973 figures).

Table 3.4

Two Measures of the Debt-Servicing Burden of Major Third World Borrowers, 1982

	(a) All Interest Payments Plus Amortization of Medium-/Long-term Loans		(b) All Interest Payments Plus Total Amortization Payments (including short-term loans)	
	1978	1982	1978	1982
Argentina	28	103	70	179
Mexico	59	59	124	129
Ecuador		22[a]	74	122
Brazil	55	87	84	122
Chile	45	60	74	116
Venezuela	15	21	62	95
Colombia		24[a]	48	94
Philippines	23	36	53	91
Peru	32	53	142	90
Turkey	16	17[a]	164	68
S. Korea	11	21	27	53
Thailand	15	17[a]	38	48
Egypt	22	39	42	48
Yugoslavia	15	30	20	46
Algeria	29	41	42	39
Indonesia	15	11	36	27
Taiwan	6	6[a]	16	21
Nigeria	6	5	7	20
Malaysia		5	18	17
Morocco	n/a	36	n/a	65

[a]1981 Source: Organization for Economic Cooperation and Development, *Debt of Developing Countries* (Paris: OECD, October 1981).
Source: Morgan Guaranty Trust Company of New York, *World Financial Markets*, (October 1982).

of the Third World in that year. As a proportion of export earnings debt servicing rose from 18 to 24 percent over that four-year period.

Average figures for the burden of debt and its annual servicing do not, however, show the extent of the debt crisis as clearly as do figures for individual, major-debtor countries. Amortization of medium/long-term debt and payment of interest on all forms of debt (including short-term debt) rose to extraordinarily high proportions of annual export earnings for a half of the 20 major debtors and for six out of the nine largest debtors between 1978 and 1982 (Table 3.4, column a). But even those high ratios, between 30 and 100 percent of exports, understate the seriousness of the crisis. When short-term debt repayments are included, as they should be if there is any question of them not rolling over more or less automatically, then the debt-servicing burden for the nine largest debtors rose to unheard of levels of between 90 and 180 percent of exports. For seven of these the interest burden alone was in excess of 20 percent of exports.[4] By comparison, when Latin American countries defaulted on debt payments in the 1930s, debt-servicing ratios were in the range of 16-33 percent.[5]

A further, useful measure of the extent of the debt crisis is the calculation of the payments gap of Third World countries. This is the difference between their foreign reserves and unused lines of credits on the one hand and debt-service payments due plus short-term debts in excess of normal trade debts (defined as the equivalent of six months' imports) on the other. Between 1978 and 1982 this gap rose from zero to $45 billion.[6]

The immediate impact of the debt crisis was a slowing down in the rate of overall new lending to Third World countries (Table 3.5). By 1982 the increase in net lending (new loans minus amortization of old loans—short- and long-term) was barely sufficient to offset interest payments on past debt. In 1983 and 1984 it is estimated that the net flow of finance to Third World countries on account of debt transactions was negative to the tune of $24 and $31 billion respectively. This reversal is largely associated with a cut back in bank lending to Third World countries after the Mexican debt crisis, and took the form mainly of a reduction in banks' short-term loan exposure.[7] With the exception of increased lending to Mexico and Brazil as part of special arrangements with these countries, to be discussed below, bank lending to non-oil developing countries declined sharply early in 1983.[8] In the first half of that year gross new lending by banks to these countries fell to only $6.6 billion compared with $20.3 billion in the same period of 1982.[9]

While, initially, banks were responding to a deterioration in the export prospects and debt-servicing capacity of major exporters of manufactures, by 1983 they were also retreating from oil exporting countries as oil prices fell significantly. It is to be noted, therefore, that the debt crisis now encompasses both large (Nigeria, Venezuela and Mexico) and relatively small (Bolivia, Ecuador and Peru) oil exporting countries.[10]

Proximate Causes of the Debt Crisis

If the debt crisis is defined as an inability (short- or long-term) to finance debt servicing out of export earnings then one can usefully analyze the proximate causes of the crisis in terms of the various factors having a negative impact on the three components of the debt-servicing ratio; that is, on

$$\frac{\text{principal payments} + \text{interest payments}}{\text{export earnings}}$$

In short, the debt crisis came to a head in 1982 because of sharp increases in both elements of the numerator in this ratio, increases which also

Table 3.5

Net Financing Flows to the Third World

	1978	1979	1980	1981	1982	1983[a]	1984[a]
Net Flow of Lending (new borrowing minus amortization)	69	74	88	87	78	43	44
Interest Payments on Debt	21	32	47	64	72	67	75
Net Financing Flows	48	42	41	23	6	−24	−31

[a]Estimate

Source: Derived from International Monetary Fund, *World Economic Outlook* (Washington, D.C.: IMF, 1984).

coincided with absolute declines in the denominator (or in export earnings) for most major debtors.

Repayment of principal rose sharply in 1982 on account of an increase in maturing medium/long-term loans in that year, but more especially, due to marked changes in the maturity structure of bank finance dating back to 1978. In an increasingly uncertain world environment, banks sought to reduce risk by switching to short-term finance and away from longer maturities. At the same time some debtors were compelled to raise short-term borrowings to offset capital flight due to weak and inconsistent domestic policy management.[11] Evidence of this maturity shift can be gleaned from Table 3.1—short-term debt rising from 16 to 20 percent of the total between 1978 and 1982, and from the equivalent of 60 percent to 70 percent of long-term debt of financial institutions over that period. Data from other sources confirm this development. Thus the flow of short-term bank finance jumped from 25 percent of total non-European LDC bank flows in 1978 to 55 percent in 1981 and 53 percent in 1982.[12] The World Bank also reported that in Latin America short-term debt rose from 18 percent of the total in 1970 to 30 percent in 1982.[13] Between 1978 and 1982, the excess of short-term debt of ten major borrowers over the equivalent of six months imports (a rule of thumb for 'normal' short-term debt requirements) rose from $6 billion to $59 billion.[14] In summary, therefore, by 1982 Third World countries were facing particularly large debt maturities as well as the problem of 'rolling over' record levels of short-term debt.[15]

Compounding the problem was the sharp rise in interest rates from 1979, already discussed in Chapter 1. Since practically all bank debt (95 percent) has been contracted at variable interest rates,[16] the doubling of the London Inter-Bank Offered Rate (LIBOR—which governs the rate paid by Third World countries), from 8.7 percent in 1978 to 16.5 percent in 1981, had serious consequences for borrowing countries. Interest payments more than tripled during this period to $64 billion in 1981 (Table 3.3) and for the first time in the decade exceeded amortization payments. The share of interest payments in total debt servicing has risen steadily from 38 percent in 1978 to 56 percent in 1982 to an anticipated 61 percent in 1984. For Third World countries as a whole, every percentage point increase in LIBOR adds a further $6 billion to their annual debt-servicing burden.

Finally, this peaking of amortization and interest payments coincided with a sharp fall in the growth of Third World export earnings in 1981 and with an absolute decline in those earnings in 1982. Thus the *ability* of Third World countries to meet this massive increase in debt-servicing liabilities was undermined on the export side. It is interesting to note that for the period in question, only once before (1975) had export growth rates been lower than the interest rate on debt. The relationship between these two rates provides a rough guide to whether or not a country's debt burden is easing or deteriorating (the so-called Simonsen criterion).[17] Table 3.6 highlights the dramatic shift in this relationship in 1981–82 for non-oil LDCs and for some major debtors.

In order to fully comprehend the significance of the debt crisis, however, it is necessary to go beyond the simple arithmetical imperatives of the debt burden on borrowers and examine the vulnerability of the international banking system to a possible failure by borrowers to repay their debts.

Bank Vulnerability to the Debt Crisis

Direct Exposure

The inability of debtors to meet their debt-servicing commitments first surfaces in the form of growing arrears of principal and/or interest payments, and, subsequently, in the form of requests to renegotiate payments obligations. The ultimate danger for banks, of course, is that their debts will not be repaid at all and for many large transnational banks this danger is an extremely serious one.

Table 3.7 gives some indication of the direct exposure of North American banks, U.S. and Canadian, in Latin America. It shows that outstanding loans to the three largest debtors in that region are in excess of their shareholders' equity and reserves for the banks as a whole. All major banks are heavily exposed in this sense, some (e.g., Citicorps and Chase Manhattan), extremely so. It is to be borne in mind that this excludes loans to smaller Latin American debtors and to foreign debtors elsewhere. Exposure to Third World and Eastern European debt, two-thirds of which was subject to servicing problems in 1982/83, was closer to 300 percent of capital for the nine largest U.S. banks and to 200 percent for all U.S. banks in 1982.[18] European and Japanese banks are similarly exposed to major Third World (not to mention Eastern European) debtors. Indeed, at the end of 1981, 60 percent of total Third World bank debt was held by non-U.S.A. banks.[19] Non-payment of debt by one or more large borrowers would, therefore, directly threaten the financial stability of major banks in creditor countries.

Systemic Sources of Potential Instability

Direct exposure by banks is an obvious measure of creditor vulnerability to the debt crisis but it is far from being a complete one. International banking has become so complex and national banking systems so interdependent over the period of this study, that any threat to one bank can be rapidly transformed into a threat to the international banking system as a whole. In order to explain why this is so it is necessary to examine the structure of the world banking system and its evolution since the late 1960s.

The explosion of bank lending to Third World nations and the emergence of the banks as the principal source of international liquidity in the 1970s, could not have taken place without the existence of a transnational financial market—the Euromarket.[20] Only a quarter of international bank lending takes the form of domestic currency loans—that is, loans denominated in the national currency of the country where the lending bank is located.

Table 3.6

Export Growth Compared with Interest Rates, 1978–1982

	1978	1979	1980	1981	1982
LIBOR+ %	**9.7**	**13.0**	**15.4**	**17.5**	**14.1**
Nominal Export Growth (%)					
Non-Oil LDCs	**17.2**	**28.9**	**26.1**	**5.8**	**– 3.8**
Brazil	7.2	24.2	29.3	15.7	–13.4
Mexico	39.1	40.2	54.3	21.9	7.3
Argentina	16.3	26.6	13.0	5.1	–15.7
Korea	31.3	13.8	15.6	21.7	2.3
Venezuela	– 0.8	50.2	36.4	10.1	–22.0
Chile	13.8	59.0	32.2	– 2.6	– 3.8

Source: William R. Cline, *International Debt and the Stability of the World Economy* (Washington D.C.: Institute for International Economics, 1983), p. 19.

Table 3.7

Bank Exposure in the Top Three Latin American Countries: Outstanding Credit as Ratio of Capital[a]

	Brazil	Mexico	Venezuela or Argentina	Total Capital
U.S. Bank Holding Companies at 30/09/83				
Bank of America	0.48	0.54	0.31	1.33
Bank of Boston	0.30	0.23	0.27	0.80
Bankers Trust N.Y. Corp.	0.45	0.69	0.23	1.37
Chase Manhattan Bank	0.70	0.43	0.34	1.47
Chemical Bank	0.57	0.61	0.16	1.36
Citicorp (at 30/06/83)	0.82	0.62	0.20	1.64
Others	0.38	0.38	0.20	0.96
Canadian Banks				
Canadian Imperial Bank of Commerce	0.38	0.39	0.13	0.91
Bank of Montreal	0.50	0.63	0.23	1.36
Royal Bank of Canada	0.33	0.39	0.16	0.88
Bank of Nova Scotia	0.40	0.51	0.27	1.18
Toronto Dominion Bank	0.37	0.44	0.15	0.96
National Bank of Canada	0.84	0.84	0.20	1.88
Total	**0.44**	**0.43**	**0.20**	**1.07**

[a]These ratios have been adjusted to allow for errors in the source data in terms of addition and of converting Canadian dollars to U.S. dollars.

Source: Calculated from Dominion Bond Rating Service data in *The Globe and Mail* (Toronto), March 19, 1984.

Most international lending is denominated in currencies foreign to the country where the lending bank is located and the market for such loans, and the foreign deposits which finance them, is the Euromarket. Regardless of the original country of parentage, any bank which by authorization of the national banking authority where it is located, conducts business in foreign currencies is part of the Euromarket. Thus a London branch of a U.S. bank dealing in dollar deposits and loans is conducting Euromarket operations whereas when it deals in Sterling deposits and loans, even with foreign customers, it is not.

The Euromarket had its origins in London and the U.S. dollar was, and still is, the currency accounting for most transactions. The Euromarket has grown phenomenally since 1960 when estimates of its size were between $1 and $3 billion. By 1971 it had reached $100 billion and a decade later it had shot up to $1500 billion.[21] At that time it comprised an estimated 520 banks with 4,400 branches, 440 subsidiaries and 1,200 affiliates outside their headquartered counties.[22] In recent years, offshore banking centres in the Caribbean (Bermuda, the Bahamas, The Cayman Islands and Panama), Asia (Hong Kong and Singapore) and elsewhere have begun to draw Euromarket business away from London by offering lower taxes, easier regulations and other operating advantages. In an attempt to regain a share of international banking business it had lost to the Euromarket, in 1981 the U.S.A. allowed extraterritorial jurisdictions to be created within banks located in the U.S.A. (International Banking Facilities); in other words, Euromarkets have been set up within its borders. As a result of these developments, London now accounts for only about a third of all Euromarket activity.[23]

The growth of the Euromarket is best seen as a reflection of and, at the same time an important component of, the internationalization of capital that has characterized the post–World War II global economy. Its origins can be traced back to the expansion of U.S. transnational activities and the growth of the U.S. dollar as a reserve currency. Large and persistent U.S. balance of payments deficits and a desire of U.S. dollar holders to avoid government regulatory restrictions explain its genesis. At various times, U.S. domestic policy initiatives have inadvertently prompted a massive shift of dollars to the Euromarket. Regulation Q which limited interest rates to be paid on domestic bank deposits, the 1963 interest equalization tax, and the voluntary credit restraint program (1965) each had this effect.[24] Banks themselves find the Euromarket attractive because it is not subject to legal minimum reserve requirements and hence they can earn interest on deposits which would otherwise be idle. In fact, there is no machinery to regulate Euromarket transactions and while this is an attractive feature to banks, it is also a potential source of system vulnerability.

The Euromarket is attractive for other reasons too. It is a competitive market dealing in large transactions and as a result margins are lower than in domestic markets. Interest rates can be 'shaved' therefore to appeal both to depositors and to borrowers. Most deposits are typically short-term with a maturity of less than six months; one-fifth are for less than eight days. In practice, however, deposits are continually 'rolled over' or renewed at the interest rate prevailing at the time of maturity. Most deposits originate in industrialized capitalist countries, and although the Euromarket was given a significant boost by the inflow and recycling of petrodollars in 1973–74 and 1979–81, it must be stressed that even at their height, OPEC deposits never constituted more than 10 percent of total Euromarket deposits.[25]

Ninety percent of Euromarket lending has taken the form of loans, the balance of bonds,[26] loans being considered more flexible and easier to assemble. Unlike those on bonds, interest rates on loans are variable and adjusted throughout the life of the loan in line with market conditions. In practice, while loans are contracted for between three to eight years, they are 'rolled over' every three to six months to adjust interest to changes in LIBOR. Given the fact that the average maturity period of loans is so much greater than that for deposits, the roll-over technique serves to enable banks to shift onto the borrower some of the earnings risks inherent in this *mismatching* of maturities. The volatility of deposits relative to loans remains, however, yet another potential source of system vulnerability.

In lending to Third World countries, individual banks have sought to minimize their risk by participating in loan syndicates. Many banks take a 'piece' of a given loan syndicate thereby spreading risk widely. At the same time cross default clauses are written into these loan agreements to maintain discipline among creditors both within and across syndicates[27] and, moreover, to serve as a powerful sanction against would-be recalcitrant debtors. It is conceivable, however, that the existence of such clauses could themselves prompt an irrational herd response by banks to debtors encountering servicing difficulties; in particular, fears have been expressed that precipitate action by smaller regional banks might undermine the stability of larger banks participating in syndicates and, therefore, destabilize the banking system as a whole.

Most syndicated loans are arranged by an elite group of 'lead manager' banks which are typically the point of contact for Third World countries and which act as middlemen negotiating with the borrower on behalf of other syndicate members. In 1981, 20 banks lead-managed over 60 percent of all syndicated loans, putting up roughly one-third of the finance themselves.[28] Lead managers collect a one time syndication fee and usually act as repayment agent for which a further small fee is levied. Otherwise, syndicated loans carry a lending margin over LIBOR which varies with the debtor. In 1980, this margin or 'spread' was between 0.5 percent and 1.5 percent for major debtors, but with the onset of the debt crisis it has risen significantly to between 1.63 percent and 2.5 percent.[29] This added margin applied mainly to Third World debt which has been renegotiated, since new syndicated lending has virtually collapsed since 1982.[30]

At the heart of the Euromarket is the *inter-bank market* believed by some to be the Achilles' heel of the whole international banking edifice.[31] It is here that deposits are transferred or taken in from domestic commercial banks, transnational corporations, central banks, states, governments and public enterprises and then lent and relent throughout a large network of banks, thereby expanding the original liquidity base. Its size is now roughly $1 trillion and comprises 60 percent of total Euromarket operations. It is 10 to 12 times the size of the syndicated loan market and it is here that the reference price for syndicated loan transactions is set, LIBOR being the average interest rate at which the large 'money centre' banks located in London offer funds to other banks.

The 'money centre' banks include the eight or nine largest New York banks and a limited number of banks headquartered in Britain, Germany, Japan, France and Canada. Their defining characteristic is that they contribute surpluses to the inter-bank market. In doing so, they earn a return without contravening prudential limits of assets to deposits (since these assets are highly liquid and, therefore, constitute reserve assets), nor country lending exposure limits (since the country destination of funds is non-specific). These 'money centre' banks also determine which banks will have access to the inter-bank market and the terms on which they will be allowed access. By determining the volume and price of funds available to other banks, the 'money centre' banks play a key role in determining the liquidity creating potential of the inter-bank market. For many banks the inter-bank market is the dominant source of Euro-deposits, and especially so for Canadian, Swiss and Japanese banks.[32] Some Eastern European and Third World countries have also been allowed to participate in this inter-bank market using borrowings to finance balance of payments deficits. Hungary suffered a major financial crisis when inter-bank funds were withdrawn following the Polish debt debacle.[33] Mexican banks were revealed to have borrowed $6 to $7 billion on this market when its own debt crisis broke in 1982.[34] Its threat to freeze repayment of these inter-bank loans (i.e., lumping them in with the rest of its debt), spread panic as the banks pondered scenarios for a chain reaction of defaulting banks all tightly interlocked in the inter-bank market. The conflict was resolved when the transnational banks agreed, under prompting from their central banks, not to withdraw their inter-bank deposits with Mexican banks once they matured. Interest spreads were, however, raised significantly. Brazil has experienced similar problems with its inter-bank borrowing but has been, seemingly, less successful in retaining them.[35]

The Euromarket is closely integrated with the major national money and financial markets and is especially sensitive to U.S. economic conditions. Eurodollar certificates of deposit of U.S. money centre banks compete with American government Treasury Bills for dollar savings. When U.S. interest rates rose after 1979, rates in the Euromarket quickly followed them. Ultimately, therefore, it is the U.S. authorities who have the final rein on Euromarket liquidity since they control its cash base. They also exercise a brake on finance to Third World debtors because of their influence on interest costs, on global economic conditions, on export earnings and, hence, on bankers' perceptions of creditworthiness.

The U.S.A. does not, however, *regulate* the Euromarket and neither does any other state. Transcending national jurisdictions, the inter-bank market and the Euromarket as a whole are in a quasi-regulatory limbo. In particular, there is no formally declared official lender of last resort in the event of a collapse of international banking. In 1974, following the collapse of the Herstaat Bank in Germany and the Franklin National in the U.S.A., the Bank for International Settlements established a Committee on Banking Regulations and Supervisory Practices (The Cooke Committee). This has attempted to introduce a uniform approach to bank regulation and supervision within the Group of Ten (plus Switzerland and Luxemburg) and to establish responsibility for ensuring solvency and liquidity among parent and host country authorities.[36] But its recommendations are non-binding and have in practice been subject to a wide variety of conflicting interpretations.[37]

The Euromarket is a highly competitive market and banks oppose any moves by government which have the effect of reducing their competitiveness, and therefore their profits, in this market. In the U.S., state intervention has been confined to controlling only those Euromarket flows which transparently affect the Federal Reserve's ability to regulate domestic money supply and even then, in the face of strong bank opposition.[38] While the Federal Reserve believes that Euromarket transactions should be subject to reserve requirements, along the lines of domestic banking transactions, it has refrained from imposing them on U.S. banks because European states have not agreed to them. Any unilateral imposition on U.S. banks would, therefore, "simply (force) the removal of U.S. banks from this lucrative market,"[39] shifting business to 'softer' centres.

Whether or not parent country central banks would assume responsibility in practice and assist banks experiencing solvency problems is unclear. There is a good deal of opposition to 'bailing out the banks' and certainly the Bank of Italy refused to assist a Luxemburg affiliate of the Banco Ambrosiano when their bank collapsed.[40] Compounding this uncertainty and heightening the vulnerability of the system globally is the fact that there is no uniformity internationally in deposit insurance arrangements. Coverage varies greatly with respect to amounts, ownership, type of currency, territorial scope and treatment of inter-bank deposits. The impact of default or repudiation on the system as a whole would depend very much on how national arrangements affect inter-bank and other forms of international business and, of course, on the speed with which the state undertook lender-of-last-resort functions if these were required.

In summary, the Euromarket mechanism on which international bank debt rests, is a very precarious one. The highly integrated nature of world banking, the potential volatility of the deposit base of the inter-bank market, the fundamental mismatching of maturities within the Euromarket generally, the unregulated nature of that market and the absence of any clear lender of last resort, all combine to suggest that debt difficulties encountered by one or more large debtors or creditors could quickly reverberate throughout the whole world banking system, exposing all banks to risk and causing chaos in the world trade and payments system.

Before turning to an analysis of how the debt crisis has been managed since the early 1980s to head off the possibility of an international banking collapse, it is important to examine why and on what basis transnational banks channelled so much credit to the Third World in the 1970s and why Third World countries were attracted to a debt-led growth strategy.

The Attractiveness of the Third World Debt Market

Transnational bank lending to Third World countries was not great before 1970. It was confined to short-term trade finance. A few countries, notably Brazil and Mexico, were gaining access to the international (Euro-) bond market in the late 1960s. Several factors changed this in the early 1970s. The Euromarket was expanding rapidly. Its higher, risk-adjusted yields were attracting funds and it was beginning to discover the enormous potential for expanding its own lending capacity.

In 1972 there was a huge speculative outflow of dollars from the United States pulled by the prospect of a weakening dollar exchange rate under the Smithsonian exchange rate system and through differential monetary policies being pursued by Germany (tight) and the United States (loose). Most of those dollars ended up in the Euromarket. This was followed closely by the oil price increase and a surge of petrodollars into the Euromarket. At about the same time Europe and Japan imposed regulations on U.S. bank branches which curtailed their lending to corporate co-nationals in these countries. Increasingly, 'cash rich' transnational corporations were using intra- and inter-company financing as an alternative to bank financing. Meanwhile, the 1974–75 recession reduced credit demand in industrialized capitalist countries. The Euromarket was, therefore, a market in search of profitable outlets for surplus funds.

The decline of traditional Euromarket profit opportunities for U.S. banks was paralleled by a commodities boom and the rapid expansion of export manufacturing in some Third World countries. Bankers' attention to these Third World markets was also attracted by larger interest spreads than those prevailing in existing markets and, for the largest banks, the additional management fees and commissions. (Although the importance of the latter in overall profits is widely recognized, it is difficult to precisely determine their role. Several observers have pointed out that they were a more important source of revenue for these banks than interest spreads.)[41] Moreover, having low external debt levels, they were virtually untapped markets and thus attractive targets in terms of banks' asset diversification objectives.

Publicized medium- and long-term lending by transnational banks to Third World countries rose from $0.8 billion in 1970 to $8.6 billion by 1973.[42] In the next three years it doubled and by 1981 was running at $50 billion p.a. By that year, large U.S. and Canadian banks were earning almost half their total profits from Third World debt.[43] Most such debt was either to the public sector or guaranteed by the public sector with the result that between two-thirds and three-quarters of all debt owed by the Third World to private lenders is guaranteed.[44] Ultimately, however, in times of acute foreign exchange scarcity, the distinction between guaranteed and non-guaranteed borrowing blurs, since the monetary authorities control access to foreign exchange. It is significant that during the 1983 Chilean debt rescheduling, the government agreed to guarantee repayment of its huge private non-guaranteed debt.[45]

Underlying the expansion of bank lending to the Third World was, therefore, a belief that 'countries do not go bankrupt' and that a guarantee, explicit or otherwise, would be meaningful. This was bolstered by a widely held view that default on loans had become unacceptable internationally since it carried with it damaging economic sanctions. Debt rescheduling had replaced default as an acceptable way of dealing with debt-servicing difficulties and new international mechanisms, with participation by creditor states and international institutions, had evolved to deal with rescheduling (discussed later in this chapter). Since World War II only North Korea (1949) has actually defaulted, although Ghana underwent a partial default in 1966. In this situation, transnational banks were able to lend massive sums of money to Third World countries without paying too much attention to the details of what 'creditworthiness' might imply.

The Assessment of Creditworthiness

Creditworthiness embodies the bankers' assessment of the debtors' ability and willingness to pay off their loans. The concentration of Third World debt in a handful of countries rich in natural resources and/or with dynamic export manufacturing sectors reflects the priority banks attach to foreign exchange earnings as a measurement of creditworthiness. The creditworthiness of these countries implied that debt servicing would be assigned top priority in allocating foreign exchange, and that the political structure was sufficiently stable (often, as shown above, through the use of state repression) that an economic crisis or change in leadership would not jeopardize the continuity of existing economic priorities or policies.[46] Bankers' assumptions regarding Third World creditworthiness were conditioned, above all, by an expectation that growth prospects were sound and that access to industrial country markets would be maintained or even expanded. It is not surprising that bankers emerged as champions of freer trade and greater market access in the 1970s.

Systematic approaches to country risk analysis only became commonly used in the mid–1970s, after much lending had already taken place. A 1976 survey found that nearly three-quarters of responding banks were using a 'structured qualitative' system involving an annual country report (more frequent for the largest borrowers) with a statistical analysis.[47] Countries were rated usually on a five-point scale. Some banks use, in addition, a 'checklist system' to further enhance cross country comparisons of risk. Points are assigned for foreign exchange performance and stability, for debt burden, economic policy, etc., each of which has a different weight, and overall risk is embodied in a single summary score reflecting the sum of weighted partial scores.

After the Nicaraguan and Iranian revolutions (1978), political risk analysis gained importance as part of banks' evaluation apparatus. With the onset of global recession it has become the most important part of country risk analysis.[48] Many banks now communicate extensively with their home government foreign affairs departments in developing their country risk profiles.[49] During periods of high debt-servicing burdens and declining earning capacity, the will and ability of governments to compress imports and economic activity in order to maintain service payments has become crucial. Sensitivity to political 'breaking points' was necessary since political turmoil would almost surely, as it had in the past, bring about a disruption in debt service flows.

The record of country risk analysis has been somewhat less than impressive. Even bankers themselves admitted that the approach was problematic and had failed to detect important trends.[50] Country risk evaluations were not generally used for determining the quality of specific loans nor for determining spreads or fees. Their main purpose was to assist in establishing overall lending or country exposure limits. Risk analysis techniques and assessments were not themselves subjected to independent evaluation, nor were they compared with past repayment experience. They were not used as part of a global asset management strategy and few banks examined the world political-economic environment as it affected the lending risk to individual economies.[51]

One of the most telling statements about the nature of bankers' creditworthiness evaluations came from a senior staff member of Morgan Guarantee Trust at a 1977 conference on sovereign risk. His reading of banks' creditworthiness assessments during the 1920s' wave of private lending to the Third World led him to the realization that:

> bankers in the 1920's used almost exactly the same basic factors in determining credit worthiness that are being used by most international lenders today. The defaults of publicly issued bonds which occurred in the early 1930's were not the result of inadequate country-by-country analysis by the bankers, but rather of their assumption that the favourable world economic trends of the early 1920's would continue forever. The faulty judgement led to over exuberance on the part of bankers during the second half of the 1920's and to a substantial number of defaulted bonds in the next decade.[52]

From the perspective of the present crisis, this statement was a remarkably, if unwittingly, prescient account of history repeating itself.

During periods of abundant liquidity, fashion and the herd instinct seemed to have dominated banks in the aggressive competition for borrowers, and risk considerations were relegated to a position of secondary importance. Banks' personnel incentive structures linked advancement to surpassing asset targets.[53] Particularly among medium-sized growth-oriented banks, when objectives of growth and risk conflicted, the latter was invariably sacrificed as they sought to break into new markets. Furthermore most banks relied heavily on risk assessments provided by lead managers. "In all but the five to ten largest banks, the most common decision for the majority of international loan officers in sovereign risk lending is whether or not to take a share of another bank's Eurocurrency credit."[54] The quality and objectivity of the information memorandum the lead manager prepared and circulated among potential participants in a given syndicated loan was suspect if only because of its vested interest in selling down the syndicate.[55] Finally, banks with sizeable commitments to borrowing countries in relation to their overall portfolios were under pressure to keep on lending due to mutual vulnerability considerations. These tended to override any contrary advice provided by risk assessment.

Thus, among the creditworthy and not so creditworthy, considerations of risk were understated; little attention was paid to the uses of borrowing or the potential yield of specific investment projects.

Only with generalized economic contraction, when creditworthiness perceptions tended to decline across the board as debtors faced growing repayment problems, did risk analysis departments gain prominence in bank decision making. Thereafter, new lending became more closely scrutinized but, by that time, with herd instinct working in reverse, little new lending was being made to Third World countries.

The Attractions and Shortcomings of Bank Finance to Third World Countries

Compared with other types of finance, bank credit has characteristics which are extremely appealing to Third World countries. It is disbursed very quickly and is available for almost immediate use. It can be used to finance the import costs of projects or a deficit on the balance of payments generally. In any event, it is *fungible* in that even where acquired for one specific purpose, it frees existing foreign exchange for other uses. At the same time, bank credit can equally be used to finance government budget deficits or the local costs of projects. Once a country has been declared creditworthy, there is no overt 'conditionality' applied to steer economic policy in a direction deemed desirable by the lender. Banks' conditionality is implicit in their standards of creditworthiness. Once committed to a country, if they feel a change of economic policy is required, they rely on the IMF, World Bank or informal pressure to bring this about. Having tried, unsuccessfully, in the past to impose conditionality on a borrower (Peru 1976), banks have come to realize that they lack the technical expertise, data and monitoring capabilities to do the job properly.[56] Above all they shy away from the political implications of this role. Political considerations are, however, less of a factor in the initial decision to lend than they often are for official bilateral and multilateral sources of finance.

For these reasons, bank credit has been a much more flexible form of finance for Third World countries than almost all other options. Equally importantly, throughout the decade of the 1970s banks had an enthusiasm to lend that was matched by no other source of finance. Kindleberger's graphic description of the first wave of bank finance (1972–73) was as valid at the end of the decade as at the beginning: "multinational banks, swollen with dollars, tumbled over one another in trying to uncover new foreign borrowers and practically forced money on the less developed countries."[57]

In the 1970s, bank finance invariably provided Third World borrowers a greater range of policy options. Many relied heavily on bank credit to diversify their economies, building infrastructure or factories that supported outward-oriented strategies. These longer-term *structural adjustments*, in countries like Brazil, Mexico and South Africa, would simply not have occurred at the same rate, if at all, without access to bank credit. Bank finance has also been used (by these as well as other countries) to enlarge the financial cushion traditionally provided by international reserves. Borrowers have used it to *finance* the maintenance of import levels and, therefore, of output and employment, during periods of cyclical downturn or external shocks. Credit has also permitted debtors to finance government and public enterprise budget deficits and, on occasion, has been pursued as a means of reducing inflation. At times, it has been instrumental in enabling Third World governments to expand their military spending. For most borrowers, credit has been used for more than one such purpose.[58]

Thus, bank credit was drawn upon both for financing short-term stabilization programs and for facilitating longer-term adjustment. On occasion it was used to avoid the painful adjustments needed to rectify imbalances and sometimes, squandered on obvious non-productive purposes occasionally permitting large scale capital flight by the private sector.[59] On the whole, however, taking large borrowers as a group, the evidence appears to show that for the decade of the 1970s, foreign borrowing was associated with increases in both the domestic savings rate and the investment rate—crude indications that, on balance, foreign borrowing was generally used productively.[60]

Some writers seem to suggest a close relationship between Third World bank borrowing and increases in their oil import costs. At best this relationship was a weak one in the first oil shock and non-existent in the second, largely because 11 of the 18 major debtors are net oil exporters and because for the others, export earnings and import substitution policies helped cushion the negative impact of higher oil prices.[61]

By the end of the 1970s, most new credits were being used to service older ones and by the early 1980s the net flow of bank finance had become negative. By that time the debt-led strategies of most major borrowers were in a shambles. Rather than helping to offset cyclical fluctuations in the world economy, as they had during both oil price increases through the prompt and, at a technical level, 'efficient' recycling of OPEC surpluses, banks acted in a manner that accentuated them. The volatility of bank flows and the herd instinct shaping them combined with high interest rates to make bank debt least available and most expensive at the very time when, for current account balance of payments reasons, it was most needed and when high costs could be least afforded. Servicing the mountain of debt has now become the chief preoccupation of debtor governments, deflecting attention and resources away from longer-term growth considerations.

During the early borrowing euphoria, many Third World policy-makers ignored the basic structural constraint within which transnational banks operate; namely, that they are profit-making institutions whose investments require immediate commercial rates of return. They played down the obvious asymmetries between bank finance and the needs of development projects which often require long gestation periods before they yield returns and, even then, returns which may only be measured in social terms and not in hard currency.[62] Thus, a Third World country which has become heavily indebted to the banks must either focus on investment projects with high short-term commercial yields and wait for benefits to 'trickle down' to the population, a strategy with a decidedly dubious success rate; or it may include a mix of longer-term development projects on the assumption that the banks will roll over maturing medium-term credit on reasonable terms. The present reality bears witness to the dangers of this assumption.

A closely related consequence of a debt-led strategy (one might call it the essence of bank conditionality) is that debtors must assign top priority to maintaining external balance or to achieving it within the short- to medium-term. A strategy of heavy reliance on bank debt means, therefore, that policies and projects are chosen with a view to ensuring a strong debt-servicing capacity. These may well supersede or detract from other equally, or even more, desirable national objectives; for example, of meeting basic needs or of laying down longer-term yielding infrastructure. When bank flows turn negative, this conflict can be expected to become acute. The structural and political reservations concerning a generalized commitment to an outward-oriented strategy, raised in Chapter 2, are of crucial relevance here. This should not be taken to imply a critique of the conditionality implied in bank creditworthiness standards; after all, one would not expect profit-making banks to behave any differently. Rather, the point is to question the suitability of commercial bank finance to strategies other than those emphasizing the short-run expansion of foreign exchange earning or savings opportunities.

In a similar manner, one can legitimately question the desirability of allowing private commercial banks to determine how balance of payments surpluses, OPEC or otherwise, are to be distributed throughout the world. As was shown in Chapter 1, poorer Third World countries have not had access to bank debt and, as a result, for some years now have had to meet acute foreign exchange crises through import compression. What is more, on closer inspection, this group of countries as a whole was a consistent net depositor to the world banking system during the period 1979–82, in effect providing a small part of the financing of credit to the handful of larger debtors.[63] From the point of view of need, therefore, the global distribution of bank credit has also been perverse.

Concern over the privatization of the process of international liquidity creation in the 1970s was expressed in many quarters, both in the Third World and the industrial world. At issue was the perceived disparity between liquidity and adjustment needs of the international financial system as a whole and the lending priorities of transnational banks. The marginalization of the IMF, the international organization charged with this role, was particularly distressing to many. An OECD committee, the McCracken group, reported on the phenomenon in 1977:

> the limits of reserve creation have become ill defined and fluid, being set now by the private market's judgment of the creditworthiness of individual countries rather than the official multilateral evaluation of the needs of the system as a whole.[64]

However, U.S. monetary authorities repeatedly resisted proposals for collective international action to deal with the growing and persistent payments imbalances among nations. They believed that the recycling of funds through the marketplace was efficient and in line with national interests. They also believed that the activities of U.S. transnational banks would enhance U.S. financial power in the world and foreign policy generally.[65]

Since the beginning of this decade, this debate has taken on a new urgency, as both the poorer Third World countries *and* the major borrowers grapple with enormous foreign exchange constraints. Ironically, in the process of managing this global crisis, the IMF has emerged as a key institution with enormous leverage over the lending policies of transnational banks and over the economic policies of most Third World governments.

Managing the Debt Crisis

Since the onset of the debt crisis in 1982, a generalized breakdown of the world banking system has been avoided only by a remarkable degree of cooperation between industrial capitalist states, international organizations, private transnational banks and debtor governments. Emergency arrangements have been made to deal with specific country problems as they have arisen and there has been some bolstering of bank supervision and provisions for bad debt. At the same time, as will be shown in the following chapters, the lending capabilities of the international institutions have been strengthened.

Emergency rescue packages for such large debtors as Mexico, Brazil, Argentina, etc., have contained four principal, interlocking elements; namely, restructuring of maturing debt, temporary bridging finance, additional commitments of credit by transnational banks, and finally, IMF financial assistance in return for adherence to a fund stabilization program. For other countries, the approach has entailed a blend of debt restructuring and IMF (and to a lesser extent, World Bank) conditional assistance.

Debt restructuring has been common to the efforts of most countries to come to grips with their economic difficulties. This involves spreading out the repayment of maturing principal over a number of years into the future; it can also entail rolling over short-term debt. It covers official as well as private debt, short as well as long. The rescheduling of official debt is normally carried out by what is called the 'Paris Club', a multilateral forum of major creditor countries which, in recent years, has involved between 5 and 20 creditors.[66] The rescheduling of bank debt, and private debt generally, is a more complicated affair, often involving hundreds of creditors (e.g., over 500 banks in the case of Poland, over 1000 in the case of Mexico). In recent years the incidence of rescheduling both types of debt has increased dramatically as have the amounts of debt involved. During 1974–78 an average of four countries rescheduled about $1.25 billion per year. By 1978–82, these figures had risen to some nine countries and about $4.5 billion per year. In 1983, no less than 30 countries rescheduled their debts for a total in the region of $60 billion: these included 5 of the 10 largest bank debtors and 11 out of the largest 25.[67] While most restructurings prior to 1982 involved official debt, since that time they have mainly involved private debt.

Most of the *official* debt-restructuring exercises involve low-income or other net oil importing countries (i.e., the poorer countries), but in 1983 countries like Mexico, Peru and Ecuador participated. Rescheduling covered between 80 and 90 percent of principal and interest (including arrears) over a period of seven to nine years with a grace period of two to three years. Interest rates were negotiated bilaterally but on non-concessional terms "to preserve a clear distinction between debt relief and development assistance."[68]

Bank debt rescheduling covered 80 to 90 percent of the principal (only) on medium-term debt and, in about half the cases, provided for short-term debt rescheduling or roll-over. The rescheduling period was generally between seven and eight years with grace periods similar to those on official debt rescheduling. Banks have refused to reschedule interest payments falling due and, aside from exceptional cases such as Nicaragua,[69] have also refused to capitalize interest arrears, instead insisting that they be made good.

Since rescheduling is a clear indication that the borrower is having trouble meeting debt commitments, it might be thought that logic would dictate an easing of the terms of that debt once it is restructured. In fact, the very opposite happens. Interest spreads have increased by .75 percent to 1 percent more than they were prior to the onset of crisis so that Brazil's margin moved from 1.5 percent over LIBOR in 1980 to 2.5 percent in 1983, Mexico from 0.5 percent to 1.89 percent.[70] In addition restructuring often attracted commissions of between 1 and 1.5 percent of the amount rescheduled. The odd borrower has managed to negotiate much easier terms (e.g., Nicaragua obtained 12-year rescheduling at 0.5 percent over LIBOR with no commission) but for exceptional reasons. By mid-1984 Mexico succeeded in bringing down the spread on its rescheduled debt; whether this was a reward for a satisfactory economic adjustment or an attempt by the banks to split the larger Latin American debtors to pre-empt a common front approach to debt problems remains controversial.[71] On the whole, though, debt rescheduling remains lucrative for banks. One estimate of their *additional* earnings from increased margins and commissions on 1982/83 reschedulings is as high as $1.75 billion.[72] It must be stressed, however, that if, as some fear, debt rescheduling becomes a recurrent exercise into the forseeable future, it will represent 'default by attrition' or 'default in all but name'.[73] If this were to happen then these additional earnings, which have a counterpart in expanded debt obligations, will be seen at that time to be simply paper or fictional profits. For the time being, however, they serve to boost the profit records of a number of transnational banks.

While, during the 1982/83 crisis, reschedulings provided immediate foreign exchange relief in the form of reduced amortization payments, the really large bank debtors needed an additional infusion of credit largely to pay for interest and commission costs of debt. As an interim measure, until these debt arrangements could be finalized, short-term emergency bridge-financing was provided by the Bank for International Settlements, the central bankers' bank. In 1982/83 this amounted to commitments of over $4 billion for five major borrowers.[74] The U.S. Treasury and the Federal Reserve between them also advanced $2.8 billion in emergency bridge-financing to Mexico and Brazil alone.[75]

Although these loans were outstanding for only 90 days, they played a crucial role in keeping the rescue package together while longer-term loan commitments could be put in place. These commitments took the form of trade and commodity credits from governments and others and, primarily, of additional credit from the banks themselves. Thus, at a time when the banks were withdrawing, generally, from lending to the Third World, they increased their exposure in 1983 by 8 percent in Mexico, 12.4 percent in Brazil and possibly 10 percent in Yugoslavia.[76] This is all the more remarkable because, in the past, banks have not only moved away from countries not meeting debt commitments, but have also tended, as the case of Turkey demonstrates, to stay away for many years.

This change in approach is explained by the new relationship between transnational banks and the IMF which has emerged since 1982. In the past, it was assumed that when a debtor country agreed to an IMF stabilization program, this might be useful in helping it to attract further bank credits. There was, however, nothing automatic in this and certainly the lending decisions of the Fund and the banks were taken quite independently. Now the Fund is assuming a much more active role in both the debt-rescheduling process and in the putting together of rescue packages as a whole. In the case of Mexico, or Brazil, for instance, the Fund, under pressure from the U.S.A. government, more or less dictated the terms of rescheduling as well as the amount of new credits to be advanced by the banks. This was an unprecedented development; without such an intervention, prudential banking practice would have suggested that banks reduce credit exposure in these countries.[77] The banks have, therefore, surrendered (with reluctance) some autonomy in decision taking in return for an IMF-enforced debtor commitment to keep interest payments regular and current. Some even go so far as to suggest that state and IMF involvement in these rescue packages suggests that new lending to major debtors carries an *implicit* government guarantee, though officials deny this.[78]

The supervision and regulation of banking business by state authorities has been pulled in two quite conflicting directions since 1982. On the one hand, the very existence of the debt crisis suggests a need for tightening up on regulations concerning bank exposure, bad debt provisions and the measurement of earnings and non-performing assets. On the other hand, if bank withdrawal from major debtor countries and the collapse of the world banking system that would inevitably ensue are to be avoided, then a relaxation of bank regulations in certain areas presents itself as a necessity. State policy in major creditor countries since 1982 reflects this dilemma. In the U.S.A., for instance, legislators laid down five regulatory and supervisory conditions for expanding IMF resources in 1983.[79] These require that procedures for examining and evaluating country risk be strengthened; that regulators consider country exposure and transfer risk in assessing capital adequacy of banks; that a system of special reserves be established for debtors facing a "protracted inability . . . to make scheduled payments";[80] that restructuring fees above administrative costs be amortized over the life of the loan rather than shown entirely as current earnings; and that cooperation with regulators in other countries and with the IMF be strengthened.

Earlier that same year, U.S. regulatory authorities were informing banks that new loans to large debtors "should not be subject to supervisory criticism."[81] The Federal Reserve Board then relaxed its loan classification standards so that such credits would not be automatically classified as "non-performing assets."[82] Similar 'relaxation' of standards has applied to the treatment of overdue interest payments and to interest blocked in escrow accounts in debtor countries.[83] There is evidence too that U.S. banks have been under much less pressure to raise reserves than have banks elsewhere.[84] These factors combine, of course, to raise bank exposure and vulnerability in the event that current crisis management efforts prove inadequate and it remains to be seen whether, or how, the legislative initiatives above will address them.

One further development prompted by the debt crisis has been the formation by transnational banks of the Institute of International Finance, located in Washington, D.C. Established in 1983 by 38 banks from 10 countries, this institute now has 187 member banks from 39 countries which together account for more than 80 percent of Third World bank debt. Its prime function is declared to be that of improving the quality of economic intelligence on major debtor countries with a view to shoring up the flagging confidence of smaller banks, and especially regional U.S. banks which are reported to hold between 30 and 44 percent of the bank debts of large borrowers. Members explicitly deny that the intent of the Institute is to form a creditors' cartel to influence terms of lending and rescheduling but it would be understandable if debtors remain skeptical.

Medium-Term Prospects

Rescue efforts to date have been remarkably successful in heading off a collapse of the banking system. Through debt rescheduling, the debt-servicing burden of 25 major debtors was reduced by over $45 billion between 1982 and 1984[85] and debt-servicing ratios began to fall in 1983 as interest rates declined[86] (Table 3.8). It seems legitimate to ask, however, whether recent initiatives are not simply palliatives which delay the day of reckoning for a few years at best. Such a question seems particularly pertinent after a recent sharp turn around in interest rates to levels approaching those of 1982—a development causing great alarm among debtor nations.

Using the same assumptions as those outlined in Chapter 2, and allowing for recent reschedulings, the IMF has projected the likely debt-servicing burdens of different Third World countries in 1987 and 1990. These are summarized in Table 3.9 and show that the ratio of outstanding debt to exports will decline steadily to 1990 for all country groups except the poorest. Debt-servicing burdens will, however, rise to 1987 and significantly so for 'net oil exporters' and 'other net oil importers'. Thereafter, however, these ratios will decline to 1990 for all country groups. These findings would suggest that if the underlying assumptions hold and if the rising debt-servicing pressures to 1987 can be contained, then the debt problem will begin to correct iself, steadily, over time.

It should be emphasized, however, that debt burdens will remain high to 1990 and especially, that debt-servicing burdens will be no lower in 1990 than they are in 1984. Also, these findings are very sensitive to changes in the underlying assumptions. If, for instance, growth rates in OECD countries are 1 percent p.a. lower than assumed in the base case, then both the debt burden and the debt-servicing burden will be higher in 1990 than in 1984. Likewise, a 1 percent p.a. increase in LIBOR over its 1984 level could leave debt-servicing burdens higher in 1990 than in 1984. It is to be noted that the assumption in the study that interest rates in 1984 and 1985 would not exceed those prevailing at the end of 1983 looked already dubious by June 1984 (Table 3.8).

Such projections assume that short-term debt, which is excluded from the debt-servicing ratio, will continue to roll over. They also hide great disparities between individual debtors, some of which are going to face enormous difficulties in servicing their debt, whatever assumptions are made.[87]

Nevertheless, at their face value, the medium-term projections of the IMF indicate that the macro-debt problem might just be manageable if debtor countries can survive the peaking of their servicing liabilities to 1987. Underlying them, however, is the very crucial additional assumption that IMF stabilization policies which underpin recent rescue efforts are capable of being sustained and that the pursuit of "financial policies aimed at the restoration of domestic and external stability," called for in the projections, will be acceptable politically to the people of debtor countries

Table 3.8

Movements in LIBOR, 1981-1984

	1981	1982	1983	1984 (June)
LIBOR (%)	16.63	13.48	8.82	12.68

Source: International Monetary Fund, *International Financial Statistics;* (Washington, D.C.: IMF, 1984); *The Globe and Mail* (Toronto), June 26, 1984.

Table 3.9

IMF Projections of Debt and Debt-Servicing Burdens to 1987 and 1990 (% exports)

	1984	1987	1990
All Non-Oil Developing Countries			
Debt Ratio	144.7	132.2	123.8
Debt Service Ratio	21.1	24.4	21.3
Major Debtors			
Debt Ratio	187.0	165.0	150.4
Debt Service Ratio	29.2	34.1	30.1
Net Oil Exporters			
Debt Ratio	189.0	177.7	167.5
Debt Service Ratio	30.6	40.0	30.4
Major Exporters of Manufactures			
Debt Ratio	135.3	123.1	115.5
Debt Service Ratio	19.0	21.3	19.6
Low-Income Countries			
Debt Ratio	300.3	298.2	307.7
Debt Service Ratio	22.8	24.2	22.2
Other Net Oil Importers			
Debt Ratio	170.2	161.4	159.7
Debt Service Ratio	22.6	27.5	25.6

Note: Debt Ratio includes short-term debt; debt service ratio does not.
Source: International Monetary Fund, *World Economic Outlook* (Washington, D.C.: IMF, 1984), p. 219.

in the years ahead. It is to a consideration of these and related issues that we now turn.

Notes

[1] W. H. Bolin and J. del Canto estimate that 94% of all transnational bank lending to LDCs has been conducted by the 60 largest banks: see their "LDC Debt, Beyond Crisis Management", *Foreign Affairs* (Summer 1983). See "The Growth of Third World Debt and the Debt Crisis" in this chapter for data on borrowing countries.

[2] World Bank, cited in A. W. Clausen, "Let's not Panic about Third World Debts", *Harvard Business Review* (November-December 1983), p. 106.

[3] See Morgan Guaranty Trust Company of New York, *World Financial Markets* (February 1983), p. 3. This figure excludes offshore banking centre liabilities.

[4] Ibid. (October 1982).

[5] Dragoslav Avramovic, "The Debt Problem of Developing Countries at end of 1982" (Geneva: December 1982, mimeo.). For some countries these ratios rose sharply *after* the year of default, to 102.6% for Chile, 50% for Bolivia and 45% for Brazil.

[6] *The AMEX Bank Review*, Vol. 10, Nos. 8/9 (September 15th, 1983), p. 5.

[7] IMF, *World Economic Outlook* (Washington, D.C.: IMF, 1984), p. 65.

[8] *IMF Survey* (August 22, 1983), p. 241.

[9] Bank for International Settlements, quoted in *The Globe and Mail* (Toronto), December 3, 1983.

[10] IMF, *World Economic Outlook*, p. 65.

[11] Mexico and Venezuela were particularly affected by capital flight in the period immediately preceding the debt crisis. See William R. Cline, *International Debt and the Stability of the World Economy* (Washington D.C.: Institute for International Economics, 1983), p. 27.

[12] Bank for International Settlements, *Maturity Distribution of International Bank Lending* (various years).

[13] World Bank, *Annual Report*, 1983, p. 99.

[14] *The AMEX Bank Review*, p. 5.

[15] Short-term debt roll-over of private banks was estimated to be $99 billion in 1982 compared with $68 billion in 1980 and $42 billion in 1978. See *The AMEX Bank Review*, Vol. 9, No. 4 (April 26th, 1982).

[16] Pablo Newhaus, "Floating Interest Rates and Developing Country Debt", *Finance and Development* (December 1982).

[17] For an elaboration of this criterion, see Cline, *International Debt*, pp. 18–19.

[18] Ibid., p. 36.

[19] Salomon Brothers, *U.S. Multinational Banking* (December 1982).

[20] Much has been written about the Euromarket. Of particular relevance to the relationship between Third World Debt, the Euromarket and system vulnerability are: Charles Lipson, "The International Organisation of Third World Debt", *International Organisation*, Vol. 35, No. 4 (Autumn 1981); E. J. Frydl, "The Debate over Regulating the Eurocurrency Market", *Federal Reserve Bank of New York Quarterly Review*, Vol. 4, No. 4 (Winter 1979–80); E. J. Frydl, "The Eurodollar Conundrum", *Federal Reserve Bank of New York Quarterly Review* (Spring 1982); C. Hardy, "Commercial Bank Lending to Developing Countries: Supply Constraints", *World Development*, No. 7 (1979); Group of Thirty, *How Bankers See the World Financial Market* (New York, 1982); and R. McKinnon, "*The Eurocurrency Market*",

Princeton Essays in International Finance, No. 125 (December 1977). The most authoritative financial periodicals which cover the Euromarket include: *Euromoney*; Morgan Guaranty Trust Co. of New York, *World Financial Markets*; and *The AMEX Bank Review*.

[21] The early estimates were made by A. Holmes and F. Klapstock, "The Market for Dollar Deposits in Europe", *Federal Reserve Bank of New York Monthly Review* (November 1960), cited in B. J. Cohen, *Banks and the Balance of Payments—Private Lending in the International Adjustment Process* (London: Croom Helm, 1981). This book is an important source of information on international bank lending. Since 1964 the Bank for International Settlements has been publishing figures on Euromarket activities. These are to be found in the BIS *Annual Reports* and in *International Banking Developments Quarterly*.

[22] Geoffrey Bell, "Debt Rescheduling: Can the Banking System Cope?" *The Banker* (February 1982), p. 17.

[23] Cohen, *Banks and the Balance of Payments*, p. 54.

[24] See, for example, J. D. Aronson, *Money and Power: Banks and the World Monetary System* (Beverly Hills, California: Sage, 1977).

[25] Several studies have pointed out the more modest role of OPEC deposits in Euromarket activity than conventional wisdom would lead one to believe. See, for example, E. F. Bacha and C. F. Diaz Alejandro, "*International Financial Intermediation: a Long and Topical View*", Princeton Essays in International Finance, No. 147 (May 1982); *Bankers Trust* (January 1983); and Lipson, "Third World Debt".

[26] OECD, *Financial Statistics Monthly*, 1973–82. This figure relates to lending to Third World countries.

[27] Cross default clauses stipulate that if one creditor participating in the syndicate declares the loan in default, then automatically, so do all other participants. This ensures discipline *within* the syndicate. Usually, however, there is provision for a syndicate to have "discretionary power to call its loans in default even if all payments are current when another syndicate has called default." Lipson, "Third World Debt", p. 615. This ensures some discipline *across* syndicates. Above all, of course, it is the debtor who is disciplined by these clauses.

[28] *Euromoney* (March 1982).

[29] See "Borrowers fight a losing battle to keep the bankers happy", *South* (July 1983), p. 63.

[30] "Syndicated Lending", *Euromoney* (February 1983).

[31] See *Euromoney* (October 1982). What follows draws heavily on this source.

[32] See United Nations, Centre on Transnational Corporations, *Transnational Banks, Operations, Strategies and Their Effects in Developing Countries* (New York, 1981), p. 56, which states that Swiss and Canadian banks obtain more than half their foreign currency deposits from the inter-bank market. A Bank of England study also found that London branches of Japanese banks obtained 75% of their deposits from the inter-bank market. *Financial Times* (London), May 23, 1983.

[33] David Shirriff, "Hungary and the Shadow of 1985," *Euromoney* (March 1982), pp. 132–141.

[34] John Dizard, "International Banking—The End of Let's Pretend", *Fortune* (November 29, 1982), p. 73.

[35] Brazil lost an estimated $3 billion in such deposits in 1982 and was unsuccessful in attempting to reverse the loss. See Edmar L. Bacha, "The IMF and the Prospects for Adjustment in Brazil" in *Prospects for Adjustment in Argentina, Brazil and Mexico: Responding to the Debt Crisis*, ed. John Williamson (Washington, D.C.: Institute for International Economics, June 1983), pp. 32–33.

[36] See Hugo Colje, "Bank Supervision on a Consolidated Basis", *The Banker* (June 1980); Richard Dale, "Safeguarding the Banking System", *The Banker* (August 1982); and W. P. Cooke, "The Role of the Banking Supervisor", *Bank of England Quarterly Bulletin* (December 1982). This section draws heavily on John Loxley, "Regulation and Restructuring: Responses to the International Financial Crisis", *Journal of Contemporary Crises* (1984) (forthcoming).

[37] In a letter to the *Financial Times* (London), May 17, 1983, Fernand J. St. Germain, Chairman of the U.S. House of Representatives Committee on Banking, Finance and Urban Affairs, quotes official statements which suggest that monetary authorities in the U.S.A., England, Switzerland, and West Germany each have separate and quite different interpretations of the meaning of the 1975 Basle Concordat which laid down the division of responsibility between parent and host authorities concerning problems of bank liquidity and insolvency.

[38] Frydl, "The Eurodollar Conumdrum". See also Cynthia C. Lichtenstein, "U.S. Banks and the Euro Currency Markets: The Regulatory Structure", *The Banking Law Journal*, Vol. 99, No. 6 (June/July 1982); Dale, "Safeguarding the Banking System"; and (author not named) "Supervising the Euromarket Dinosaur", *The Banker* (August 1978).

[39] Lichtenstein, "Euro Currency Markets", p. 499.

[40] Loxley, "Regulation and Restructuring", from which this paragraph is drawn.

[41] K. Lissakers, *International Debt, the Banks and U.S. Foreign Policy*, A staff report prepared for the United States Senate Sub-Committee on Banking and Finance (Washington, D.C., 1977), p. 11. See also, Jane D'arista, "Private Overseas Lending: Too Far too Fast?", in J. D. Aronson, *Debt and the Less Developed Countries* (Boulder: Westview Press, 1979), p. 63.

[42] OECD, *Financial Statistics Monthly* (Various Issues).

[43] Salomon Brothers, *Review of Bank Performance*, 1982 for the U.S.A. and *Bank Profits: Report by the House of Commons Standing Committee on Finance Trade and Economic Affairs* (Ottawa: Canadian Government Printer, July 1982 for Canada).

[44] See IMF, *World Economic Outlook*, p. 205.

[45] *The Globe and Mail* (Toronto), February 12, 1983.

[46] See for example, Group of Thirty, *Risks in International Lending* (New York: Group of Thirty, 1982); Y. Maroni, "How to Borrow Reasonably", Federal Reserve Board, *International Finance Discussion Paper No. 203*, February 1982; and Cohen, *Banks and the Balance of Payments.*

[47] U.S. Export-Import Bank, *A Survey of Country Evaluation Systems in Use* (December 1976). Fabio Basagni in Cohen, *Banks and the Balance of Payments* gives an account of this study.

[48] See Group of Thirty, *How Bankers See the World Financial Market* (New York: Group of Thirty, 1982), results of a 1981 questionnaire, question 31.

[49] M. J. Seiber, *Developing Country Debt* (Boulder: Westview Press, 1982), p. 17.

[50] Group of Thirty, *Risks in International Lending*, pp. 6–9.

[51] U.S. Export-Import Bank, *Country Evaluation Systems.*

[52] Bruce Brackenbridge, "One Approach to Country Evaluation" in *Financing and Risk in Developing Countries*, ed. S. H. Goodman (New York: Praeger Special Studies, 1978).

[53] The adverse effects of this practice were candidly stated by a London banker in Q. P. Lim, "The Big Shift in Bank Strategies", *Euromoney* (November 1982).

[54] J. Thornblade, "A Checklist System: The First Step in Country Evaluation" in Goodman, *Financing and Risk*, p. 73.

[55] Basagni, in Cohen, *Banks and the Balance of Payments*, p. 102.

[56] See William R. Cline, "Economic Stabilisation in Peru, 1975–78" in *Economic Stabilisation in Developing Countries*, eds. Cline and Weintraub (Washington, D.C.: The Brookings Institute, 1981), pp. 305–06.

[57] C. P. Kindleberger, *Manias, Panics and Crashes—A History of Financial Crises* (New York: Basic Books, 1977), p. 23.

[58] Cline, "Economic Stabilisation in Peru", pp. 309–10. Cline states that bank credit to Peru financed balance of payments deficits, government budget deficits, military imports and projects which had previously been rejected by the World Bank as unproductive.

[59] Ibid.

[60] See Jeffrey D. Sachs, "The Current Account and Macroeconomic Adjustment in the 1970's", *Brookings Papers on Economic Activity, No. 1* (Washington, D.C.: The Brookings Institute, 1981), quoted in Cline, *International Debt*, pp. 28–29.

[61] Bruce Campbell, "Transnational Bank Lending, Debt and Balance of Payments Deficits in Third World Countries" (Ottawa: North-South Institute, April 1984, mimeo.).

[62] For an elaboration of these asymmetries, see Robert Devlin, "Transnational Banks, External Debt and Peru: Results of a Recent Study", *CEPAL Review* (August 1981); and Robert Devlin, "Commercial Bank Finance from the North and Economic Development of the South", *CEPAL Review* (December 1979).

[63] John Loxley, "The Less Developed Countries and the International Financial Crisis" in *Background Technical Reports for 'Towards a New Bretton Woods*, ed. B. Persaud, Vol. 11 (London: Commonwealth Secretariat, 1984).

[64] OECD, *Towards Full Employment and Price Stability* (Paris: OECD, 1977), paragraph 161.

[65] Minos Zombanakis, "The International Debt Threat—A Way to Avoid a Crash", *The Economist* (April 30, 1983), pp. 11–13.

[66] IMF, "Recent Multilateral Debt Restructurings with Official and Bank Creditors", *Occasional Paper*, No. 25, 1983. For a summary of this study, see *IMF Survey* (January 23, 1984).

[67] These figures and details of terms of reschedulings below, are taken from IMF, *World Economic Outlook*, pp. 65–66. The figure for 1983 value of reschedulings is taken from *IMF Survey* (January 23, 1984), p. 28.

[68] IMF, *World Economic Outlook*, p. 66.

[69] The Nicaraguan case, in which banks were relieved to receive any payment at all, is described in detail in *South* (July 1983), pp. 63–64.

[70] Ibid.

[71] See "Bank Concessions Show Long-Term View", *The Globe and Mail* (Toronto), June 18, 1984.

[72] See M. S. Mendelsohn, *Commercial Banks and the Restructuring of Cross-Border Debts* (New York: Group of Thirty, 1983), Summarized in *IMF Survey* (July 25, 1983).

[73] *IMF Survey* (July 25, 1983), p. 213.

[74] Loxley, "Regulation and Restructuring".

[75] See Cline, *International Debt*, pp. 40–44 for a good description of the rescue packages of the major debtors.

[76] Loxley, "Regulation and Restructuring".

[77] Peter Field, David Shirreff and William Ollard, "The IMF and Central Banks Flex Their Muscles", *Euromoney* (January 1983), pp. 35–44.

[78] Karen Lissakers, "Dateline Wall Street: Faustian Finance", *Foreign Policy* (Summer 1983), p. 166.

[79] Geoffrey Bell and Graeme Rutledge, "How to Account for Problem Loans", *Euromoney* (January 1984), pp. 43–46.

[80] Ibid., p. 43.

[81] Paul Volker quoted in Field, Shirreff and Ollard, "The IMF and Central Banks", p. 40.

[82] Samuel Alberto Yohai, "How the World Bank Might Recycle Assets", *Euromoney* (January 1983).

[83] Bell and Rutledge, "Problem Loans", p. 44.

[84] Lissakers, "Dateline Wall Street", p. 171.

[85] IMF, *World Economic Outlook*, p. 67.

[86] *World Financial Markets*, p. 5. For Argentina, Mexico and Brazil the overall debt-servicing ratio (including short-term debt principal) had fallen in 1983 to 154%, 126% and 117% compared with 179%, 129% and 122% respectively in 1982 (see Table 3.4).

[87] This is brought out very clearly in a similar projection exercise by William Cline who, incidentally, reaches conclusions very close to those of the IMF study. See Cline, *International Debt*, Chapter 3. Though cautiously optimistic, his findings indicate that countries like Venezuela, Algeria, Israel, Egypt, Ecuador and Peru can be expected to encounter, or to continue to encounter, severe debt-servicing difficulties by 1986. The debt-servicing ratios of such major debtors as Brazil, Mexico and Argentina will continue to be in excess of 40% (*excluding* short-term debt) to that date. Also, it is to be noted that Cline's base-case assumption is that LIBOR would be no higher than 9% in 1984!

4

THE INTERNATIONAL MONETARY FUND

Introduction

The IMF was created at the end of World War II to help regulate the international economy. Its main purpose is to ensure that national economic policies do not restrict or inhibit the international flow of commodities and payments as they did, so disastrously, in the 1930s. By requiring members to subscribe to a common set of rules regarding exchange and payments arrangements, the Fund attempts to prevent the narrow pursuit of national interests from impeding international growth and stability. The need for an institution to play this role stems from the fact that while capital and trade have become increasingly internationalized, economic policy continues to be formulated essentially by individual nation states whose interests often do not coincide.

To enable members to adhere to its rules during periods of economic difficulties and to restore balance in their economies without resort to restrictive policies detrimental to other members, the Fund is empowered to advance them credits to smooth the process of adjustment. Above a certain level, credits are made available only on condition that the borrower agrees to follow a prescribed program of economic policy adjustment. Because acceptance of this 'conditionality' is often perceived to be an admission of some loss of national autonomy over economic decision taking, and because the required adjustment measures are sometimes painful and politically unpopular, governments are often reluctant to borrow from the Fund. Hence, over the years, the use of Fund conditional resources has come to be viewed as desirable only when other alternatives have been exhausted. It is, therefore, an indication of the seriousness of the current economic crisis that, since 1979, no fewer than 68 Third World countries and 12 of the 20 major Third World debtors, have turned to the IMF for financial assistance, and accordingly, have had their economic policies shaped by Fund conditionality.[1] In the process, the Fund has emerged as an immensely powerful institution. The pivotal role it has played and continues to play in arranging rescue packages for the world's largest debtor countries (and banks) further underscores the importance of the Fund at this time in the management of the global economy.

As more governments have turned to it for help, the Fund has become the centre of controversy. At issue is the appropriateness of its approach to the problems being faced by Third World countries. Specifically, the amounts and terms of its financial assistance and the nature and desirability of the conditions it attaches to its credits have been the subject of intense debate in recent years. This chapter will examine these questions at some length but first, by way of context, it is necessary to describe briefly how the Fund is structured.

The Structure of the Fund

The organization of the Fund has been dealt with extensively elsewhere,[2] and only those features will be sketched out here which are necessary to an understanding of the role of the Fund and its potential for reform.

Although the Fund was originally intended to be a *world* monetary institution, one that Keynes hoped might function on purely technical, non-political lines, this was not to be. The politics of the 'cold war' led to separate monetary institutions being established in both the capitalist and socialist camps.[3] For most of the years preceding 'detente' the sole socialist member was Yugoslavia, and it was acceptable only because of its rift with the U.S.S.R. Since the early 1970s, however, Romania, China and Hungary have also become members. The dominant influence in the IMF has always been the United States on account of its centrality in the world capitalist system as measured by its share of international trade and capital flows and by the importance of the dollar in the world reserves and payments.

In formal terms, power in the Fund is determined by the votes each member has which in turn are linked to the size of members' quotas in the ratio of one vote for every SDR 100,000 of quota plus a basic allotment of 250 votes. Quotas were and still are arrived at by a judicious mixture of economic calculation and political expediency, with the distribution in Table 4.1 being the outcome.[4]

A Board of Governors meets annually to determine Fund policy but most important decisions are handled by the Executive Board. The latter has 22 members; the five large industrial capitalist countries each have an appointed member as does Saudi Arabia on account of its special contribution to Fund finances. The other 16 are elected although, in effect, a seat has been reserved since the beginning of this decade for the People's Republic of China. In theory, decisions are taken in the Executive Board by votes on the basis of quota, with each of the elected members representing a group of countries and exercising votes on their behalf. In both bodies relatively unimportant decisions require a simple majority, more important ones a 70 percent majority while on such crucial matters as the structure of the Fund, allocations of SDRs, quota changes, etc., a 'high' majority of 85 percent is required. In practice, in the Executive Board, decisions are usually arrived at by consensus and hence informal influence and lobbying is more important there than the exercise of formal voting power.

It can be seen from Table 4.1 that the U.S.A. is the only single country to have effective veto power over 'high' majority votes, while industrial

Table 4.1

Quotas and Voting Rights in the IMF (SDR millions)

	June 1983			January 1984		
	Quota	**%**	**Votes** (%)	**Quota**	**%**	**Votes** (%)
U.S.A.	12,608	20.7	19.5	17,919	19.9	19.2
U.K.	4,388	7.2	6.8	6,194	6.9	6.6
West Germany	3,234	5.3	5.0	5,403	6.0	5.8
Japan	2,489	4.1	3.9	4,223	4.7	4.5
France	2,879	4.7	4.5	4,483	5.0	4.8
Italy	1,860	3.1	2.9	2,909	3.2	3.1
Canada	2,036	3.3	3.2	2,941	3.3	3.2
Other Industrial	7,919	13.0	12.8	12,017	13.3	13.2
All Industrial	37,410	61.3	58.6	56,089	62.3	60.4
Major Oil Exporters	6,662	10.9	10.8	10,393	11.5	11.4
All Other Countries	16,987	27.8	30.6	23,553	26.2	28.2
Total	**61,059**	**100.0**	**100.0**	**90,035**	**100.0**	**100.0**

Source: Calculated from data in A. W. Hooke, *The International Monetary Fund: Its Evolution, Organization and Activities* (Washington, D.C.: IMF, 1983), pp. 71–75.

capitalist countries as a whole dominate the vote. The share of the vote held by the U.S.A. has declined steadily since the Fund's inception but this has not significantly weakened that country's influence because of the voting structure of the Fund. The growth of the share of OPEC, and in particular Saudi Arabia, is the most striking development since 1973 but one which does not appear to have had much of an impact on the policies of the Fund.

It is to be noted that the collective vote of the Third World, at about 39 percent of the total,[5] is a minority one which prevents it from independently shaping IMF policies through 'bloc' action. While the Third World, nevertheless, still holds a large enough proportion of votes to veto important decisions, this power is not exercised because the reality is that such a move would jeopardize the financial base of the Fund which rests largely on contributions from industrialized capitalist nations. In addition, as will be argued in Chapter 7, on many issues there is no coincidence of interest between different groups of Third World countries, the concerns of OPEC, for instance, often being quite different from those of the least developed countries. Where common concerns do arise, these are usually advanced through means other than the exercise of a unified negative vote, such as lobbying, argumentation and propagandizing. While this is generally an ineffective means of dealing with major Third World concerns, it has not been totally futile. Third World members were successful in achieving an allocation of Special Drawing Rights (discussed later in this chapter) in proportion to quota, overturning an earlier decision which would have restricted SDRs to industrialized capitalist countries only. Even so, this fell far short of the goal of 'linking' SDR allocations to the needs of Third World countries—a goal widely supported by the poorer members of the IMF.[6]

The Third World can also exercise some limited influence on IMF policies and practices through the Interim Committee, which advises on the management of the international monetary system and the amendment of Fund articles and, more especially, through the Development Committee which, in conjunction with the World Bank, deals specifically with real resource transfers to Third World countries.

Because of the realities of the distribution of world economic and political power, the Fund perspective on global issues largely mirrors that of the industrialized capitalist nations and, especially, that of the United States government. On occasion, the Fund has been seen to project narrow U.S. interests in a particularly crude manner. This was so in the case of the withdrawal from membership of Czechoslovakia and Cuba and the blocking of Poland's application for membership.[7] At times, loans have been granted to U.S. client states even when normal Fund requirements appear not to have been followed (e.g., in the case of El Salvador and South Africa),[8] while at other times assistance to governments opposed by the U.S. administration (e.g., Vietnam and Bishop's Grenada)[9] has either been denied or delayed.

It would be incorrect, however, to see U.S. influence in the Fund as being unrestrained or unchallenged. While the common interests of industrialized nations are strong, so are the tensions between them as they compete with each other for markets, investment opportunities and influence. The growing strength of some European nations and Japan has clearly given rise to friction between them and the U.S.A. on a number of fronts. This inevitably finds reflection from time to time, in disputes surrounding Fund decisions. Thus, West Germany would prefer to see Poland as a member of the Fund because its ties with that country in the form of debt and trade are very strong—much stronger than those between the U.S.A. and Poland.[10] Several European nations were unhappy with the way in which the U.S. pushed through the 1982 loan to El Salvador,[11] while U.S. opposition to the Fund giving assistance to pre-invasion Grenada was ultimately overruled.[12] The efforts of the Reagan administration to reassert the influence of the dollar (and of the U.S.A. generally) in world affairs have also been resisted by France which has repeatedly called for a conference on international monetary reform.[13] The question that arises, therefore, is whether and to what degree these tensions and the current climate of global disorder might offer Third World countries an opportunity to assert a greater influence over IMF policies in the foreseeable future than their formal proportion of votes appears to allow them. We shall return to this complex question in Chapter 7 when discussing proposals which have been advanced for reform of the Fund.

Fund Resources and Facilities

Resources

It has been shown that the Fund played only a minor role in financing Third World balance of payments deficits in the years 1973–83, providing no more than 4 percent of total financing (Table 1.4). What this figure hides, however, is the sharp rise in the absolute *and* relative importance of Fund assistance since the onset of the current crisis. While the net contribution it made to financing the current account deficits of non-oil developing countries was *negative* in 1977 and 1978, it has risen steadily since then to over $10 billion in 1983, equivalent to no less than 18 percent of total deficits (Table 4.2). All country groups are now much more dependent on Fund credit than they were in 1977 but especially the major exporters of manufactures. Their dependence coincides with the debt crisis and postdates that of the poorer income groups by a full two years.

IMF credit flows are not, however, a good indicator of the influence the Fund wields over the Third World. Because governments tend to exhaust all other options before turning to the Fund, its power to influence economic policy is out of all proportion to the financing which accompanies its programs. Also, compliance with an IMF program was, until quite recently, often taken by banks to be a sign of 'good housekeeping' and rewarded by flows of bank credit which might be well in excess of borrowings from the IMF. For many countries these two indirect effects are likely to be more important than any direct balance of payments relief that borrowing from the Fund will provide.

The Fund obtains most of the resources for its credits from members' subscriptions which are based on quotas. Its other major source of financing is borrowing which, by a decision of the Executive Board, is also restricted by the size of quotas—outstanding borrowing and unused credit lines being limited to 50–60 percent of total quotas.

Historically, members paid their subscriptions to the Fund partly (25 percent) in gold or convertible currencies and the rest in the form of their own domestic currencies. More recently the SDR has become an acceptable substitute for the 'gold tranche' portion of subscriptions, now termed the 'reserve tranche'. Domestic currencies are, however, the main form of subscription capital. Selected currencies considered 'usable' are loaned to members in need in exchange for an equivalent deposit of their own currency. In effect they 'purchase' currency from the Fund but since there is a requirement to repurchase their own currency, the transaction is really one of a loan. In the earlier years of the Fund's life, the U.S. dollar was the only convertible currency and hence was the only currency borrowed (purchased) from the Fund. Other domestic currencies were simply not usable in this way even though they constituted the bulk of the Fund's capital. Over time, as other currencies became convertible the proportion of the Fund's capital that could be loaned rose from about 37 percent in

Table 4.2

Non-OPEC Third World Countries' Use of Fund Credit, 1977–1983

	1977	1978	1979	1980	1981	1982	1983
Non-Oil Developing Countries							
($ billion)	−0.2	−0.3	0.2	1.5	6.1	7.1	10.2
% Current Account Debit	−0.6	−0.7	0.3	1.7	5.6	8.6	18.0
Net Oil Exporters							
($ billion)	0.2	—	—	−0.3	0.1	0.5	1.0
% Current Account Deficit	3.2	—	—	−2.9	0.4	3.5	14.5
Major Exporters of Manufactures							
($ billion)	−0.1	−0.6	−0.4	0.5	1.1	2.0	4.2
% Current Account Deficit	−1.1	−5.6	−1.7	1.5	2.9	5.8	24.6
Low-Income Countries[a]							
($ billion)	0.1	—	0.2	0.3	1.3	1.1	0.8
% Current Account Deficit	1.9	—	2.0	2.5	10.4	9.2	8.2
Other Net Oil Importers							
($ billion)	—	0.5	0.5	0.6	2.9	1.8	3.2
% Current Account Deficit	—	3.3	2.6	2.2	8.8	7.6	13.2

[a]Excluding India and China

Source: International Monetary Fund, *World Economic Survey* (Washington, D.C.: IMF, 1984).

the early 1950s to about 51 percent in 1983.[14] Even now, the number of currencies which are 'usable' is still quite small; only five of them account for about 80 percent of 'usable' currency holdings.[15] The currencies of non-oil developing countries remain inconvertible so that while the quotas of these countries amount to over 20 percent of the total, drawings from the Fund in their currencies were less than 2 percent of the total by 1983.[16]

Since its creation both the subscriptions and the lending power of the Fund have gradually increased as more countries have become members (100 more since 1946) and as both specific and general adjustments have been made to quotas. Thus between 1946 and 1983 quotas were raised from $8.8 billion to SDR 61.06 billion, equivalent to about $66 billion.

The Articles of Agreement permit the Fund to supplement subscription capital by borrowing from governments, central banks and the private sector, subject only to obtaining permission of the member whose currency is being borrowed. Under the General Agreement to Borrow (GAB) the Fund has a line of credit with the 10 major industrial capitalist countries. By early 1983 this amounted to SDR 6.4 billion and was available for use by any of the 10 so that possible large borrowings by them would not impede the Fund's ability to meet the needs of members with smaller borrowing entitlements. The Fund also borrowed to finance its 1974 and 1975 Oil Facilities in amounts totalling SDR 6.9 billion and its Supplementary Financing Facility (SDR 7.8 billion). In May 1981, it made arrangements to borrow up to SDR 12.0 billion from the Saudi Arabian Monetary Authority to finance its Enlarged Access Policy.[17] The nature of these various facilities, financed by borrowing, is described below.

By late 1982 it became apparent that the Fund's resources were rapidly becoming inadequate to meet the huge increase in Third World demands being placed upon them. Clear evidence of this was to be seen in a sharp deterioration, in excess of SDR 11 billion, in the Fund's own liquidity in 1982/83.[18] As the large debtor countries began to line up for Fund assistance, debate began to rage as to how best the Fund might raise the additional resources it so clearly required.

Many Third World countries and sympathizers believed that the best way to expand Fund resources was to significantly raise quotas. The Brandt Commission, for example, argued that they should be doubled.[19] This would not only double the lines of credit to which borrowers might have access but it would also double the amount they could borrow on non-conditional and low conditional terms. As well, expanding the Fund's ordinary resources in this way would permit members to borrow much more cheaply than they could if drawing on resources which the Fund had borrowed under special arrangements (6.6 percent p.a. as opposed to between 13.2 and 14.9 percent p.a. in 1982).[20] In support of an increase of this magnitude, it was pointed out that in spite of their growth in absolute terms, quotas had fallen dramatically relative to world trade, from around 14 percent in 1950 to around 3 percent in the early 1980s. When allowance is made for the growth in convertibility and, therefore, of loanability of Fund resources during that time, the fall was from 5.2 percent to 1.5 percent of world trade—figures which serve to emphasize the limited direct capital base of the Fund. It was argued that as a result, not only was world trade inhibited by the lack of liquidity but that, in addition, the distribution of existing liquidity was badly skewed in favour of those with privileged access to bank credit and gold reserves or those few fortunate enough to possess domestic currencies acceptable as reserve currencies. A large increase in quotas would go some way toward providing less fortunate, poorer Third World countries, with greater access to badly needed imports and, in the process, expand world trade.

The U.S.A. government in particular was opposed to such a move. Being reluctant to support expansionist financing of this magnitude, it preferred instead to see a greater emphasis on 'adjustment' and avoidance of measures that would dilute conditionality. It was not particularly sympathetic to arguments about the declining relative importance of IMF quotas, being content to see an expanded role for privately generated liquidity, especially when the bulk of it involved the dollar. Originally, it seemed to reject all but very small quota increases but eventually, under pressure both from European members of the Fund who tended to take an intermediate position, and from the U.S. banking community which was grappling with what appeared to be an imminent threat of default by Mexico, it relented. In February 1983, the Interim Committee agreed to a 47.5 percent increase in aggregate quotas, to SDR 90 billion.[21] Obtaining congressional approval for this increase proved, however, to be no easy task as the Fund became the object of attack from both ends of the political spectrum. The left wing argued that it was a tool of U.S. imperialism, inflicting hardship on the poor of the Third World, and giving support to conservative regimes guilty of human rights abuses. The right wing argued that it was supporting communist regimes guilty of human rights abuses and was a tool of world socialism. Critics of all political stripes charged that the quota increase would simply bail out the banks, enabling them to avoid paying the price for their past irresponsibility.[22] Delays in approving the U.S. contribution became so protracted that the Fund announced it was cancelling all new lending.[23] The Managing Director of the Fund warned of the "incalculable consequences for economic and financial stability world-wide" of not approving the quota increase—an increase which the President of the World Bank described as "the highest financial priority on planet Earth—bar none."[24] Yet it was not until November that the increase was finally approved carrying, as we have seen, a rider tightening up the supervision of the foreign lending business of U.S. banks.

The increase in quotas was accompanied by an expansion of the GAB to SDR 17 billion and access to these funds was broadened beyond the 10 contributors to other members of the Fund. These borrowings can now be used for lending on high conditional terms if "the Fund's resources are inadequate to meet requests for financing of exceptional balance of payments situations of members that could threaten the stability of the international monetary system."[25] In other words, this special fund is geared specifically to deal with possible crises in large debtor countries only. It was supplemented by further such loans of SDR 1.5 billion from Saudi Arabia in 1983 and of SDR 6 billion from Saudi Arabia and the Bank for International Settlements in 1984.[26] The quota increase and additional borrowings raised usable Fund resources by some SDR 33 billion.

For the time being at least, this seems to solve the IMF's liquidity problem, but only because the Fund has adopted a policy which requires most Third World countries to 'adjust' their balance of payments, essentially by contracting domestic demand. It cannot be assumed that it has in any way satisfied the Third World's own perceived needs for balance of payments financing. In particular, countries that are not large debtors will gain little from the increase in Fund resources. Not only will they not benefit from the special fund, but also the impact of the quota increase was largely offset by a U.S.-inspired adjustment in the percentage of quota that members might borrow. The strengthening of Fund finances in 1983/84 was designed, therefore, to preserve the stability of the international banking system and failed to address the needs of the poorer Third World countries for additional balance of payments assistance.

In the past the Fund has also supplemented its ordinary and borrowed resources by selling the original gold contributions of members at prices well in excess of those prevailing when they were acquired. Profits made on these transactions were in part channelled, in 1976, into a Trust Fund to be loaned to developing countries. Out of its total holdings of gold of 150 million ounces, the Fund sold 50 million and made a profit of $4.6 billion of which $1.3 billion was distributed directly to members.[27] The Fund retains the balance of its gold holdings, valued at over $30 billion more than its book value,[28] despite pressure from Third World countries for it to engage in further sales. There have also been proposals that the gold be used as collateral for more aggressive borrowing by the IMF.[29]

Types of Facilities

The oldest and most important financial facilities of the IMF 42e drawings in the *reserve* and *credit tranches.* Members are allowed to draw up to 125 percent of quota in five tranches of 25 percent each. The first of these is called the reserve tranche because it is, notionally, a drawing against the gold, SDR or hard currency portion of quota subscriptions. No interest is payable on reserve tranche drawings and members are not required to repay drawings (repurchase their currencies). The other four tranches are termed 'credit tranches', drawings under which are interest bearing and repayable within three to five years. The conditionality attached to credits is minimal in the reserve tranche and the lower (first) credit tranche but becomes more demanding in the upper (second to fourth) credit tranches.

Members can either purchase foreign currencies immediately under the credit tranche facility or, as is quite common, conclude a standby arrangement with the Fund which allows them to borrow a negotiated amount as and when needed within a stipulated period. Such arrangements are often used as a lever to secure commercial bank financing. For most of the lifetime of the Fund, standby arrangements were in effect for a maximum of one year but with the growing economic crisis in the 1970s a decision was taken in 1979 to extend them to three years where circumstances warranted.

The pressure of global economic difficulties has forced the Fund to adapt its facilities in other directions too.[30] In 1974 it introduced the *Extended Facility* which provides members with longer-term funding for supply-oriented programs designed to meet balance of payments problems. Funds can be drawn in phases over three years and repaid between four and a half and ten years afterwards. Conditionality is similar to that in upper credit tranches of the regular lending facility but covers a broader range of policies reflecting the fact that programs are longer and geared more to production. The maximum that could originally be borrowed under this facility was 140 percent of quota subject to a combined total borrowing under this and the credit tranches of 165 percent of the member's quota.

Toward the end of the 1970s it was apparent that what could be borrowed from the Fund under these facilities was much too limited relative to the size of balance of payment deficits that members were experiencing. Accordingly, additional facilities were introduced, financed by borrowing from surplus countries. Between 1979 and 1982 the *Supplementary Financing Facility* provided additional credit to members whose needs exceeded what was available in the credit tranche and extended facilities. It has since been replaced by the *Enlarged Access Policy* which (apart from carrying no interest subsidy to low-income borrowers—see below) works in almost identical fashion and is also financed by borrowing. Drawings under either (since commitments made before 1982 under the SFF with funds undrawn at that time continue to be available) are fixed in proportion to funds being made available under the regular or extended facilities. For example, if a member is drawing on the Extended Facility, then funds are made available from these facilities in the ratio of 1:1 until the combined use of upper credit tranches and Extended Facility reaches 140 percent of quota (202.5 percent under a standby arrangement).

The Fund is prepared to go beyond these limits using only borrowed resources and, under the Enlarged Access Policy could, until 1984, lend up to 150 percent of quota under a one-year arrangement and up to 450 percent of quota over three years. This, together with access under credit tranches and the Extended Facility could raise cumulative borrowing to a possible maximum of 600 percent of quota. In exceptional circumstances members could borrow even more. The conditionality attached to these facilities is the same as that for the upper credit tranches and Extended Facilities and repayment is to be made between three and a half and seven years. Since the resources are borrowed, interest rates on drawings tend to be higher than those on ordinary facilities.

In order to prevent increases in quotas under the 1983 Eighth General Review of Quotas from enabling individual countries to have greater access both to unconditional IMF financing and to IMF financing in general, the U.S. sought to limit borrowing under the Enlarged Access Policy to 102 percent of quota in any one year with a declining proportion in subsequent years. Third world countries fought to maintain the 150–450 percent arrangement so that quota increases would give them an increase in borrowing ability proportionate to their increase in quota, while other industrialized capitalist countries took a middle position arguing for a limit of 125 percent of quota p.a. which would give borrowers an average increase of 22.5 percent in access to resources.[31] Eventually, and despite Third World opposition, it was agreed that the 102 percent p.a. maximum over three years (and a cumulative limit of 408 percent) would apply in most cases,[32] effectively reducing the borrowing ability of 108 of the 146 IMF members to below what they could borrow at old quotas and old limits. Since the increased quota allocation was not a proportionate one across the board (see Table 4.1), Third World countries had in any case ended up with a lower share of total quota than previously. The net result of these two developments is that 'low-income' countries, for instance, have had their annual borrowing ability reduced from a theoretical maximum at SDR 6.5 billion to SDR 5.8 billion or by 11 percent; and this at a time when their import compression is at its worse!

Provision was also made, however, for countries "with serious debt problems caused by circumstances beyond their control"[33] to borrow 125 percent of quota p.a. to a maximum of 375 percent over three years (and 500 percent cumulative). Once again the threat that the debt crisis poses to international capital and the narrowly perceived interests of the industrialized capitalist world took clear precedence over the urgent needs of the Third World as a whole.

The Fund also operates a *Compensatory Financing Facility*, established in 1963, which allows members who are primary producers to offset purely temporary deterioration in current account balance due to export shortfalls, or, since 1979, due to shortfalls in travel receipts or workers' remittances and, since 1981, due to an excess in the cost of cereal imports. In each case balance of payments deterioration is measured as a deviation from a five-year trend. Until 1984 the maximum that could be borrowed was 100 percent of quota under *either* the export shortfall facility *or* the excess in cereal import cost facility, subject to a joint limit of 125 percent in total. With the Eighth General Review of Quotas coming into effect these limits were reduced to 83 percent each or 105 percent in total. For the low-income countries the net effect of these reduced maxima, the expanded quota and their reduced quota share was to leave their potential drawing on the joint facilities of the CFF almost exactly unchanged from its 1983 level.

Drawings under the CFF are payable between three to five years afterwards. They do not reduce the ability of members to borrow under facilities discussed earlier since those are designed to deal with longer-term balance of payments problems. CFF drawings also carry less conditionality though, once they exceed 50 percent quota, members are required to satisfy the Fund that they are taking appropriate steps to rectify their balance of payments problems.

Other facilities provided by the Fund include assistance to members contributing to approved buffer stock schemes (the limits to which were also trimmed back after the quota increase), interest rate subsidies on its oil facilities (discussed in the next section) and on the Supplementary Financing Facility, and a Trust Fund for low-income developing countries financed by its gold sales.

Apart from its conditional credit activities the Fund has the power to generate *unconditional* international liquidity by allocating *Special Drawing Rights* (SDRs). These are a form of reserve assets created by the Fund as and when it deems their creation is warranted by the international liquidity situation. Between 1970 and 1972 the Fund allocated SDR 9.3 billion and between 1978 and 1981, SDR 12 billion. Members received allocations in proportion to their quotas. Since 1981 the value of the SDR has been fixed as a weighted average of the values of the five most important currencies in world trade. Before that time it was tied to 16 currencies and, in the very early years, from 1970 to 1974, to gold. In May 1984 it had a value of $1.04.[34]

The SDR acts as a reserve asset simply because all IMF members accept it in settlement of international transactions. Members can obtain the currency of others in return for transfers of SDRs. Originally not all SDR allocations could be drawn down as members had to hold an average balance of 30 percent of their cumulated allocations. To that extent there was a credit element in this instrument since when balances fell below that limit SDR holdings had to be reconstituted. This minimum balance was lowered in 1979 to 15 percent and, in April 1981, was abolished. SDRs now operate fully as a reserve asset and represent grants to member countries. Since 1980, however, they carry 100 percent interest calculated as a weighted average of the short-term rates prevailing in the five countries whose currencies are used to determine the value of the SDR. This considerably reduces the attractiveness of SDRs to Third World users, who up to that point, had paid less than market rates of interest. The same rate of interest is paid to holders of SDRs as is levied on those making use of them for payment.

Two Approaches to Crisis Management: The Fund Before and After 1981

There is clear evidence that the Fund's approach to the management of the most recent phase of the global crisis, since 1981, is qualitatively different from that which it adopted during the 1974–75 crisis and during 1979–81. This is reflected most graphically in the variety of facilities offered to Third World countries, in the mix of high and low conditionality of facilities and, as suggested earlier, in the changes in borrowing limits on specific facilities associated with the Eighth Quota Review. The implication of each of these is that the Fund is now placing much more emphasis than previously on the necessity of borrowers to adjust their economies to the changed world conditions, offering quite restrictive amounts of financial assistance to any *individual* borrower and asserting, in return, powerful leverage over economic policy.

In 1974–75 the Fund set up two *Oil Facilities* to help members meet payments difficulties resulting from oil price increases. The emphasis in the first facility was on financing deficits rather than demanding adjustment to eradicate them. In the second there was more emphasis on oil conservation and substitution but no performance criteria were set and drawings were not phased. The facilities were purely temporary and were not continued after 1975–76. While drawings under these facilities accounted for only 14 percent of total drawings between 1974 and 1983, in calendar years 1974–75 they were by far the most important form of drawing, accounting for over 70 percent of the gross total of credits advanced by the Fund. Members also drew heavily on reserve tranches, the first credit tranche and the compensatory finance facility. As a result, in the year ending April 1975, only 23 percent of all IMF financing was on 'high' conditional terms. If a $1 billion standby credit to a single large borrower, Italy, is excluded, the proportion falls to a mere 2 percent. In the following year high conditional finance was only 3 percent of the total (see Table 4.3).

During 1979/80 and 1980/81 the proportion of high conditionality finance rose to 17.7 and 27.1 percent respectively.[35] While no oil credits were offered during this time, allocation of SDRs provided relief to many countries[36] while Third World countries benefited also from Trust Fund Loans and gold profit distributions. These helped to offset a pronounced increase in drawings on upper credit tranche facilities and the EFF.

While high conditionality drawings continued their strong increase in 1981/82 and 1982/83, no allocations of SDRs were made and oil facility credits and Trust Fund loans were no longer available. Large debtors drew heavily on their reserve tranches and the CFF but the proportion of high conditionality drawings registered a huge increase, to 65.7 percent and 53.7 percent respectively. If drawings on the CFF by countries already drawing in the upper credit tranches are designated 'highly conditional' as one could argue they should be,[37] this trend is greatly reinforced. In 1982/83, for example, only 1 percent of CFF drawings were by countries *not* being conditioned by an IMF stabilization program.[38] If allowance is made for this then the proportion of high conditionality finance rises from 81 percent in 1981/82 to 86 percent in 1982/83. The equivalent figures for 1979/80 and 1980/81 are 23.8 percent and 29 percent respectively. If one then deducts drawings on the reserve tranche, which are really part of members' foreign reserves, then virtually 100 percent of IMF finance in 1982/83 was highly conditional compared with 24 percent in 1979/80 and 6.6 percent in 1975/76.

This marked increase in conditionality has been explained in various ways. The Fund denies there has been a change in policy, arguing that the

Table 4.3

Conditionality and IMF Financial Assistance 1975/76, 1980/81, 1982/83

(year ending April 30)	**1975**	**1976**	**1980**	**1981**	**1982**	**1983**
Zero Conditionality						
Reserve Tranche	0.98	1.32	0.22	0.47	1.08	1.13
SDR Allocations	—	—	4.03	4.05	—	—
Oil Facility Subsidy	—	0.01	0.03	0.05	0.01	—
Gold Profit Distributions	—	—	0.30	0.40	—	—
SFF Subsidy	—	—	—	—	0.02	0.04
	0.98	1.33	4.58	4.97	1.11	1.17
Low Conditionality						
First Credit Tranche	0.20	0.29	0.16	0.78	0.02	0.03
Oil Facility	2.50	3.97	—	—	—	—
CFF	0.02	0.83	0.86	0.78	1.64	3.74
Buffer Stock Facility	—	—	0.03	—	—	0.35
Trust Fund Loans	—	—	0.96	1.06	—	—
	2.72	5.09	2.01	2.62	1.66	4.12
High Conditionality						
Credit Tranche	1.10	0.17	0.93	1.90	2.73	3.68
Extended Fund Facility	—	0.01	0.22	0.92	2.58	2.46
	1.10	0.18	1.15	2.82	5.31	6.14
Total Assistance	4.80	6.60	7.74	10.41	8.08	11.43
% High Conditionality	22.9	2.7	17.7	27.1	65.7	53.7
% Total Assistance to Non-OPEC LDCs	**53.1**	**52.5**	**67.3**	**76.2**	**96.4**	**99.4**

Source: Derived from International Monetary Fund, *Annual Reports* (Washington, D.C.: IMF, various years).

global crisis simply warrants tougher adjustment measures by members. Observers have been quick to retort that this suggests the Fund has declined to pursue the kind of *countercyclical* policies that many believe crisis management requires. The most plausible explanation for why it has done so would seem to lie in the coming to power, in January 1981, of the Reagan administration, which has a strong belief in non-expansionist, monetarist solutions to the international crisis. Since that time, both the U.S. government and the Fund have adopted a rigid doctrinaire view of the type of policy action required to deal with the problems of the world economy, one that leaves no room for the kind of flexibility and innovativeness the Fund demonstrated in the 1970s, when U.S. policy was less clear and assertive and the dollar weaker.

Third World countries are most directly affected by this conservative IMF orthodoxy because, *without exception*, all countries borrowing from the Fund since 1979 have been Third World countries, the transactions of other countries since that time (in the figures in Table 4.3) being limited to reserve tranche and SDR, or non-credit drawings. This is to be contrasted with the situation from 1946 to 1973 in which three-quarters of all drawings on the Fund were by industralized capitalist countries.[39] The Fund has, therefore, emerged from the decade of the 1970s, and survived the great uncertainties surrounding its function after the collapse of the Bretton Woods fixed exchange rate system, with a clear role in the world economy—that of policing the economic policies of the Third World. It is to a consideration of the nature of this role and the disputes surrounding it that we now turn.

Conditionality in Fund Stabilization Programs

Background

The *term* 'conditionality' refers to the policy measures a member is required to take as a 'quid pro quo' for borrowing from the Fund. The intent of conditionality is to maintain the revolving nature of Fund resources by ensuring that members' drawings are purely temporary. More importantly, conditionality is a regulatory device which disciplines members to solve their balance of payments and other problems by pursuing policies consistent with the IMF Articles of Agreement. This being so, before discussing the specifics of conditionality, it is necessary to review the main obligations of members under the Agreement.

In pursuit of its objectives of a stable, multilateral payments system, members are required under Article IV to "collaborate with the Fund to promote exchange stability, to maintain orderly exchange arrangements with other members and to avoid competitive exchange alterations."[40] Under Article VIII of the Agreement, members must avoid restrictions on current account payments or transfers, discriminatory currency arrangements and multiple currency practices. Restrictions may, however, be placed on capital account transactions. The currencies of members are to be convertible both internally and externally and members are required to furnish data on various aspects of their monetary and economic situation.

When the Fund was established it was recognized that very few of the original members could meet the requirements of Article VIII due to the reconstruction problems they were facing in the aftermath of the war. Accordingly, provision was made in Article XIV of the Agreement for a transitional period in which it would be permissible to maintain exchange restrictions on current account. During this period governments were to take all possible measures to liberalize their systems. It is under these transitional arrangements that the majority of Third World countries join the Fund. Indeed, most members of the Fund cannot meet the requirements of Article VIII and by April 1983 only 54 out of 146 claimed to have done so,[41] the majority of which were industrialized countries (18) or oil exporters (12). Only one of the 39 low-income countries in the Fund, Haiti, declared itself to be meeting these requirements and only 3 out of 10 major exporters of manufactures, compared with 22 out of 49 'other net oil importers'. In reality, however, most signatories to Article VIII continue to maintain a variety of exchange restrictions. Even so, these conditions stand as an important indication of the *general direction* in which the Fund seeks to move the system when called upon for advice or credit assistance. Otherwise the Fund exercises general surveillance over restrictions through regular consultations (under Article IV) and through periodic special reviews.

The *practice* of conditionality emerged in the late 1940s at the insistence of the U.S.A. which was the principal creditor nation.[42] It was a practice not envisaged in Keynes' original proposal for an international monetary institution and was bitterly opposed by the European nations, the main debtors at the time, who believed that the IMF should not interfere in this way with national autonomy. But U.S. influence prevailed. Conditionality was formally accepted as a *principle* by the Executive Board in February 1952 but was not written into Articles of the Fund until 1969. Current guidelines on conditionality were issued by the Fund only in 1979.[43]

These guidelines urge members to approach the Fund for assistance before their problems become too acute. In recognition of the deteriorating world situation, and formalizing what was already current practice in 1979 under extended and supplementary financing facilities, they permit standby arrangements to be extended from their normal one year up to three years, if needed. Due regard is to be paid by the Fund "to the domestic, social and political objectives, the economic priorities and the circumstances of members, including the causes of their balance of payments problems." The guidelines confirm long-standing arrangements for consultation, phasing and performance clauses, restricting the latter two to purchases beyond the first credit tranche. They provide, in addition for 'preconditions' or corrective measures to be taken by governments before, and as a requirement for, the receipt of IMF assistance. The Fund is not to discriminate in its treatment of different members but at the same time it may impose performance criteria which vary between them because of the "diversity of problems and institutional arrangements" they face. Performance criteria will generally be limited to a small number of macro-variables and only exceptionally to others "when they are essential for the effectiveness of the member's program because of their macro-economic impact." Provision is also made for periodic reviews of longer-term programs, for analysis and assessment of performance under individual programs, and for evaluation of the effectiveness of standby programs in general.

Conditionality is exercised in the upper credit tranches and in drawings under the extended facility (whether financed from ordinary Fund resources or under the Supplementary Facility or Enlarged Access Policy). Members negotiate a stabilization program with the Fund and embody this in a formal 'letter of intent' which is sent by the member to the Fund but which, in practice, is normally drafted in advance by the Fund itself. Undertakings by the member can be of three sorts; *preconditions* which are not normally written into the letter of intent, and *performance criteria* and *other conditions*, which are. Unless the preconditions are met, the program and assistance will not be put in place. Once the program has taken effect, performance criteria must be met if phased IMF credits are to continue. These inevitably include the *qualitative* criterion that members must not introduce or intensify restrictions on trade or current payments or transfers, nor introduce multiple currency practices.[44] In addition, they encompass a small number of *quantitative* macro criteria. If performance criteria are not met then drawings will be suspended and resumed only if members obtain a waiver of exemption, a modification of the criteria or the replacement of the whole arrangement with a new one.[45] The 'other conditions' can be numerous and quite varied but non-compliance in itself brings no direct sanction though it may, of course, indirectly lead to performance criteria not being met. Any evaluation of conditionality must, therefore, encompass each of these three aspects in full and not simply the quantitative performance criteria on which attention tends to be focused, understandably, because of the rather obvious implications of non-compliance with them.

If one looks *only* at the quantitative performance criteria then the content of IMF programs, in practice, is quite limited. On the basis of a small sample of standby arrangements between 1964 and 1979, these criteria would seem to consist largely of ceilings on total domestic credit, public sector credit and new external debt.[46] Sometimes minimum levels of foreign exchange reserves will be indicated, but hardly any other criteria. Only when preconditions and other conditions are brought into the picture does a collection of conditions resembling the popular conception of an IMF package emerge. Devaluation is apparently the most common precondition though Killick has argued that this measure does not appear to be demanded as frequently as is often assumed, being a feature of only between about a quarter and a third of all standbys.[47] It is perhaps a measure of the degree to which conditionality has been tightened up in recent years that in 1983 the incidence of devaluation had risen to between 40 and 50 percent.[48]

'Other conditions' are as numerous as they are varied. They cover fiscal targets of various kinds, different aspects of the activities of non-financial public enterprises, policies on pricing, subsidies,[49] wages and interest rates and assorted 'liberalization measures'.

There is much discussion in the literature on whether or not there is in fact a standard IMF package. Those strongly dissatisfied with the Fund's performance, including representatives of Third World countries, argue that in spite of Fund guidelines to the contrary, there is,[50] while those less critical of the Fund argue that there is not.[51] Certainly the Managing Director of the IMF seems to have a standard list of corrective measures in mind when discussing adjustment—demand management policies (including a "major effort on the fiscal side"), a realistic exchange rate, adequate prices for producers and exporters, the use of the interest rate to mobilize savings and investment, and the liberalization of exchange and trade systems.[52] This list is repeated frequently in IMF publications,[53] and mirrors the stylized 'orthodox' stabilization package discussed in Chapter 2. Undoubtedly, while programs do vary considerably from country to country in terms of their *detailed composition*, there does appear to be a *general thrust* to each which follows quite closely the Fund's own published conception of the content of its programs. What is at issue, therefore, is really not the existence or otherwise of a standard package but rather the relevance and appropriateness of the 'general thrust' behind even the 'diversified' packages that are applied; this is the essence of the conditionality debate.

The Debate

A number of closely related issues are involved in the conditionality debate. At the highest level of abstraction there is the question of which countries should bear responsibility for adjusting to global payments imbalances—countries in deficit or those in surplus. Next there is that of the appropriate blend of finance and adjustment and, therefore, of high and low conditionality sources of finance—a blend which some argue should be determined by reference to the structural characteristics of the borrower as well as to the precise origin of payments imbalances. Finally, if it is agreed that *some* conditionality is required, there is the complex matter of the form it should take.

Under the present world monetary system the obligation to adjust to world current account imbalances falls squarely on the shoulders of deficit countries. Adjustment for countries in balance of payments surplus is an entirely optional matter, but deficit countries *must* adjust unless they have guaranteed long-term sources of financial support or are in the privileged position of their currency acting as a reserve currency. Since Third World countries, which account for most of the global deficit do *not*, with the possible exception of Saudi Arabi, meet either of these conditions, the existing world order can be said, to use the words of Keynes, to "throw the burden on the countries least able to support it, making the poor poorer."[54]

Yet this was not the intention when the IMF was being established. Keynes had argued, unsuccessfully, for a system in which countries in surplus would be penalized for *not* adjusting by being charged interest on their foreign reserve balances held in his proposed monetary institution.[55] Instead, the Fund Agreement provided, under Article VII, for currencies of countries in surplus to be declared 'scarce' but gave the Fund few powers to deal with the situation other than to force members to buy gold from it or authorize other members to restrict transactions in the scarce currency. The Fund does not act as a repository for the reserves of countries in external surplus and when it borrows from them, as it has increasingly in recent years, it does so at commercial rates of interest which are then passed through to borrowers. This is quite the *opposite* of what Keynes intended.

A more rational and equitable global order would not only require a shared responsibility to adjust, it might also necessitate the allocation of surpluses on criteria other than the narrowly commercial ones which have characterized bank financing of global deficits since the early 1970s. Banks cannot be faulted for focusing their credits on a handful of what looked like creditworthy countries in the 1970s—that is the nature of commercial decision taking. What is at issue here is, rather, the *appropriateness* of privatizing world liquidity management in this way. With hindsight, of course, it is now apparent that what was applauded earlier as an efficient global recycling of surpluses contained the seeds of a possible collapse of the world banking system and with it, the world economy. Yet apart from this inherent instability in the way in which surpluses were recycled, there was also a distributional bias against poorer Third World countries, which finds reflection, as shown in Chapter 1, in a serious stagnation of their import purchasing capacity.

The IMF position on dealing with this bias *within* the existing general framework of international monetary management is a highly ambiguous one with important implications for the application of conditionality. On the one hand, it recognizes that poorer Third World countries need an "exceptionally high level"[56] of concessional external finance to meet what Williamson would describe as, their "structural deficits".[57] It acknowledges that, for structural reasons, orthodox stabilization programs might not work as quickly or effectively there as elsewhere and that structural adjustment will, therefore, take longer and require high levels of financing. On the other hand, it does not feel that as a monetary institution, it is the appropriate body to provide the concessional aid that is needed. It protests that "Fund financing must never be confused with development assistance. The Fund has neither the resources nor the authority to provide development aid."[58] It is, however, questionable whether such a clear line can be drawn between financing for "structural adjustment" and financing for "economic development" generally.[59] Also, the Fund has certainly accepted the *principle* of providing finance on concessional terms to low-income Third World countries as the Trust Fund, gold profit distributions and interest-subsidy schemes testify—and what is aid if it is not merely concessional financial assistance? Moreover, it could be argued that the Fund is, in any case and in spite of itself, moving in the very direction it wishes to avoid. The larger sums that it permitted members to borrow over the 1970s, the allocations of SDRs, the longer maturity periods of loans and the veritable explosion in the number of countries seeking assistance are all making unprecedented, *secular*, demands on Fund resources; demands which many would argue are quite appropriate for the Fund to meet.

Nevertheless, the Fund is now resisting any new initiatives to satisfy the pressing financing requirements of low-income countries—requirements which would be even greater, of course, if non-orthodox adjustment approaches of the type outlined in Chapter 2 were being pursued. What is more, it admits that these needs are unlikely to be met from other sources.[60] In consequence, the Fund arrives at a position where it can justify "inevitably sharper and more intense" adjustments in these countries than elsewhere because their external deficits are large "relative to the availability of financing."[61] What this ignores, of course, is the discretion the Fund can exercise over the flow and terms of its own finance, a discretion it has exercised in the past. It also ignores the numerous proposals which exist for the Fund to facilitate the kind of adjustment which it accepts as being desirable. The Fund has the legal mandate to greatly expand financial assistance on low conditional terms to these countries—which have a low "capacity to adjust"[62] —and could find the resources to do so if it so chose. That it prefers not to can be explained by the viewpoint of its dominant members, and especially that of the U.S.A., on what constitutes appropriate global economic policy at this time. These reform proposals and IMF-U.S.A. responses to them are discussed in Chapter 7.

Turning to the 'form' of conditionality, the Fund has often been accused of applying simplistic monetarist analysis to the problems faced by its members. It gives credence to this critique by imposing credit restraint ceilings in almost all its programs whatever the causes of the instability they seek to address.[63] Also the Fund has been the source of much theoretical and applied work on monetarist models for Third World countries. This finds expression in its publications[64] *and* in its training manuals.[65] What is more, the Fund is quite explicit that the monetarist approach to the balance of payments underlies the credit ceiling guidelines it imposes.[66] Its penchant for liberalization measures and market pricing is also quite in keeping with a monetarist philosophy.

On top of this underlying monetarist approach the Fund then draws on others such as the absorption and, more recently, supply-oriented approaches.[67] The result is, unquestionably, ecletic[68] but with, nonetheless, a strong underlying monetarist bias. The uneasiness with which these lie together has increased in recent years as the Fund has come to the view that adjustment is not going to be possible in the short-run for most Third World countries. It seems to have reached this conclusion with some reluctance and without clearly understanding its implications because, while it talks of supply factors and *structural* adjustment, its principal performance criteria continue to be short-term, demand-oriented and very monetarist in character. Even those who are quite sympathetic to the Fund see these inconsistencies.[69]

There have been numerous critiques of the theoretical and political appropriateness of those aspects of the Fund's programs that are monetarist, generally in line with the ones discussed in Chapter 2. Sidney Dell has been especially vigorous in emphasizing that the Fund ignores its own guidelines by refusing to recognize the very different origins of balance of payments deficits and by seeking to cure all of them by demand restraint. Where deficits are entirely out of the hands of the country involved and are caused by global crisis, this is a costly way of attempting to deal with them. It would, he argues, be more appropriate to provide unconditional financing for these, possibly by widening the scope of the Compensatory Finance Facility to include the financing of general import price increases.[70] The Fund and its more sympathetic observers deny the relevance of the origin of payments imbalances. They see a need to adjust to all disturbances that are not transitory or self-reversing whatever their origin. Implicit in this position, again, is the Fund's view of the limited nature of its resources. As Mikeselle has put it, "(t)here is nothing in the cause of a country's payments imbalance that relieves it of the necessity for adjustment, given the limitations on the availability of external finance."[71] The Fund also sees demand restraint as an "indispensable ingredient" to adjustment programs,[72] vital to the switching of expenditures from consumption and imports to investment and exports. There is more than a suggestion here that domestic mismanagement is always a major factor in Third World economic crises.

A further point of contention is the Fund's analytical preference for large, sudden adjustments in exchange rates, interest rates, subsidies and prices. It makes no apologies for this 'shock treatment' even though "it may sometimes involve rather high initial costs in terms of growth and employment," since "it can be expected that import benefits will follow in short order, and over time the net benefits may be greater than if a more gradual course had been chosen."[73] The costs of this 'overkill', to use Dell's term,[74] have been documented in a number of specific country case studies[75] and have given rise to what have become known as 'IMF riots' in recent years in countries such as Peru, Egypt, the Sudan and the Dominican Republic.[76]

Whatever the degree or speed of adjustment demanded, the Fund is exposed to criticisms of excessive policy intervention and paternalism. President Nyerere of Tanzania speaks for many Third World governments when he asks "when did the IMF become an International Ministry of Finance? When did nations agree to surrender to it their power of decision taking?"[77] In defence, the Fund and sympathetic observers reply that no country is compelled to borrow from it, that the degree of intervention is a function of the timeliness of government action to address problems and that governments often use the Fund as a scapegoat for their own shortcomings.[78] There is undoubtedly some truth in each of these responses but they are less convincing during a period of global crisis stretching over several years in which policy maneouvrability and access to other external sources of finance by many Fund members are both severely restricted.

The 'pin-point targetry' of Fund conditionality is another source of irritation among borrowers.[79] Performance criteria are set quite rigidly and failure to meet them leads quickly to a withdrawal of IMF funding. This has given rise to the proposal that the assumptions underlying performance criteria be clearly specified so that if they are not met for reasons outside of the borrowers' control, then the criteria could be amended to take this into account. Rigid ceilings might thus be replaced by targets with provisions being made for contingencies.[80] The Fund response is that the advantage of current performance criteria is that they are "subject to unambiguous reading"[81] and cover, in any case, variables subject to routine monitoring by all governments.

Critics charge that Fund programs do not explicitly address the question of how the burden of adjustment will be distributed among different social groups. No attempt is made to guarantee employment levels nor the preservation or extension of basic needs provisions.[82] Some claim with justification that Fund programs have a strong bias toward shifting income from workers to property owners.[83] There is, indeed, some evidence of programs causing sharp falls in real wages.[84] The mechanisms by which this occurs are the imposition of ceilings on money wages in the face of general inflation, the removal of subsidies or price controls on basic consumption items, the raising of taxes or fees and reduction of government services, and an increase of unemployment due to demand compression.

It is for this reason, primarily, that the IMF has itself spoken of the need for strong governments to implement its programs effectively.[85] We have already remarked, in Chapter 2 on the close relationship between 'successful' adjustment programs and authoritarian regimes.

While the direct impact on wages is reasonably predictable, the way in which overall income distribution will be affected is less clear. As argued, again in Chapter 2, this will depend on the extent to which income is shifted from the urban to the rural areas and on the structure of property relationships and economic power in the rural areas. This explains why the one study Fund staff have made on income distribution offers few generalizable conclusions except that Fund programs should be more sensitive to the issue.[86] Yet one can hardly believe that the Fund is *not* aware of the general distributional consequences of specific programs, especially as they affect wage earners. Also, it is certainly not a difficult task to design programs with different distributional implications. A more plausible explanation is that sharp cuts in real wages fit into the IMF's profit-restoration approach to economic recovery. From its point of view, therefore, taking steps to ameliorate that impact would, as Williamson has argued about distributional implications in general, "inevitably neutralize the effects one was seeking in the first instance."[87]

Since urban workers have political influence disproportionate to their numbers, and a geographical proximity to the decision makers themselves, governments ignore the effects on their real income at their peril—'IMF riots' are strictly an urban phenomenon. The fact that real wages might have been steadily eroded in any case in the absence of the program, as the IMF claims in defence, is usually correct but hardly relevant when the alternative is presented in the form of shock treatment. The point at issue here is that there is no evidence that IMF programs have ever redistributed income in a progressive direction[88] even though, as evidence from Malaysia and Tanzania shows, it is theoretically possible to do so, and especially in a stabilization-with-growth program.[89]

For its part, the Fund takes the position that it has no mandate to interfere in matters of income distribution or basic needs which are the clear political prerogative of member governments. It maintains, however, that by switching the terms of trade in favour of rural areas Fund programs are, if anything, biased in favour of the poorer sections of society.[90]

IMF conditionality clearly pushes members into integrating more fully into the world economy through trade and payments liberalization. On the trade side the emphasis is, as in the typical conventional model of Chapter 2, very much on export promotion and the equalization of domestic prices with world prices. In effect, when applied to the large number of countries seeking IMF assistance in recent years, the price adjustments associated with this trade emphasis serve to help restore the global rate of profit, and especially that in the industrialized capitalist countries, by reducing the real wages of workers in the Third World and by turning the terms of trade against Third World countries. On the payments side, IMF policies serve to enhance the internationalization of capital in the form both of bank debt and of direct investment.[91] Indeed, it is now a basic theoretical position of the Fund that "(e)xpanded flows of direct investment to the developing countries are in everybody's interest. . . . Thus the Fund is encouraging developing countries to remove obstacles to such flows and to place greater emphasis on policies designed to attract foreign direct investment as part of their development strategy."[92] Fund conditionality would, therefore, be quite inconsistent with development strategies which emphasize national economic integration or convergence and would open up these economies to the very market forces and foreign influences that such strategies seek to neutralize. For Third World countries in the early stages of transition to socialism pursuing these types of strategy, a pro-market emphasis might be particularly difficult to accommodate. Such countries have, on occasion, been excluded from the Fund for refusing to dismantle controls (e.g., Cuba 1966) or have been denied credits (e.g., Vietnam and Grenada 1981).[93] They have protested vigorously at this treatment. Nevertheless, Fidel Castro has perhaps spoken for all of them when saying that, given the nature of Fund conditionality, Cuba is not sure whether being deprived of IMF credits is a punishment or a privilege.[94] This is a particularly telling statement given Cuba's relatively strong reliance on external trade and external bank debt—

a reliance which has been the object of criticism by those advocating a more pronounced emphasis on convergence,[95] but one which does not in general terms seem to conflict with the strategic thrust underlying IMF conditionality.

The debate on conditionality is, therefore, a very wide-ranging one touching upon the efficiency and equity of the world payments system, on policy approaches to solving the global crisis and on the development strategies being pursued by member countries. The question remains, however, of what kind of an impact IMF programs have had in practice on Third World countries and how successful conditionality has been in meeting objectives laid down by the Fund.

The Performance of IMF Programs in Terms of Their Own Objectives

Assessing the performance of Fund stabilization programs is no easy task. Relatively little is known about their content because of the Fund's commitment to confidentiality in its dealings with members. Also there are several different yardsticks of evaluation, each with its own attractions and weaknesses.[96] Most of the few empirical studies that have been made either compare the situation in terms of the balance of payments, growth and inflation *after* the implementation of the program with the situation *before*, or they compare the performance in these terms of countries with programs with that of other countries without programs. The shortcomings of both methods are that it is not known to what extent programs were actually implemented and it is impossible to say whether the program or other exogenous factors were responsible for actual performance. The studies in question tend to aggregate all or most countries together, expressing results in broad percentage terms, which hides the extremes and the different performances by different country groups. Most such studies also do not undertake tests of the significance of their findings.

Another approach is to assess performance in terms of the extent to which performance criteria have been met. This is useful information but is of second order importance except where performance criteria measure directly the extent to which the *objectives* of the program are being met (e.g., the rate of inflation, the balance of payments, etc.). Otherwise performance criteria such as credit ceilings are linked to objectives only indirectly and, as we have seen sometimes, on the basis of dubious analysis. While such studies can throw light on the relationship between performance and performance criteria, their usefulness is limited in this regard by their exclusion of countries whose programs were cancelled because of failure to comply with agreed terms. This shortcoming is shared by most studies, regardless of their methodology.

Ideally it would be useful to know what might have happened in the absence of programs or what might have happened if alternative programs had been implemented. Understandably, there is nothing in the literature on this except the odd piece of theoretical modelling. It is generally accepted, however, that most countries turn to the Fund for assistance only when their economic situation is deemed untenable and that few of them develop any alternative programs even when they disagree strongly with the one presented to them by the IMF. This is partly because when foreign exchange is the critical constraint, there *are* few alternatives but to turn to the Fund. In addition, a characteristic of acute crisis appears to be the paralysis of governments in terms of innovative policies so that negotiations with the Fund become *defensive* rather than creative. The inflexibility of the Fund in terms of its 'general thrust' also does not help to stimulate alternative programming.

With these reservations in mind, we can summarize the evidence of the extent to which Fund programs have met their objectives expressed as "the restoration and maintenance of viability to the balance of payments in an environment of price stability and sustainable rates of growth."[97]

The Balance of Payments

On the basis of studies undertaken by Connors[98] and by the ODI, Killick has concluded that, in terms of improving the current account balance, "the most that can be claimed is some modest short-run tendency for the programme to move in the desired direction but a tendency which has only low claims to statistical significance."[99]

Drawing on studies by Reichman and Stillson,[100] Reichman,[101] and the ODI, Killick concludes that the basic, or overall, balance of payments responded more strongly than the current account which suggests that IMF programs do have a catalytic effect in attracting capital.[102] Once again, however, the results were not very significant statistically.

These findings appear to be disputed by a more recent study by Donovan covering the 1970s.[103] This shows that, as a percentage of GNP, the current account balance of countries drawing in the upper credit tranches improved both in absolute terms and *relative* to that of all non-oil developing countries. This improvement was registered in the year following the agreement and was sustained over a three-year period as well (see Table 4.4). The absolute and relative improvement in the overall balance of payments as a percentage of exports of Donovan's country group was even more pronounced than that in the current account. On the basis of these findings the IMF now claims that its programs bring 'significant' absolute and relative improvements in the balance of payments.[104]

The author has reworked Donovan's study using only poorer Third World countries with a per capita income of $690 or less in 1980.[105] The results show that the LLDCs did not enjoy the improvement in current account performance registered by Donovan's country group—indeed their current account position worsened after implementing IMF programs. Their overall balance of payments record was also inferior to that of Donovan's countries and although their three-year performance on this measure was

Table 4.4

Performance of LLDCs Actively Drawing on Upper Credit Tranche Facilities (average % change in performance indicators, 1971–1980)

		Upper Tranche Program LLDCs	All LLDCs	Donovan Countries	All NODCs
Current Account	1 Year	−0.8	−0.9	1.5	−0.4
	3 Year	−2.4	−2.2	1.2	−0.8
Overall Balance	1 Year	−3.8	−1.1	5.6	−0.3
	3 Year	3.3	−2.1	7.1	0.1
Inflation	1 Year	0	1.1	1.8	3.2
	3 Year	−2.8	2.8	2.3	6.9
GDP Growth	1 Year	−0.4	−0.3	−0.3	−0.2
	3 Year	−0.1	−0.6	0	−0.4

Source: John Loxley, *The IMF and the Poorest Countries*, (Ottawa: The North-South Institute, 1984), p. 22.

strong, it was found (on three different tests) to be not significantly different at the 5 percent level from the performance of all least developed countries.

What is more, it was found that an IMF program did *not* act as a catalyst in attracting commercial bank loans to the LLDCs although it did for countries classified in Chapter 1 as 'net oil exporters' and 'major exporters of manufactures'.

It would seem, therefore, that Donovan's results are influenced very much by the superior balance of trade and payments performance of the handful of countries which successfully pursued a debt/export strategy in the 1970s. They cannot be generalized to other Third World countries, nor necessarily to other periods of time as the IMF implies they can. It is especially important to note, in this respect, that none of the above studies assesses the performance of countries borrowing from the IMF during the most recent global recession when export earnings of Third World countries *and* net flows of bank finance actually fell.

Inflation

As was pointed out in Chapter 1, the IMF places great importance on underdeveloped countries reducing the rate of inflation as a means to more rapid growth. It is interesting, therefore, that its own studies indicate that IMF programs have been singularly unsuccessful in this regard. Reichman and Stillson, Reichman and Donovan[106] report that the rate of inflation was reduced in only a minority of cases. Connors confirms the tendency for the rate of price increase to rise and only an ODI study has found evidence of a declining rate of increase in the first year of programs (but rising again thereafter).[107] In his most recent study, Donovan reports "that in only slightly more than one third of . . . program countries were inflation rates reduced. On average, the annual rate of consumer inflation rose by 2 percentage points following the adoption of the program."[108] Part of this, he concludes, was due to exchange rate measures (also borne out by Reichman and Stillson) and program adjustment in administered prices.

Donovan once again goes further than others, however, in arguing that the inflation rate rose less in those countries with programs than in those without. It is difficult to know what weight to attach to this when Donovan has deliberately excluded from his program countries "a small number of countries with exceptionally high rates of inflation . . . in excess of 35 percent per year."[109]

The inflation record of poorer Third World countries borrowing from the IMF in the 1970s was, however, noticeably better than that of other country groupings (Table 4.4): indeed in the three years following the introduction of IMF programs, inflation actually fell on average. The performance of LLDC borrowers on this three-year measure was found to be significantly different from that of all LLDCs at the 5 percent level.[110] Unfortunately, this finding is ambiguous because of the presence of serial correlation. To the extent that it *is* statistically significant, one could argue that IMF programs could be expected to have a positive impact on inflation in these countries if, as argued in Chapter 2, the import constraint is a major cause of inflation. IMF credits could, in this situation, have a significant impact on prices by relaxing domestic supply constraints.

In countries on flexible exchange rates and where social struggles over income shares are more important than import constraints in fuelling inflation (i.e., in essentially middle-income Third World countries), IMF programs could be expected to have less success. IMF representatives claim that reducing inflation in such countries is now given less emphasis in Fund programs than it was in earlier years.[111]

Real Growth

A number of studies have shown that IMF programs have little impact on economic growth. Reichman and Stillson concluded that "there is no evidence that programs systematically affected the level of economic activity within the period considered."[112] Connors and the ODI reached very similar conclusions.

Most studies (Reichman and Stillson, Donovan 1981, Donovan 1982) seem to show a roughly 50–50 split between the number of countries experiencing accelerated growth and those experiencing decelerated growth. Donovan also argues that the growth performance of those with programs was slightly worse in the first year and slightly better over three years than those without programs, but not significantly so. These findings are confirmed by the author's own study of LLDC performance (Table 4.4); the changes in the rates of growth of LLDC program countries were found to be not significantly different from those of all LLDCs during the 1970s.

A further finding of this last study, of great relevance to any objective evaluation of the effectiveness of IMF programs, is that the growth performance of countries borrowing from the IMF follows closely that of nonprogram countries. This simply affirms the enormous importance to individual Third World countries of overall trends in the global economy.[113]

Performance Relative to Targets

Much of the literature deals not with the meeting of objectives but with the extent to which Fund targets were met in terms of performance indicators. On this measurement, the record seems to show a steady deterioration during the 1970s. Thus, for the period 1963–72, Reichman and Stillson reported that 76 percent of programs were considered successfully implemented.[114] This fell to 33.33 percent between 1973–75.[115] In 1978–79 only 5 out of 23 programs were successfully implemented without modification or waiver.[116] More recently the Managing Director of the Fund reported that of the 34 standby and extended arrangements in effect in mid-1982, no fewer than 10 had been "interrupted",[117] resulting in a movement away from longer-term programs, toward one-year standbys.

The Fund's record is particularly bleak in sub-Saharan Africa, where 60 percent of the LLDCs are located. By the Fund's own reckoning its programs there have fallen well short of targets. Thus, it has disclosed that growth targets were reached in only 5 out of 23 African programs, inflation targets in only 13 out of 28 and trade targets in only 11 out of 28.[118] With such an abysmal record it is not surprising that the appropriateness of the Fund's approach to stabilization and structural adjustment has been the subject of much acrimonious debate by the central bankers of that continent.[119]

The main problem area is generally that of restraining credit to governments due to the difficulty of controlling recurrent expenditure and to unfulfilled expectations of foreign capital inflow.[120] But there is also evidence of governments being reluctant to devolve or to implement liberalization programs.[121]

Reichman has argued that even partial implementation of programs "prevented the crisis situation that would have developed had no program been in effect,"[122] but Killick's assessment of the evidence is that there is at best only "a moderate connection between program execution and the achievement of desired economic results and very little connection at all between results and compliance with credit maxima."[123]

It would appear, therefore, that Fund programs had a poor and deteriorating record of implementation over the 1970s (one which, incidentially, may have improved since 1983) and whether implemented or not experienced little success in meeting their objectives. By the same token there is no systematic evidence of programs causing any great hardship in terms of depression and/or inflation or perverse balance of payments results. This has led some to raise the question of whether or not the disputes surrounding IMF programs are really "much ado about nothing."[124]

In contemplating IMF programs, governments are not likely to be guided, however, by the 'average' program elsewhere or by the 'average' results elsewhere. Underlying these 'averages' are the extreme situations which give rise to political instability. Thus, while Third World countries borrowing from the Fund in the 1970s showed, on average, no significant declines in growth, individual countries experienced declines in growth rates of between 4 and 10 percentage points in a single year.[125] This is not to say that IMF programs were responsible for this but the *association* may help explain why many governments are reluctant to borrow from the Fund. Also, and perhaps more importantly, there is the question of how programs *redistribute* income since this can be crucial to political stability.[126] It tends, therefore, to be the extreme examples where IMF riots have taken place that rightly or wrongly, shape the views of Third World governments toward the IMF. Also, Fund inflexibility toward governments such as those of Tanzania, Argentina and the Dominican Republic, which in recent years have considered proposed programs to be too harsh or unacceptable on distributional grounds, has not improved the IMF's image. For these countries, the debate about IMF conditionality is certainly 'much ado about *something*'.

The Fund, the Major Debtors and the Banks

The question of the political acceptability of IMF programs is nowhere more crucial than in the major debtor countries. The key element in current strategies to contain the debt crisis is an assumption that the IMF adjustment programs, which debtors had to accept as the price for debt rescheduling and for the receipt of additional financial resources, are workable. Not only that, they must be sustainable throughout the current decade if anything approaching internal and external balance is to be achieved in these countries or, more to the point, if debt servicing is to proceed smoothly as projected by the IMF and others.

By mid-1984, many of the major debtors had experienced dramatic improvements in their balance of payments performance relative to 1982. For most of them, however, this had been achieved by drastically cutting back import demand. Thus, in 1982, Argentina cut back its imports in real terms by about 50 percent and Mexico by 40 percent; in 1983 Venezuela reduced its imports by about 30 percent while between 1980 and 1983 Brazil cut them by a third. The result was a sharp decline in imports as a percentage of GDP and the eradication of all but essential food and raw materials, leading the World Bank to conclude that future growth prospects had been damaged by the inability to import investment goods. Among the larger debtors only Mexico, Korea and Turkey succeeded in raising real export earnings between 1981 and 1983.[127]

The domestic costs of the adjustment packages of large debtors have been enormous. After rising steadily between 1970 and 1981, per capita consumption fell by 10 percent in Argentina, 6 percent in Mexico and 3 percent in Brazil in 1982.[128] Real growth rates declined by 4.5 percent in Mexico, 6.6 percent in Brazil and 5 percent in Argentina, in that year while unemployment soared in all three countries.[129] Only in Mexico has the rate of inflation begun to fall since the onset of the stabilization program, from over 100 percent in 1983 to the still very high rate of 65 percent by mid-

1984. In Brazil the inflation rate has risen steadily and now stands at over 200 percent p.a., while in Argentina it reached 650 percent p.a. in 1984.[130] The distributional consequences of these rates and the accompanying adjustment packages have been staggering. Real wages have fallen quite dramatically as the link between wages and prices has been relaxed; for example, in Mexico trade unions negotiated a 22 percent fall in real wages in 1983 while, by that year, real wages in Argentina were estimated to be only 40 percent of their 1975 level.[131] In each of these countries, excess capacity and bankruptcies have risen as domestic demand has fallen and local credit costs risen, while government spending has been slashed with negative consequences for basic needs expenditures.[132]

Thus, while a debt collapse has been avoided and the balance of payments has improved significantly, domestic austerity has been severe. In Argentina and Brazil this has led to widespread, visible public discontent, while in Mexico it has undoubtedly strained the special corporatist relationship the state enjoys with the trade union movement. Debtor governments have spoken bitterly about the burden of austerity and particularly so with the latest round of interest rate increases.

Smaller debtor countries have also found it politically difficult to adhere to IMF programs and service their debts as planned. There has been rioting over IMF-inspired austerity in Chile.[133] In June 1984, Ecuador unilaterally announced it was suspending payments on debts to foreign governments.[134] At the same time the Bolivian government, which was also implementing an adjustment program (though not under IMF auspices), was pressured by the national trade union movement to cancel all payments on its commercial bank debts until the financial situation of the country improved.[135]

The record of IMF programs is at best a chequered one and while one might expect debtor countries to have a better 'capacity to adjust' than poorer Third World countries, there are clear economic and political limits to how far and how quickly they can adjust in the present context. Oil producers are catering to a depressed and uncertain export market while those exporting manufactured goods are confronting sluggish world demand and an increasingly hostile, protectionist environment.[136] At the same time, as shown in Chapter 3, debt-servicing burdens will remain very high throughout the decade even on optimistic assumptions about interest rates, world trade growth, etc. Debtor countries face, therefore, the medium-term prospect of devoting large proportions of uncertain export earnings entirely to servicing foreign debt while their governments have the unenviable task of restraining, severely, the consumption standards of their people for years to come. The social and political pressures to which this will give rise can be expected to grow as debt-servicing burdens peak to 1987, but they will remain acute for many years thereafter.

The IMF has emerged from the debt crisis in the role of debt collector or repayment enforcer for the transnational banks. In the process, the Fund and the banks have become mutually dependent upon one another, each being indispensable to the other in the management of the debt crisis. The basis of this new relationship is the Fund's supposed ability to impose economic adjustment programs on borrowers that are both workable and, if necessary, sustainable over a period of time. The evidence that IMF programs are effective in meeting their objectives is not strong and there are grounds for questioning the wisdom of applying IMF conditionality to a large number of countries simultaneously and especially in the context of a depressed world trade environment. Moreover, the severity of the domestic austerity which seems to be required to guarantee debt servicing on existing terms, raises serious questions about the political sustainability of current approaches to economic adjustment in a number of debtor countries. Should IMF programs prove unsustainable, then reforms of a more fundamental nature would be required to shore up the world banking system; reforms that would have to alleviate more directly the burden that servicing is imposing on debtor countries (see Chapter 7).

Preoccupation with the debt crisis should not, however, deflect attention from the critical economic problems being faced by the poorer Third World countries. They too are being forced, increasingly, to rely on IMF credits. Under existing IMF policy these credits are expensive and highly conditional and the appropriateness of the conditionality which accompanies them is the subject of controversy. The IMF record in these countries is at best a poor one and while a strong case could be made for alternative approaches to adjustment, along the lines of that sketched out in Chapter 2, the Fund seems inflexibly committed to the 'conventional' approach. Only as evidence mounts of the failure of IMF programs in these countries is the Fund and the countries that control it likely to reconsider its approach to economic adjustment.

Notes

[1] IMF, *Annual Reports* (Washington, D.C.: IMF, 1979 to 1983).

[2] See for instance, Deborah M.R. Coyne, *Monetary and Financial Reforms: The North-South Controversy* (Ottawa: The North-South Institute, 1984).

[3] For the early history of the Fund see J. K. Horsefield, *The International Monetary Fund 1945–1965: Twenty Years of International Monetary Cooperation* 3 Volumes (Washington, D.C.: IMF, 1969), and M. G. de Vries, *The International Monetary Fund, 1966–71: The System Under Stress* 2 Volumes (Washington, D.C.: IMF, 1976).

[4] Figures on quotas and information on organization and financing of the Fund are to be found in A. W. Hooke, *The International Monetary Fund: Its Evolution, Organization and Activities* (Washington, D.C.: IMF, 1982).

[5] Coyne, *Monetary and Financial Reforms*, p. 23, puts the figure at 43%.

[6] Ibid., pp. 26–28.

[7] On Czechoslovakia and Cuba leaving the Fund, see Horsefield, *The IMF 1945–1965*, pp. 359–364 and pp. 548–550. On Poland, see *The Times* (London), August 19, 1981.

[8] See *The Globe and Mail* (Toronto), September 13, 1982 on the El Salvador Loan and November 4, 1982 on the South African loan.

[9] *The Times* (London), August 19, 1981.

[10] *The Globe and Mail* (Toronto), September 13, 1982.

[11] Ibid., August 27, 1983.

[12] Ibid., May 14, 1984.

[13] Calculated, for the earlier period, as the U.S. quota as a percentage of total quota minus that for the U.S.S.R. from figures in Horsefield, *The IMF 1945–1965*, and for 1983 as the estimate of the quotas of countries whose currencies are deemed usable as a percentage of total quotas using data taken from Hooke, *The IMF*, pp. 71–75.

[14] IMF, *Annual Report*, 1983, p. 93. It is to be noted that the criterion of usability is that "the members concerned have a balance of payments and reserve position that the Fund considers 'sufficiently strong' for that purpose", so that currencies so considered could vary from year to year depending upon the economic situation of the country concerned. See ibid.

[15] Calculated from IMF, *International Financial Statistics*, various issues.

[16] Hooke, *The IMF*, pp. 27–31.

[17] IMF, *Annual Report*, 1982, p. 84 and 1983, p. 93.

[18] The Brandt Commission, *Common Crisis North-South: Cooperation for World Recovery* (London: Pan, 1983), pp. 51–53.

[19] IMF, *Annual Report*, 1982, Chapter 3.

[20] *IMF Survey* (February 21, 1983).

[21] See, for example, *The Globe and Mail* (Toronto), October 3, 1983.

[22] Ibid., September 21, 1983.

[23] Ibid., September 29, 1983.

[24] IMF, *Annual Report*, 1983, p. 94.

[25] See Hooke, *The IMF*, p. 28–30 for reference to Saudi loan and *IMF Survey* (May 1984) for Saudi/BIS loan.

[26] Hooke, *The IMF*, pp. 53–54.

[27] As of June, 1984.

[28] *North-South: A Programme for Survival*, Report of the Independent Commission on International Development Issues, Brandt Commission I (London: Pan, 1980), p. 220.

[29] Developments in the lending capability of the Fund in response to the crises of the 1970s are described in Manuel Guitian,*Fund Conditionality: Evolution of Principles and Practices* (Washington, D.C.: IMF, 1981), as well as in Hooke, *The IMF*.

[30] See *The Globe and Mail* (Toronto), September 10 and September 27, 1983.

[31] *IMF Survey* (January 9, 1984).

[32] *The Globe and Mail* (Toronto), September 27, 1983.

[33] *IMF Survey* (January 9, 1983).

[34] *IMF Survey* (June 4, 1984).

[35] IMF, *Annual Report*, 1983, p. 86. Table 21 is the basis for this data.

[36] SDR allocations to non-OPEC Third World countries were estimated at 27% of the total in each of these years.

[37] See *Towards a New Bretton Woods*, Report by a Commonwealth Study Group (London: Commonwealth Secretariat, 1983), p. 52 which speaks of "the increasing practice of linking CFF drawings with the acceptance of upper credit tranche IMF credit."

[38] IMF, *Annual Report*, 1983, pp. 120–121. Of the 29 countries drawing on the CFF in 1982/83 only 2 countries accounting for only 1% of drawings did not have standbys or extended fund arrangements with the IMF.

[39] Calculated from IMF, *International Financial Statistics*, 1973.

[40] The Articles of Agreement of the Fund are reproduced in Horsefield, *The IMF 1945–1965*, and de Vries, *The IMF*. These should be read in conjunction with J. Gold, *The Second Amendment of the Fund's Articles of Agreement* (Washington, D.C.: IMF, 1978).

[41] IMF, *Annual Report*, 1983, p. 95. The list of countries that have accepted Article VIII obligations is on p. 118.

[42] See Sidney Dell, *On Being Grandmotherly: The Evolution of IMF Conditionality*, Essays in International Finance, no. 144 (New Jersey: Princeton University, October 1981) and J. Gold, *Conditionality* (Washington, D.C.: IMF 1979), for the historical background of conditionality.

[43] Gold, *Conditionality*, deals with the guidelines in detail.

[44] Ibid., p. 33.

[45] Guitian, *Fund Conditionality*, p. 16.

[46] T. Killick, "IMF Stabilization Programmes", *ODI Working Paper No. 6*, London, September 1981, p. 14. The ODI research project on the IMF is the most comprehensive ever undertaken and readers are urged to consult the various papers for their wealth of data on and insights into conditionality.

[47] Ibid., pp. 15–18.

[48] Derived by applying Killick's methodology. Data source: *IMF Survey*, (1984). The 50% figure is arrived at by deducting the French Franc.

[49] See W. A. Beveridge, and M. R. Kelly, "Fiscal Content of Financial Programs supported by Standby Arrangements in the Upper Credit Tranches, 1969–78", *IMF Staff Papers*, Vol. 27, No. 2 (June 1980), for a full discussion of the fiscal aspect of programs, content and performance.

[50] See, for example, "The Arusha Initiative—A Call for a United Nations Conference on International Money and Finance"—a policy resolution of the South-North Conference on the International Monetary System and the New International Order, Arusha, Tanzania, June 30th-July 3rd 1980, in *Development Dialogue*.

[51] See Killick, "IMF Stabilization Programmes"; B. Nowzad, "The IMF and its Critics", *Essays in International Finance*, No. 146 (New Jersey: Princeton University, December 1981); and J. Williamson, "The Lending Policies of the International Monetary Fund", Institute for International Economics: Policy Analyses in International Economies, No. 1, August 1982; also reprinted in *IMF Conditionality*, ed. John Williamson (Washington, D.C.: Institute for International Economics, 1983).

[52] J. de Larosiere, *Economic Adjustment in the Developing Countries and the Industrial Countries: The Need for Complementarity* (Washington, D.C.: IMF, 1982), p. 9.

[53] See for example, Guitian, *Fund Conditionality*, pp. 5–13, or his earlier publication "Conditionality—Access to Fund Resources", reprinted from *Finance and Development* (December 1980, March 1981 and June 1981), or S. Mookerjee, "Countries Tackling Large Payments Imbalances Often need a Medium-Term Adjustment Strategy", *IMF Survey* (August 30th, 1982).

[54] Quoted in Dell, *On Being Grandmotherly*, p. 17. Dell argues cogently against the burden that payments asymmetry places on Third World countries. See also S. Dell, and R. Lawrence, *The Balance of Payments Adjustment Process in Developing Countries* (New York: Pergamon, 1980), pp. 96–100. This latter publication reflects the views of the Group of Twenty-four on this issue as it is based on a report prepared for and accepted by that group.

[55] Keynes' proposal is dealt with at length in Horsefield, *The IMF 1945–1965*, pp. 18–21.

[56] IMF, *Annual Report*, 1982, p. 39.

[57] Williamson defines a "structural deficit" as one "caused by a presumably permanent external shock which cannot be eliminated without structural change except by a permanent departure from internal balance." See Williamson, "The Lending Policies of the IMF", p. 656.

[58] J. de Larosiere, *The Role of the International Monetary Fund in Today's World Economy* (Washington, D.C.: IMF, 1982), p. 3.

[59] See, for instance, G. K. Helleiner, "The Less Developed Countries and the International Monetary System", *World Politics*, Vol. xxxvi, No. 1 (October 1983), p. 150.

[60] IMF, *Annual Report*, 1982, p. 39.

[61] IMF, *World Economic Outlook*, 1984, p. 25.

[62] For a discussion of the 'capacity to adjust' of poorer Third World countries and its implications for conditionality, see Sidney Dell, "Stabilisation: The Political Economy of Overkill" in Williamson, *IMF Conditionality*, pp. 34–35 and G. K. Helleiner, "Lender of Early Resort: The IMF and the Poorest", *American Economic Association, Papers and Proceedings*, Vol. 73, No. 2 (May 1983), pp. 351–352.

[63] Killick, "IMF Stablization Programmes", p. 28.

[64] Much of this work is published in IMF, *The Monetary Approach to the Balance of Payments* (Washington, D.C.: IMF, 1977).

[65] International Monetary Fund Institute, *Financial Policy Workshops: The Case of Kenya* (Washington, D.C.: IMF, 1981.)

[66] Guitian, *Fund Conditionality*, pp. 5–8.

[67] Ibid., pp. 8–13.

[68] John Williamson has argued that this is the best way to describe Fund policies. See his "The Economics of IMF Conditionality" in *For Good or Evil—Economic Theory and North-South Negotiations*, ed. G. K. Helleiner (Toronto: University of Toronto Press, 1982), pp. 121–131.

[69] Killick, "IMF Stablization Programmes", p. 37 and Williamson, "The Lending Policies of the IMF", pp. 633–640.

[70] Dell, "The Political Economy of Overkill", pp. 30–32.

[71] Raymond F. Mikesell, "Appraising IMF Conditionality: Too Loose, Too Tight or Just Right" in Williamson, *IMF Conditionality*, p. 60.

[72] J. de Larosiere, *Economic Adjustment in the Developing Countries and the Industrial Countries—The Need for Complementarity* (Washington, D.C.: IMF, 1982), p. 9.

[73] Mookerjee, "Medium-Term Adjustment Strategy", p. 276.

[74] Dell, "The Political Economy of Overkill".

[75] See Alejandro Foxley, "Stabilisation Policies and Their Effects on Employment and Income Distribution: A Latin American Perspective", in *Economic Stabilisation in Developing Countries*, eds. William R. Cline and Sidney Weintraub (Washington, D.C.: The Brookings Institute, 1981), pp. 198–205; or Dell and Laurence, *Balance of Payments Adjustment Process.*

[76] See, for instance, R. N. McCauley, "A Compendium of IMF Troubles: Turkey, Portugal, Peru, Egypt" in L. G. Franko and M. J. Seiber, *Developing Country Debt* (New York: Pergamon, 1979).

[77] "No to IMF Meddling"—Extract from President Nyerere's New Year Message 1980 to the Diplomats accredited to Tanzania, *Development Dialogue*, No. 2 (1980), p. 8.

[78] See, for example, J. de Larosiere, "Does the Fund Impose Austerity?" (Washington, D.C.: Pamphlet issued by the IMF, June 1984); and William B. Dale, "Financing and Adjustment of Payments Imbalances" in Williamson, *IMF Condi-*

tionality, pp. 3–16. Similar arguments are to be found in Nowzad, "The IMF and its Critics".

[79] This term is used by Sidney Dell in "The Political Economy of Overkill", pp. 40–41.

[80] See comments by Arnold C. Harberger in Williamson, *IMF Conditionality*, pp. 378–580.

[81] Sterie T. Beza, Commentary, in Williamson, *IMF Conditionality*, p. 590.

[82] See the Brandt Commission's, *North-South*, pp. 215–217.

[83] Cheryl Payer, *The Debt Trap* (New York: Monthly Review Press, 1974).

[84] Foxley, "Stabilisation Policies and Their Effects".

[85] See Rosemary Thorp and Lawrence Whitehead, *Inflation and Stabilisation in Latin America* (London: Nelson, 1980), p. 11.

[86] O. Johnson, and J. Salop, "Distributional Aspects of Stabilisation Programs in Developing Countries", *IMF Staff Papers*, Vol. 27, No. 1 (March 1980).

[87] Williamson, "The Economics of IMF Conditionality", p. 128.

[88] R. E. Feinberg, "The International Monetary Fund and Basic Human Needs" in *Human Rights and Basic Needs in the Americas*, ed. M. Graham (Washington, D.C.: Georgetown University Press, 1982).

[89] For a discussion of the Malaysian experience, see William R. Cline, "Economic Stabilisation in Developing Countries: Theory and Stylised Facts" in Williamson, *IMF Conditionality*. For Tanzania see John Loxley, "Tanzania: Origins of a Financial Crisis" in Robert L. Ayres, *Banking on the Poor: The World Bank and World Poverty* (Cambridge, Mass.: MIT Press, 1983).

[90] C. David Finch, "Adjustment Policies and Conditionality" in Williamson, *IMF Conditionality*, pp. 77–78.

[91] See Samuel Lichtensztejn, "IMF–Developing Countries: Conditionality and Strategy" in Williamson, *IMF Conditionality*, pp. 209–222.

[92] J. de Larosiere, quoted in *IMF Survey* (March 26, 1984), p. 84.

[93] See IMF, *The Summary Proceedings, Annual Meeting* (Washington, D.C.: IMF, 1980), p. 203, and 1981, p. 163, for Vietnam's protest against being refused credits; and for Grenada, the same publication 1981, p. 76.

[94] See M. Taber, *Cuba's Internationalist Foreign Policy 1975–1980: Fidel Castro's Speeches* (New York: Pathfinder Press, 1981), p. 176.

[95] See C. Y. Thomas, *Dependence and Transformation: The Economics of the Transition to Socialism* (New York: Monthly Review Press, 1974), pp. 18–20.

[96] These various possibilities are analyzed in John Williamson, "On Judging the Success of IMF Policy Advice" in Williamson, *IMF Conditionality*, pp. 129–143.

[97] Guitian, *Fund Conditionality*, p. 30.

[98] T. A. Connors, "The Apparent Effects of recent IMF Stabilisation Programs" (Washington: Federal Reserve International Finance Discussion Paper No. 135, April 1970, Mimeo).

[99] T. Killick, "The Impact of IMF Stablisation Programmes in Developing Countries", *ODI Working Paper* No. 7 (March 1982), p. 7.

[100] T. M. Reichmann and R. T. Stillson, "Experience with Programs of Balance of Payments Adjustment: Stand-by Arrangements in the Higher Tranches, 1963–72", *IMF Staff Papers* Vol. 25, No. 2 (June 1978).

[101] T. M. Reichmann, "The Fund's Conditional Assistance and the Problems of Adjustment, 1973–75", *Finance and Development* (December 1978).

[102] Killick, "The Impact of IMF Stabilisation Programmes", p. 9. This also contains the results of the ODI Studies referred to.

[103] D. J. Donovan, "Macroeconomic Performance and Adjustment Under Fund Supported Programs: The Experience of the Seventies", *IMF Staff Papers*, Vol. 29, No. 2 (June 1982).

[104] J. de Larosiere, *The Role of the IMF*, p. 5.

[105] John Loxley, *The IMF and the Poorest Countries* (Ottawa: North-South Institute, 1984).

[106] D. J. Donovan, "Real Responses Associated with Exchange Rate Action in Selected Upper Credit Tranche Stabilisation Programs", *IMF Staff Papers*, Vol. 28, No. 4 (December 1981).

[107] Killick, "Impact of IMF Stabilisation Programmes", pp. 15–16.

[108] Donovan, "Real Responses Associated with Exchange Rate Action", p. 185.

[109] Ibid., p. 182.

[110] Loxley, *The IMF and the Poorest Countries*, pp. 19–23.

[111] Finch, "Adjustment Policies", p. 81.

[112] Reichman and Stillson, "Balance of Payments Adjustment", p. 303.

[113] Loxley, *The IMF and the Poorest Countries*, p. 29.

[114] Reichman and Stillson, "Balance of Payments Adjustment", p. 308.

[115] Reichman, "The Fund's Conditional Assistance", p. 41.

[116] Killick, "The Impact of IMF Stabilisation Programs", p. 24.

[117] de Larosiere, *The Role of the IMF*, p. 6.

[118] Reported in *The Globe and Mail* (Toronto), August 25, 1983.

[119] The 'impracticability' of the IMF Solution dominated the 1983 meetings of the Association of African Central Bankers. See *Daily News* (Tanzania), August 11, 1983.

[120] Beveridge and Kelly, "Fiscal Content of Financial Programs", pp. 241–249.

[121] Killick, "The Impact of IMF Stabilisation Programmes", p. 27.

[122] Reichmann, "The Fund's Conditional Assistance", p. 41.

[123] Killick, "The Impact of IMF Stabilisation Programmes", p. 38.

[124] Ibid.

[125] Loxley, *The IMF and the Poorest Countries*, p. 28.

[126] The principal weakness of the Fund as 'global policeman' is seen by some to be its lack of means to control the working classes of borrowing countries; for this the Fund must depend upon national governments. See Ron Phillips, "The Role of the International Monetary Fund in the Post-Bretton Woods Era", *Review of Radical Political Economics*, Vol. XV, No. 2 (Summer 1983), p. 76.

[127] World Bank, *World Development Report*, 1984 (Washington, D.C., Discussions Proof), p. 226.

[128] Ibid.

[129] For a discussion of recent stabilization efforts in these countries, see William R. Cline, *International Debt—Systemic Risk and Policy Response* (Washington, D.C.: Institute for International Economics, 1984), Appendix C.

[130] *The Globe and Mail* (Toronto), September 27, 1984.

[131] See *The Globe and Mail* (Toronto), May 7, 1984; and Alejandro Foxley, *Latin American Experiments in Neoconservative Economics* (Berkley: University of California Press, 1983), p. 122.

[132] World Bank, *World Development Report*, 1984, p. 227. In Mexico's case, the public sector deficit was to be reduced from 16.5% of GDP in 1982 to 3.5% in 1985. See Ariel Buira, "The Exchange Crisis and the Adjustment Program in Mexico" in *Prospects for Adjustment in Argentina, Brazil and Mexico: Responding to the Debt Crisis*, ed. John Williamson (Washington, D.C.: Institute for International Economics, 1983), pp. 51–60. In the discussion following this article, pp. 61–63, William Cline

raises the issue of the domestic cost and political sustainability of these and other measures in Mexico.

[133] *The Globe and Mail* (Toronto), April 2, 1984.

[134] Ibid., June 6, 1984.

[135] Ibid., July 9, 1984.

[136] See IMF, *Annual Report*, 1983, pp. 58–59. According to the IMF protectionism is even more of a problem in 1984 than in earlier years. See *IMF Survey* (September 17, 1984), p. 278.

5

THE WORLD BANK AND STRUCTURAL ADJUSTMENT

In channelling resources from the industrialized capitalist countries to Third World countries, the World Bank has an importance very similar to that of the IMF.[1] The major difference between these bodies is that the Bank, which consists of two institutions, the International Bank for Reconstruction and Development (IBRD) and its soft loan affiliate, the International Development Association (IDA), has a mandate to finance longer-term 'reconstruction and development' efforts as opposed to short-run stablization programs.[2] In 1979, however, it introduced a new form of lending, the Structural Adjustment Loan (SAL) which has much more in common with IMF facilities than with conventional forms of Bank assistance.[3] These loans are distinguishable from IMF loans, though, by the form and degree of conditionality which attaches to them. While it is too early to say how SALs will perform relative to the expectations of the Bank and borrowing countries, there are already suggestions that the type of conditionality they carry might serve as a model in reforming IMF conditionality.[4]. Even if this does not transpire, World Bank initiatives tend to exercise significant influence over the theory and practice of development policy and its approach in this area can be expected, therefore, to have an impact out of all proportion to the size of its loans. Thus, while structural adjustment lending has not so far accounted for more than 8.9 percent of annual loan commitments by the Bank (Table 5.1) and has been restricted by the Executive Board to a maximum of 10 percent of its total lending in the foreseeable future,[5] (and to a maximum of 30 percent of total Bank assistance to any individual country), it nevertheless warrants careful examination.

Nature, Size and Terms of Structural Adjustment Loans

The new loan facilities were initiated by the Bank in September 1979 to enable borrowers to restructure their economies over a five- to ten-year period. The main objective of restructuring is to strengthen the balance of payments to a point where imports required for continuing development can be financed on a self-sustaining basis. The Bank holds that this restructuring requires changes in the patterns of production, trade and investment, which in turn necessitate both policy and institutional reforms, which are the object of its conditionality. In addition, however, the re-

Table 5.1

Total IBRD and IDA Loan Approvals

	1980		1981		1982		1983	
	$m	**%**	**$m**	**%**	**$m**	**%**	**$m**	**%**
Structural Adjustment Loans	305	2.7	867	7.0	921	7.1	1,285	8.9
Other Program Loans	218	1.9	155	1.1	320	2.5	150	1.0
Project Loans	10,960	95.5	11,279	91.8	11,775	90.5	13,042	90.0
Total	**11,482**	**100.0**	**12,291**	**100.0**	**13,016**	**100.0**	**14,477**	**100.0**

Source: Derived from the World Bank, *Annual Report* (Washington, D.C.: World Bank, 1983).

structuring process will itself generate additional import demands in the short run and structural adjustment loans are designed to finance these and to act as a catalyst in attracting foreign capital from other sources. The loans provide financing for general import support and are, therefore, a form of program loan.

Program lending is not new to the World Bank. In the first five years of its existence the Bank's lending activities were focused on post-war reconstruction in Europe and almost three-quarters of its loans were in program form. The proportion dropped to 20 percent in the following five years and, as the Bank's operations switched to lending to underdeveloped countries, stabilized at between 4.5 to 6.5 percent of total lending after that time.[6] The rationale for this switch is that the Articles of Agreement (of both the IBRD and the IDA) stipulate that "except in special circumstances" the Bank should confine its lending to individual projects.[7] This has meant that program lending has been largely a response to situations of crisis. Occasionally, the focus has been on easing general problems of reconstruction as in the case of Bangladesh (1972–81) or Uganda (1982) but, more frequently, program lending has been designed to alleviate serious bottlenecks in specific sectors of the economy. Thus, India has received a number of industrial program loans while other countries have received agricultural export rehabilitation credits.[8] Each such loan has been justified by exceptional circumstances and it appears that the new structural adjustment loans are being justified in the same way; that is, as a legitimate response by the Bank to the current global crisis as it affects underdeveloped countries. It is to be noted, however, that Dell has recently argued that the Bank does indeed have a general mandate to make long-term stabilization loans but that it has chosen not to exercise that mandate.[9]

Table 5.1 shows that structural adjustment lending is now the most important form of program lending in the Bank and that in 1983 it was approaching the ceiling imposed upon it by the Executive Directors. Unless this ceiling is relaxed, the size of this form of lending will be dictated in the immediate future by the rate of growth of the overall resources of the Bank and, at a maximum, is likely to be in the range of $1.2 to $1.5 billion p.a. It is to be noted, however, that Table 5.1 is a little misleading in that some project loans are in a sense 'policy-based' loans in their key characteristics. This is the case, for instance, with export rehabilitation projects. Policy-based lending, in this broader definition, including SALs, is said to have reached as much as 25 percent of total bank lending in 1983/84.[10]

Up to April 1984 the Bank had approved over $4 billion in structural adjustment loans to 16 countries. Over 85 percent of these loans were received by middle-income countries with per capita incomes in excess of $450 in 1980, and fully 29 percent (or $1.2 billion) by one country, Turkey. Only five low-income countries had received loans by that date amounting to only 13 percent of the total lending (see Tables 5.2 and 5.3).

The terms of structural adjustment loans are similar to those of other types of loans issued by the World Bank. Those advanced from the IBRD

Table 5.2

Structural Adjustment Loans by Type of Recipient, 1980–1984

	Countries	$m	% of Total Amount
Major Exporters of Manufactures	2	825	20.2
Net Oil Exporters	1	50	1.2
Low-Income Countries	5	526	12.9
Other Net Oil Importers	8	2,678	65.7
Total	**16**	**4,079**	**100.0**

Source: World Bank, "Structural Adjustment Lending Progress Report" (Washington, D.C.: World Bank, June 6, 1984), pp. 84–150.

are repayable over a period of between 15 and 20 years with between three and five years grace depending on the income level of the borrowing country. Interest is charged at 0.5 percent above the Bank's cost of borrowing and stood at 11.6 percent in June 1982, and 9.89 percent in July 1984. In addition, from January 1982 a front-end fee of 1.5 percent was introduced on new commitments. This fee has also been reduced as the Bank's financial position has improved and now stands at 0.25 percent.

Structural adjustment loans from the IDA are repayable in 50 years, including a grace period of 10 years and carry no interest. There is, however, a fee of 0.75 percent on the disbursed portion of each loan and, from January 1982, an additional 0.5 percent on the undisbursed portion. Only countries with a per capita income of less than $731 in 1980 dollars are eligible for IDA assistance and countries 'graduate' to more commercial terms as incomes rise. In 1982, 38 countries were eligible to receive pure IDA loans and a further 13, a blend of IDA and IBRD loans.[11] The remaining 'middle-income' underdeveloped countries are eligible only for pure IBRD loans.

The Conditionality of Structural Adjustment Loans and Its Rationale

It is not, therefore, the financial terms of structural adjustment loans that distinguish them from other facilities offered by the Bank. Rather, it is a combination of their flexibility and conditionality. SALs are more flexible than project and other types of program loans because they provide more general import support not tied to the requirements of specific projects or sectors. On the other hand, this flexibility carries with it the price of a much greater degree of conditionality and is itself bounded by that conditionality as the Bank specifies, up to a point, how the foreign exchange proceeds of the loan will be allocated.

The Bank sees structural adjustment loans as having three advantages over project and sectoral loans, viz:

Table 5.3

Structural Adjustment Loans Approved as of April 30, 1984

		Date of Approval	Amount ($m)	Disbursements ($m)
Kenya	I	03/25/80	55.0	55.0
	II	07/01/82	130.9	130.9
Turkey	I	03/25/80	200.0	200.0
& Supplement		11/18/80	75.0	75.0
	II	05/12/81	300.0	300.0
	III	05/27/82	304.5	304.5
	IV	06/23/83	300.8	299.9
Bolivia		06/05/80	50.0	50.0
Philippines	I	09/16/80	200.0	199.3
	II	04/26/83	302.3	302.3
Senegal		12/18/80	60.0	43.7
Guyana		02/03/81	22.0	22.0
Mauritius	I	06/02/81	15.0	15.0
	II	12/08/83	40.0	13.4
Malawi	I	06/25/81	45.0	45.0
	II	12/20/83	55.0	27.7
Ivory Coast	I	11/24/81	150.0	150.0
	II	07/05/83	250.7	125.7
Korea	I	12/17/81	250.0	250.0
	II	11/08/83	300.0	200.0
Thailand	I	03/02/82	150.0	150.0
	II	03/31/83	175.5	175.5
Jamaica	I	03/23/82	76.2	76.2
	II	06/14/83	60.2	35.2
Pakistan		06/01/82	140.0	140.0
Togo		05/17/83	40.0	25.0
Yugoslavia		06/28/83	275.0	80.7
Panama		11/15/83	60.2	40.2
Total			**4,079.3**	**3,532.2**

Source: World Bank, "Structural Adjustment Lending Progress Report" (Washington, D.C.: World Bank, June 6, 1984), pp. 84–150.

> the comprehensiveness of their coverage both in terms of macro and sector issues of policy reform; the exclusive focus on policy and institutional reform; and the detailed articulation of the precise modifications in policy necessary to adjust the economy to a changed economic environment.[12]

In short, this new type of lending affords the Bank a degree of leverage over the economic policies of borrowers greatly in excess of that afforded by its conventional lending facilities. While the Bank believes this will create an economic climate that will improve the performance and effectiveness of its other types of loans, an important consideration for an institution borrowing on world capital markets, this is merely a secondary consideration; structural adjustments are required for their own sake if member countries are to overcome their economic crises.

According to the Bank's analysis, the need for reform stems not only from the situation of global crisis but also from weaknesses and failures of domestic policies and institutions within underdeveloped countries.[13] These weaknesses impose their own costs in terms of economic performance but also act as an impediment to countries adapting to the changed international environment. In particular, the Bank sees overvalued exchange rates, inadequate price incentives to producers and waste and incompetence in state-run credit and marketing agencies as the major causes of poor export performances in many countries. It also holds state intervention responsible for such price 'distortions' as excessive import tariffs, negative real interest rates and high urban wages and feels that these impede the mobilization and/or efficient allocation of resources. Likewise, the tendency toward unproductive investment is held to reflect the failure of states to articulate or follow clear investment priorities, while inflationary budget deficits are viewed as the inevitable outcome of policies of price controls, of subsidizing urban consumption, of providing basic health, education and water supplies free of charge and of enlarging unproductive state expenditures on administration and defence. In general, growth has been held back in many countries by the replacement or restriction of the private sector by the state in all major sectors of the economy to the point where the state sector, in either its government or parastatal form, has over-reached its administrative and management capabilities.

These views of the causes of crisis are to be found in several Bank publications but are developed most uncompromisingly in the Bank's report "Accelerated Development in Sub-Saharan Africa—An Agenda for Action" (The Berg Report), the basic premise of which is that "domestic policy issues are at the heart of the crisis" in sub-Saharan Africa.[14]

The conditionality of structural adjustment loans is premised on this diagnosis of the underlying causes of economic crisis in the underdeveloped world. Accordingly, the Bank concentrates on 'getting prices right,' on altering the balance between state control and the use of market forces, on adjusting investment priorities and on improving institutional performance. That is, it focuses quite clearly on what might be termed supply-side stimulation. The Bank does not normally address issues of demand management directly even though it believes that demand restraint is often a necessary prerequisite for successful adjustment efforts. Instead, it assumes that its own programs will usually follow closely on the heels of the successful negotiation of an IMF extended facility, and, therefore, envisages its own assistance and conditionality as closely complementing, rather than replacing or competing with, those of the IMF.

Table 5.4 captures the range of policy concerns covered by the 27 structural adjustment loans that had been negotiated to April 1984. It can be seen that the measures which most frequently occur are those dealing with pricing, incentives and institutional support in the key sectors of the economy as well as with the revision and review of public sector investment priorities. Most programs contained, in addition, measures to improve public sector financial performance, budgetary policy and external debt management capacity. A minority had provisions relating to exchange rate and interest rate policies but these are the traditional preserve of IMF programs.

The main thrust of trade policy adjustment has been to promote both agricultural and industrial exports (including minerals) through diversification and improved competitiveness, and to discourage uneconomic import substitution industries. Export promotion has involved incentives in the form of higher producer prices or direct export subsidies. It has also entailed institutional reform such as the streamlining of administrative procedures and the provision of credit or insurance facilities for non-traditional exports. Import adjustment has taken the form of the modification of tariff levels and the liberalization of controls. In some cases domestic oil prices have been raised to world levels to discourage imports and, simultaneously, to encourage both energy conservation and investment in domestic energy alternatives.

With the object of raising efficiency, the private sector has been allowed to replace public sector institutions in certain areas of some countries and steps have been taken to expose the public sector to greater financial discipline.

Most programs have provided for reductions in public investment and the realignment of priorities in favour of projects yielding quick, large returns or generating net improvements in the country's foreign exchange position. Steps have been taken to employ cost-benefit analysis in the public sector and to otherwise strengthen investment planning, often with technical assistance provided by the World Bank.

Restructuring of the recurrent budget has also focused expenditure on directly productive sectors such as agriculture and exports and involved selective cut backs in non-developmental activities. "Most SALs include reductions in the budgetary impact of subsidy programs for both inputs and consumer goods by focussing these programs more sharply on the target groups."[15]

Policies designed to improve resource mobilization have included the movement toward positive real interest rates, the introduction of tax reforms and the curtailment of public enterprise deficits in favour of 'self-financing' through new pricing policies or improvements in efficiency.

Table 5.4

Key Components of Structural Adjustment Operations

	Bolivia	Guyana	Ivory Coast		Jamaica		Kenya		Korea		Malawi		Mauritius	
			1	2	1	2	1	2	1	2	1	2	1	2
Trade Policy														
Tariff Reform and Import Liberalization					●	●	●	●	●	●				●
Export Incentive and Improved Institutional Support		●	●	●	●	●	●	●			●		●	●
Resource Mobilization														
Budget Policy		●			●	●	●	●	●	●	●	●		●
Interest Rate Policy		●					●	●			●	●		
Strengthening of Institutional Capacity to Manage External Borrowing	●	●	●				●	●			●	●	●	●
Public Enterprise Financial Performance	●	●		●	●	●			●	●	●	●		

Table 5.4 **Cont'd**

	Pakistan	Panama	Philippines 1	Philippines 2	Senegal	Thailand 1	Thailand 2	Togo	Turkey 1	Turkey 2	Turkey 3	Turkey 4	Yugoslavia
Trade Policy													
Tariff Reform and Import Liberalization		•	•	•	•	•	•		•	•	•	•	•
Export Incentive and Improved Institutional Support	•	•	•	•	•	•	•		•	•	•	•	•
Resource Mobilization													
Budget Policy	•				•	•	•	•	•	•	•	•	•
Interest Rate Policy									•	•	•	•	•
Strengthening of Institutional Capacity to Manage External Borrowing					•		•	•	•		•	•	•
Public Enterprise Financial Performance	•	•			•	•	•	•	•	•	•	•	•

Table 5.4 **Cont'd**

Key Components of Structural Adjustment Operations

	Bolivia	Guyana	Ivory Coast		Jamaica		Kenya		Korea		Malawi		Mauritius	
			1	2	1	2	1	2	1	2	1	2	1	2
Efficient Use of Resources														
Public Investment Program Revision and Review of Structural Priorities	●	●	●	●	●	●	●		●	●	●	●	●	●
Pricing Policy:														
Agriculture	●	●	●	●	●	●		●	●	●	●	●	●	●
Energy	●	●			●			●	●	●	●		●	●
Incentive System:														
Industry				●	●	●	●	●	●	●		●	●	●
Energy Conservation Measures		●						●	●	●				
Energy - Development of Indigenous Sources		●						●	●	●			●	

Table 5.4 **Cont'd**

	Pakistan	Panama	Philippines		Senegal	Thailand		Togo	Turkey				Yugoslavia
			1	2		1	2		1	2	3	4	
Efficient Use of Resources													
Public Investment Program Revision and Review of Structural Priorities	•	•			•			•	•	•	•	•	•
Pricing Policy:													
Agriculture	•	•			•	•	•	•		•	•	•	
Energy	•			•		•	•	•	•	•	•	•	•
Incentive System:													
Industry	•	•	•	•	•	•	•	•	•	•			•
Energy Conservation Measures				•		•	•	•		•	•	•	•
Energy - Development of Indigenous Sources	•						•	•		•	•	•	

Table 5.4 **Cont'd**

Key Components of Structural Adjustment Operations

	Bolivia	Guyana	Ivory Coast 1	Ivory Coast 2	Jamaica 1	Jamaica 2	Kenya 1	Kenya 2	Korea 1	Korea 2	Malawi 1	Malawi 2	Mauritius 1	Mauritius 2
Institutional Reforms														
Strengthening of Institutional Capacity to Formulate and Implement Public Investment Program		•	•	•		•	•	•	•	•	•	•		•
Institutional Efficiency of Public Sector Enterprises	•		•	•	•	•					•	•	•	•
Improved Institutional Support in Agriculture (marketing, etc.)		•	•	•	•	•		•			•	•	•	
Institutional Improvements in Industry and Sub-sector Programs				•	•	•					•	•	•	

Table 5.4 **Cont'd**

	Pakistan	Panama	Philippines 1	Philippines 2	Senegal	Thailand 1	Thailand 2	Togo	Turkey 1	Turkey 2	Turkey 3	Turkey 4	Yugoslavia
Institutional Reforms													
Strengthening of Institutional Capacity to Formulate and Implement Public Investment Program	●				●	●	●	●	●	●	●	●	
Institutional Efficiency of Public Sector Enterprises	●	●			●		●	●		●	●	●	
Improved Institutional Support in Agriculture (marketing, etc.)	●	●			●		●	●		●	●	●	
Institutional Improvements in Industry and Sub-sector Programs	●	●	●	●			●						

Source: World Bank, "Structural Adjustment Lending Progress Report" (Washington, D.C.: World Bank, June 6, 1984), pp. 84-150.

Where foreign indebtedness is important, agreements have provided for its restructuring and the development of policy with regard to debt management.

Finally, there are two other aspects of conditionality. While loan proceeds are available for import support in general, some portion may be earmarked for expenditure on certain types of imports considered by the Bank to be important for specific sectors or projects. Likewise, while the local counterpart funds of adjustment loans add to government revenues, some portion of these may be earmarked for specified development projects or other uses.[16]

Formulation and Monitoring

The formulation of structural adjustment programs usually begins with the outlining of a framework of medium term objectives and, in broad terms of the measures to be taken to meet these objectives. On the basis of this a detailed action program is then drawn up one year at a time. These are all reviewed by the Bank and, once agreement is reached and the policies and programs formally adopted by borrowing governments, are incorporated into a Letter of Development Policies. The formulation of programs appears to rely heavily on Bank staff and on sectoral technical and policy studies prepared by the Bank. Often, the specific action programs also entail provision for further such studies or for the hiring of technical assistants.

The Bank monitors performance in terms of the specific policy actions and not in terms of quantitative macro-economic indicators. A small number of key policy initiatives are identified as preconditions for the release of subsequent credit tranches—each loan being disbursed in tranches at three to four-month intervals. Thus, "at all stages of the preparation, appraisal, implementation and ex-post review of the operation, the focus is on the program of policy actions."[17] It is precisely this concentration on supply side policy adjustment and the avoidance of rigid quantitative performance criteria of dubious theoretical worth, that appeals to some writers looking for suitable ways to reform IMF conditionality. On the other hand, as will be argued later, these are serious questions to be raised about the nature of the policies that constitute World Bank conditionality. At the same time, some observers fear that without quantitative criteria of some sort (not necessarily those of the IMF) conditionality can easily fall victim to subjective or political judgements leading to policy advice the results of which are not capable of verifiable measurement.[18]

Relationships Between the World Bank and the Fund

The movement of the World Bank into the area of general balance of payments support at the very time that the Fund was introducing longer-term, supply-oriented programs, has led some observers to conclude that their functions are beginning to converge. Given the very tentative nature of these developments at this time—we have already discussed the difficulties encountered by the IMF in its attempted reorientation as well as the extremely limited scope of structural adjustment lending by the World Bank—it appears that the Bank and the Fund need not fear any imminent resurrection of plans of forty years ago for a single institution to combine both their functions.[19] Yet this apparent 'convergence' process is of sufficient concern to both institutions that staff of each have been moved to emphasize both the fact and the nature of the division of labour that they see operating between them.[20] In the process of doing so, they have demonstrated that concerns over 'specialization' are really no different in principle now than they were almost twenty years ago and that, notwithstanding their recent new directions, both institutions view the division of labour between them in exactly the same terms as they did then. All that appears to have changed since that time is that more cooperative efforts are taking place between their staff at the working level.

Formal collaboration between the two institutions dates back to an exchange of memoranda in 1966.[21] These emphasized the need for close working relations and exchange of information. More importantly, it was agreed that the economic and financial evaluations and advice given to member governments by one institution should always be such as to be acceptable to the other institution. In other words, they agreed never to disagree on analysis and recommendations to members. By and large, this has been the rule to date with only a few exceptions being made public. The most notable of these was the release of the World Bank's positive and supposedly confidential assessment of developments in Grenada under the New Jewel government. This greatly embarrassed the IMF which, under pressure from the U.S., had refused to lend to that country.[22] It is also clear that in the 1970s the World Bank took a more sympathetic view of Tanzania's attempts to deal with its problems, advancing a program loan at the very time that the IMF was refusing upper credit tranche assistance.[23]

These memoranda stipulated that "the Bank is recognized as having primary responsibility for the composition and appropriateness of development priorities" while "the Fund is recognized as having primary responsibility for exchange rates and restrictive systems, for adjustment of temporary balance of payments disequilibria and for evaluating and assisting members to work out stabilisation programs as a sound basis for economic advance."[24] Provision was made for consultations and briefings to ensure that each was apprised of the other's views in their respective areas of specialization. If staff of one institution wished to discuss with member governments issues falling under the domain of the other, prior consent of the other was to be obtained.

In the 1970s more formal provision was made for the sharing of information, especially after mission visits to countries. Between 1979 and 1980, there was a very pronounced increase in the number of country missions of each in which staff from the other institution participated, as well as a doubling in the number of parallel missions.[25] This type of collaboration is expected to increase in future.

The new policy directions of the 1970s are, however, viewed as being "both complementary and mutually reinforcing."[26] Recent statements indicate that the division of labour is regarded as remaining essentially as outlined in 1966 although its detail has been refined somewhat. Thus, "the Bank should look to the Fund for views on exchange rate, monetary, fiscal, and foreign borrowing policies including the establishment of medium term targets for the current account of the balance of payments," while "the Fund should look to the Bank for views on development priorities as reflected in the size and composition of the investment program, recurrent outlays in development sectors, the efficiency of resource use and micro pricing decisions."[27]

The official view is that this specialization and collaboration works well (with only minor problems of synchronizing different policy packages and analyses requirements), and that the reason for this is to be found in the very different "orientation of each institution's staff and the experience and expertise it is capable of mustering."[28] A more persuasive explanation might be found, however, in the essential harmony of viewpoint that these institutions hold on the causes of instability, and their appropriate remedies. This, even without 'an agreement not to disagree' but expecially with it, would inevitably serve to reduce friction between the two institutions. It finds its ultimate expression in the practice of the World Bank in not advancing SALs until countries have first reached agreement with the IMF—even when countries have strong disagreements with the Fund over the 'supply side' measures it is advocating—measures which are supposedly under the purview of the Bank.

Assessment of Structural Adjustment Lending

It will be many years before any definitive evaluation can be made of the performance of the Bank's new lending program for, by its very nature, structural adjustment is a long-term process. In this section, we shall therefore confine our attention to evaluating

(i) the terms of structural adjustment loans relative to those of facilities offered by the IMF;

(ii) the nature of the adjustment model underlying World Bank conditionality; and

(iii) the constraints on the future growth of this type of lending.

Terms

The obvious attraction of structural adjustment loans is that they provide a country with quickly disbursable foreign exchange which is virtually freely usable to purchase any commodities from any country of origin. In this respect, they are superior to bilateral import support which is usually country- and commodity-specific and often bureaucratically slow in its disbursement. These characteristics are identical to IMF credits except where some of the proceeds of SALs are earmarked to certain sectors of the economy. Such earmarking has not been a feature of IMF programs except in a very general, indicative way. Also, more recently there are indications that the Bank is moving toward designating certain imports as either 'eligible' or 'ineligible' in structural adjustment programs.

Interest and repayment terms of SLAs are superior to those of IMF facilities and especially so for countries which qualify for IDA or blended loans. IBRD loans carry a lower interest rate and longer maturity period than IMF facilities so annual debt servicing is lower, which is important for countries with balance of payments constraints. Over the lifetime of the loan, however, countries pay more in interest in absolute terms, so the relative attractiveness of these loans can only be assessed if these flows are discounted back to the present. At a discount rate of 10 percent, the interest and repayment burden of IBRD loans is, in fact, no different in present value terms from that of IMF loans. For a $300m loan the present value at 10 percent would be about $280m for an IBRD loan over 20 years compared with $275m for an IMF loan over 10 years. At higher discount rates, which are surely called for when the actual rates on these respective loans are in excess of 10 percent p.a., the IBRD loan is superior in present value terms to an IMF (extended) facility. Needless to say, an IDA credit is vastly superior to both—a $300 million loan implying present value costs of only $50 million at a discount rate of 10 percent p.a. over 50 years.

Unlike IMF facilities, World Bank loans of all types are not limited in any way to the size of members' subscriptions. Within any overall financing constraint this can permit certain borrowers relatively more flexibility than they would otherwise enjoy. By the same token, it also implies a much greater skewness in the distribution of World Bank loans between countries and allows the Bank to favour countries pursuing 'acceptable' policies to a degree not possible under the IMF quota system. Thus, 15 countries account for almost 70 percent of *all* IBRD loans (project as well as program), while only 8 countries account for the same proportion of *all* IDA credits. One country alone, India, has received 40 percent of all IDA credits.[29] With the very tight financing ceiling imposed by the Exceutive Board, the multi-year nature of programming and the absence of borrowing limits tied to subscriptions, it is apparent that the skewness of distribution already observed in structural adjustment lending is likely to persist even if in moderated form.

Conditionality and the World Bank Model

What is unique about structural adjustment lending is that it carries with it an unprecedented degree of conditionality; firstly, because in practice (even if not in principle) it assumes IMF conditionality as a *precondition*[30] and secondly, because it then erects a variety of exacting, detailed conditions on top of that. In the process, it implicitly underwrites the IMF approach to stabilization with all its shortcomings. Even where certain senior Bank officials disagree with conditions being demanded by the IMF, they are bound by the collaboration agreements to defer to Fund opinion in areas where it is deemed to have 'primary responsibility.' This can lead the Bank into situations of conflict with countries requesting structural adjustment assistance. The clearest case of this sort is the Tanzania one where in 1981/82 a team of international experts appointed jointly by Tanzania and the World Bank to advise on a structural adjustment loan gave advice on the exchange rate, interest rate, food subsidies, minimum wages and the structure (not the level) of government recurrent spending which differed markedly from that given by the Fund. Yet the Bank continued to insist that an agreement with the Fund was necessary *before* it would negotiate a structural adjustment arrangement with Tanzania on the basis of the experts' report.[31] The result was a stalemate for several years with no adjustment funds from either source. As the economic situation of the country continued to deteriorate, and the IMF position became more intransigent, the stance of the World Bank was interpreted as an attempt to apply pressure on Tanzania to accept the Fund's terms. Yet, privately, a number of Bank officials would have been happy to see an agreement in place on terms closer to those recommended in the report than those demanded by the IMF; but the collaborative arrangements meant that this was never a possibility.

By and large, though, the Bank does not disagree with the general approach of the Fund, sharing its emphasis on the need for demand management and 'realistic' exchange rates, interest rates and prices. The Bank's own view of its conditionality as 'reinforcing' that of the Fund is undeniably accurate but understates both the qualitative and the quantitative difference between their conditionality. The Fund concentrates as we have seen on only a handful of macro-performance targets. Bank conditionality, on the other hand, encompasses a very wide range of *policies* at all levels of the economy and also, embraces institutional structure and enterprise operations. This comprehensive form of conditionality gives the World Bank an unprecedented degree of leverage over the policies of its debtors; in its own words, "structural adjustment lending has provided a unique opportunity to achieve a more comprehensive and timely approach to policy reforms."[32]

Bilateral donors and most other multilateral donors would be hesitant to seek, let alone openly confess to, wielding this degree of leverage. Indeed, it is only a dozen years ago that the prospect of publicity being given to the Bank using its money to influence donor policies was a cause for controversy, prompting indignant responses from Bank officials that it would reduce the effectiveness of the Bank.[33] At the same time, of course, the Bank's ability to exert influence was limited by the dominance of project lending, which is "the least well adapted for use as a 'lever'."[34] Since then, the Bank has more openly spoken of the need to shape economic policy in member countries and on more than one occasion has itself bemoaned the limited leverage that project and sectoral/program aid permit.[35] It was the crisis of the late 1970s which presented the Bank with the opportunity to extend those limits via structural adjustment lending.

This increasing frankness on the issue of leverage is itself partly an honest reaction by the Bank to conditions of crisis and the frustration of having to conduct project and sector lending operations within these conditions. More especially, however, it is a reflection of the coming to maturity of a coherent, clearly articulated, Bank view of what constitutes 'correct' economic policies to speed development. After studying recent Bank publications one would not be able to say, as Teresa Hayter could in the early 1970s, that "it is hard to discover what the Bank's views on development policies are."[36] These views are spelled out clearly in the World Development Reports and in specialist publications of the Bank.

We have seen that the World Bank 'model' which is embodied in structural adjustment lending to date is one which emphasizes externally oriented growth (except for energy which is the focus of import substitution), greater reliance on price and other incentives and an expanded role for the private sector at the expense of the state sector. It is, indeed, entirely complementary to the IMF model, but defined in greater detail and asserted even more forcefully. Yet, as spelled out in the Berg Report, it is a model which rests on questionable theoretical and empirical foundations and one which is likely to create far-reaching political repercussions if implemented.

To begin with, it suffers from the same weakness of the IMF model in its prescription for export-oriented strategies, that of the fallacy of composition. The price projections of the Berg Report for primary exports have been rejected by a number of writers as being inconsistent with its volume projections,[37] while the projections for manufacturing exports also appear to be overly optimistic.[38] At the root of these errors is to be found a conviction, widely held in the Bank, that those countries that performed best in the 1970s were ones which adopted externally oriented growth strategies and that this prescription is not only equally valid in the 1980s, but also is one to be applied across the board to all countries.[39] Once the special circumstances of the rapid export growth countries in the 1970s are taken into account, once allowance is made for the impact of world crisis on demand, and once the Bank's own export projections are adjusted downward to fit more realistic elasticity assumptions, then the need for a much more cautious, case-by-case approach to adjustment is readily apparent. In a situation of relative stagnation of world demand, of rising protectionism, and for many underdeveloped countries, the most serious deterioration in their terms of trade since the 1930s, potential borrowers can be excused for not quickly and uncritically embracing the export-led growth model.

In placing failures of domestic policy "at the heart of the crisis" the Bank not only underestimates the degree to which domestic policies have been conditioned over the years by the structure of relationships which countries maintain with the outside world, it also overlooks entirely its own role, and that of other aid donors, in shaping these policies. Thus, if inefficient import substituting industries are a problem, as they are, should it not also be said that for many years the Bank played an active role in promoting them?[40] If export crops have been neglected in favour of food crops, could this not be because an earlier overconcentration of resources in export production, often inspired and usually supported by the Bank, led to acute food supply problems in many countries which in some of them at least, is now being addressed?[41] If high cost, capital intensive, bureaucratically managed agriculture is impeding growth, is this not in some part due to its support by donors like the World Bank, sometimes at the clear expense of small-scale, cooperative farming that was ideologically unacceptable to the Bank?[42] The point is not to damn the Bank's current directions by pointing out complicity in past errors; rather, it is to make a case that more humility is required on the part of the Bank in its approach to policy advice, given its own chequered performance in the past and the uncertainties surrounding many of the assumptions in its model.

Many of the policy thrusts of the Bank would have far-reaching political implications if acted upon with vigour. In some countries the pronounced shift of emphasis in agriculture from food to export crops that the Bank is calling for "would probably be a recipe for starvation."[43] The removal of tariff and other forms of protection for local industrial goods would in many countries lead to drastic deindustrialization,[44] especially in a world situation of under-capacity production which renders underdeveloped countries extremely vulnerable to low cost imports. It would create urban unemployment and cause disaffection among local owners of industry. In both these areas any policy changes would need to be gradual with careful attention to planning at the micro level so that, where feasible, food supplies would not be prejudiced by attempts to raise foreign exchange earnings, and so that the long-run dynamic benefits of industrialization can be maintained at the same time that efficiency is improved. This would imply a very different approach to adjustment, in terms of both speed and policy measures, from that advocated by the Bank.

The Bank's attitude toward the relative roles of the state and the private sector also calls for comment. That the Bank actively promotes the expansion of private enterprise should surprise no one, given its control by the major capitalist countries (who control 63 percent of IBRD votes and 61.3 percent of IDA votes) and its Articles of Agreement which enjoin it, among its other functions, "to promote private foreign investment by means of guarantees or participation in loans and other investments made by private investors; and when private capital is not available on reasonable terms to supplement private investment."[45] The articles also require it to "conduct its operations with due regard to the effect of international investment on business conditions in the territories."[46] With this in mind those critiques of the Bank which conclude that it "has deliberately and consciously used its financial power to promote the interests of private, international capital in its expansion to every corner of the 'underdeveloped' world"[47] seem to be a little naive, suggesting only that the Bank has been highly successful in carrying out its mandate.

Given that the Bank lends *through* governments or on the basis of government guarantees, its support of private enterprise is not, however, as readily apparent as it might otherwise be. It was for this reason and because, under McNamara's leadership in the 1970s, the Bank adopted a well publicized 'antipoverty' policy, that the Bank became a target of attacks from the U.S. political right for being a 'pro-socialist' and, therefore, an anti-American institution.[48] In response to these attacks the U.S. Treasury Department conducted a study which concluded that the World Bank (and other multilateral banks in which the U.S. participates) has "been most effective in contributing to our global economic and financial objectives, and thereby also serving our long-term political/strategic objectives."[49] On occasion this has meant the Bank refusing loans to governments which are out of political favour with the U.S.A. (Egypt, Chile, Vietnam and Afghanistan). At other times, the U.S. administration has used Bank funds to replace its own bilateral aid when Congress has cut back on it to specific countries for human rights violations or other reasons, the case of the Philippines being the best documented one.[50] In general, the report of the Treasury Department confirmed a view long held by left critics that the loan portfolio of the Bank parallels very closely U.S. foreign policy interests. While this makes a mockery of those articles of the IBRD (IV,10) and the IDA (V,10) requiring them to operate apolitically, it is to be expected given the power structure in the Bank.

The Treasury report also found that the private sector was the major beneficiary of Bank lending and is rarely 'crowded out' by Bank projects. Nevertheless, it still recommended a 30–35 percent cut in real terms in U.S. contributions to IDA replenishment and a policy of confining increases in IBRD capital to callable capital only.

These recommendations have a number of implications for the Bank's finances which will be discussed later, but one of them is to increase pressure on the Bank to enter into more cofinancing arrangements with other donors and the private sector. This will simply strengthen directions that the new President, Mr. Clausen, has, in any case, been advocating.

Starting from the premise that "those countries that have demonstrated the best economic performance have encouraged their private sectors"[51] (a dubious premise; even the Bank's own figures show the People's Democratic Republic of Yemen and Romania as having the highest per capita growth rates in the world between 1960 and 1980, while non-market industrial economies easily outpaced industrial market economies over the same period!),[52] Mr. Clausen has given the Bank a pro-private enterprise boost, advocating more speedy 'graduation' of countries (from IDA concessional to IBRD loans, to cofinancing, and then to independent resort to capital markets) and a much greater degree of cofinancing with banks; he has also supported expanding the activities of the International Finance Corporation (IFC), doubling its capital in 1984, and of encouraging private foreign investment by creating a multilateral investment insurance agency under World Bank auspices.[53] All of this means the World Bank will be following its mandate with more vigour than in the past.

It is in this broader context that the emphasis on the private sector in structural adjustment programs should be situated.

There is a tendency in Bank literature to grossly oversimplify the problem of state involvement in the economy. State ownership of the means of production is not merely a matter of efficiency. In many countries it was a reaction to perceived abuses in the private sector; in some countries it forms part of a socialist ideology; in yet others, it satisfied nationalist aspirations or met the frustrations, personal or otherwise, of leaders who found themselves with political power but with no economic power. Other forms of state intervention have similarly diverse and complex roots. Nor can it be said that efficiency was always lost by this intervention or that it will necessarily be restored by 'liberalizing' the economy. Indeed, as argued in Chapter 2, there is a case to be made that the success stories of the 1970s were based on "extensive state intervention" of various kinds.[54]

What is clear is that altering the balance between state and private sector activities to the degree deemed desirable by Berg would have profound political and social implications. In many countries it would mean a significant increase in the level of activity of foreign capital since there is no local capitalist class ready to fill the gap. In others, the removal of protection for local industry would threaten the *replacement* of the influence of local capital by that of foreign capital. In all cases there would likely be important changes in the distribution of income and wealth, which would also have political ramifications.

Distributional issues receive only passing reference in Bank statements on structural adjustment, but reading between the lines there is a recognition that programs are likely to sacrifice equity in pursuit of growth and efficiency. Thus, the Bank seems to feel that incentives to agriculture, exports and labour intensive production will benefit the poorest, but these benefits will be more than offset by adverse movements in the terms of trade and reductions in consumption as resources are shifted into investment and exports. For this reason it expresses concern that programs be designed so that "their impact on the poorest members of society and on programs of basic needs and human resource development are minimised."[55]

The Berg Report is less nuanced in its prescription for Africa. It proposes that urban wages be cut and that user fees be levied for government services such as health, education and water supply. It openly advocates that rural investment be concentrated on larger 'progressive' farmers, as well as on the most productive regions. Since all of this is in the context of opening up whole areas of the economy to the private sector, the overall result would be unambiguously a deterioration in the living standards of the poor and growing inequities in general. Structural adjustment lending as currently conditoned would run directly counter to the Bank's professed concern for alleviating poverty and meeting basic needs.

This concern evolved in the 1970s as a reaction to the realization that rapid economic growth did not necessarily, nor normally, imply an increase in the well being of the majority of the population of Third World countries.[56] The alleviation of poverty became an objective of Bank programs, one that was welded onto, rather than replacing, the growth emphasis of the Bank.[57]

"Redistribution with growth" was wholeheartedly espoused by the Bank under the leadership of Robert McNamara, whose own views on aid were shaped as much by U.S. self-interest as they were by any humanitarianism ("I believe the United States buys more security by spending a dollar for development assistance than for military hardware!").[58] Over the decade of the seventies there was, in consequence, a dramatic shift of emphasis in World Bank lending away from infrastructure toward rural development, water supply and sewerage, education, urbanization and other 'basic needs' sectors (see Table 5.5). The new emphasis also found expression in a much greater rate of growth in IDA credits than in IBRD lending, and in a redirection of the Bank's overall country lending program. Thus, IDA credits were increasingly focused on, and eventually confined to, those countries with the lowest per capita incomes. IBRD loans to this group also rose, from 29 percent of its total before 1968 to 39 percent in 1981/82 "despite the credit costliness considerations which impose limits on IBRD lending to many poor countries."[59]

The shift in resources was large and indisputable. How successful it has been in alleviating poverty in underdeveloped countries is, however, a more contentious matter. The Bank itself admits that its "projects have provided few direct benefits for the landless, for tenants unable to offer collateral for loans and for the 'near-landless' farmer who finds it hard to borrow, acquire inputs, and take risks."[60] These groups account for the poorest sections of the rural population—as much as 38 percent of the total in a country like Bangladesh[61]—the very sectors of society most in need. Similarly, in urban areas the Bank admits that its programs are not accessible to the poorest 20 percent of the population.[62] Clearly these admissions are enormous qualifications to any success the Bank might claim for its poverty alleviation thrust. They highlight a fundamental limitation to the Bank's whole program which is that it is attempting to eradicate poverty while, at the same time, working within and often strengthening the very structure of property relationships that generate and reproduce it; trying to "help the poor without hurting the rich" as one sympathetic observer has described it.[63] This is only partly a question of the Bank's ideological set; it is much more a function of social and political structures in its member countries and the determination of governments themselves to deal with inequities.

Yet it is, in part, a reflection of the Bank's ideology. Robert Ayres has argued that a "redistribution with growth" strategy was adopted by the Bank because a "basic human needs" strategy, as advocated by some staff would have entailed much more radical implications.[64] The former strategy took the existing distribution of income and wealth for granted and dealt only with redistributing incremental growth. The emphasis was on "increasing the income, productivity, and output of the poor. . . . In neither a national nor international sense did (redistribution with growth) seek fundamentally to change the world in which the poor lived; it sought to improve the terms on which they related to it."[65] A 'basic human needs' approach would, inevitably, have implied far-reaching state intervention in the marketplace

Table 5.5

Trends in Lending, IBRD and IDA, by Sector, 1970–1983 ($ million)

	1970			1980			1982			1983		
	IBRD	**IDA**	**Total**	**IBRD**	**IDA**	**Total**	**IBRD**	**IDA**	**Total**	**IBRD**	**IDA**	**Total**
1. Agriculture and Rural Development	187.7	238.7	426.4	1,700.4	1,758.0	3,458.4	2,180.2	898.2	3,078.4	2,386.3	1,312.0	3,698.3
2. Development Finance Companies	191.0	25.0	216.0	743.0	74.5	817.5	957.8	135.5	1,093.3	1,177.9	60.3	1,238.2
3. Education	52.3	27.6	79.9	360.1	80.1	440.1	428.4	98.0	526.4	296.4	251.5	547.9
4. Energy	530.4	25.8	556.2	—	—	—	—	—	—	—	—	—
Oil, Gas, and Coal	n.a.	n.a.	n.a.	328.5	128.5	457.0	720.4	45.7	766.3	979.1	70.8	1,049.9
Power	n.a.	n.a.	n.a.	1,584.5	807.8	2,392.3	1,432.9	698.3	2,131.2	1,529.2	239.0	1,768.2
5. Industry	43.5	32.5	76.0	393.5	29.0	422.5	910.4	49.0	959.4	625.1	66.7	691.8
6. Non-Project	—	75.0	75.0	280.0	242.5	522.5	990.7	250.0	1,240.7	1,174.7	260.0	1,434.7
7. Population, Health and Nutrition	2.0	—	2.0	65.0	78.0	143.0	13.0	23.0	36.0	60.5	57.9	118.4
8. Small-Scale Enterprises	—	3.0	3.0	222.0	38.0	260.0	228.0	57.7	285.7	516.1	15.0	531.1
9. Technical Assistance	—	—	—	—	13.0	13.0	24.8	47.7	72.5	25.7	27.0	52.7
10. Telecommunications	67.9	16.7	84.6	66.0	65.0	131.0	338.3	57.5	395.8	—	57.0	57.0
11. Transportation	487.1	147.4	634.5	1,205.0	239.5	1,445.5	1,379.5	234.7	1,614.2	1,406.1	17.5	1,923.6
12. Urbanization	—	—	—	249.8	99.0	348.8	324.8	50.0	374.8	328.3	226.0	554.3
13. Water Supply and Sewage	18.5	14.0	32.5	446.4	184.7	631.1	400.2	41.0	441.2	630.9	180.0	810.9
Total	**1,580.4**	**605.7**	**2,186.1**	**7,644.2**	**3,837.5**	**11,481.7**	**10,329.6**	**2,686.3**	**13,015.9**	**11,136.3**	**3,340.7**	**14,277.0**
% 'Basic Needs' Sectors (1,3,7,12,13)	16.5	46.9	24.8	36.9	57.3	43.6	32.3	41.3	34.3	33.2	60.7	39.5

Source: World Bank, *Annual Report* (Washington, D.C.: World Bank, 1983).

and in property ownership. Thus, while staff published a number of important works in this area, the Bank never adopted the basic human needs approach for this "would have entailed a head-on clash with some key elements of traditional bank ideology."[66] Poverty alleviation entailed, in part, lending money to what might be termed 'basic needs sectors', but the methodology employed was not one of systematically measuring needs and then, equally systematically, directing resources and institutional change in such a way that these needs were met. Rather, the focus was on increasing the output of the not-so-poor and providing facilities such as water, housing, etc., for those able to pay for them.

While not reaching down to the poorest, the Bank maintains that "poverty oriented projects have been successful in meeting their primary objective of increasing the productivity and incomes of the small farmers,"[67] and in helping address the housing needs of urban dwellers in the second and third poorest quintiles of income distribution. The Bank also claims some success in its primary education programs and (while admitting that "by value, 70 per cent of benefits go to the non-poor")[68] in its urban water and sanitation lending.

Being protective of its 'triple-A' bond rating and its perfect repayment record, the Bank is careful to emphasize that returns to its poverty-focused projects are as high as those on its other projects—yet another reason why they are out of the reach of the very poor.

Critics of the Bank do not deny that some of its projects do reach the poor, even though "the figures put out for public relations purposes about the number of poor people helped are fantastic calculations that bear little relationship to reality."[69] Rather, they maintain that "poverty is not abolished, and is not even alleviated, if only a few people step up a notch or two in the hierarchy of wealth."[70] They then proceed to document examples of how World Bank projects fail to affect the poor or alternatively affect them negatively as when slum clearance schemes uproot those too poor to participate, or force them out as property values rise after redevelopment; or when commercial farming projects displace subsistence farmers. While the Bank readily admits that its activities sometimes make the poor worse off, it maintains this happens in only "a small minority" of projects.[71] One study of the Philippines claims, however, that Bank activities have unambiguously fostered inequity in both the rural and urban areas.[72]

However limited the impact of the antipoverty approach might have been, the World Bank seems now to be withdrawing from it. Table 5.5 reveals the sharp cut in IDA lending between 1980 and 1982 as the U.S. reduced its funding of the agency. In order to achieve this overall cut of 30 percent, however, lending to what might be termed 'basic needs sectors,' crudely defined as rural development, nutrition, health, urbanization, education and water supply and sewerage, were cut, on the whole, by exactly 50 percent. This, and the departure from the Bank of Mahbub Ul Haq and Paul Streeton, the chief architects of the poverty alleviation thrust, suggests that more than budgetary restraint is taking place. Admittedly, half of the cut in IDA's lending to 'basic needs' sectors was made good by expanded IBRD lending but this would not offset the decline in credits to the poorest countries and would certainly raise the borrowing costs of countries previously receiving 'blended' loans. While IDA lending to these sectors recovered strongly in 1983 and rose as a proportion of total IDA lending, it was still 10 percent below its 1980 level in current dollar terms or 25 percent or so below if allowance is made for inflation.

Two key questions arise concerning the relationship between structural adjustment lending and the alleviation of poverty. Firstly, to what extent is the Berg Report to be considered a model for the World Bank in its structural adjustment lending and, secondly, need structural adjustment policies necessarily conflict with poverty alleviation? There are no simple answers to these questions. The Berg Report *is* extreme and some observers claim the Bank has been distancing itself from it since its publication. Certainly a follow-up report was a little more nuanced in some areas—giving more weight to external shocks in explaining Africa's problems, avoiding the 'progressive farmer' emphasis when discussing rural strategies, and recognizing, forthrightly, the political problems involved in 'adjustment'.[73] At the same time, however, it maintained the essential thrust of the Berg Report in terms of espousing outward-looking growth strategies, a considerably reduced role for the state sector and 'getting prices right' in all sectors (including the imposition of user fees for 'basic needs' services). The 1984 World Development Report takes essentially similar positions. It would appear, therefore, that there is a high degree of consistency between current Bank policies and those proposed by Berg.

Only recently has the Bank begun to address, directly, the relationship between structural adjustment lending and poverty alleviation, taking a stance which is very similar to that of the IMF. It argues that adjustment will raise returns to farmers and especially low-income ones; will raise employment by discouraging capital intensive and 'prestige' projects; and, by facilitating growth, will enable resources to be devoted to poverty alleviation. It recognizes, however, that more needs to be done to address the transitional costs of adjustment and that the distributional impact of adjustment needs to be studied in individual cases.[74] In effect, therefore, distributional issues are not addressed directly as an integral part of structural adjustment programs; and there is, as yet, no empirical evidence of the distributional impact of this type of program.

Because World Bank structural adjustment programs 'piggyback' on IMF stabilization programs, the resulting impact on the structure of income and wealth could be quite far-reaching. The kind of institutional change involved in these programs is also likely to challenge or threaten many different vested interests. It is for these reasons that the Bank states that "difficulty in gaining political acceptance for the adoption and implementation of structural adjustment programs has been and remains the overwhelming obstacle to proceeding more rapidly with Bank structural adjustment lending."[75] Furthermore, it recognizes that these difficulties are likely to be greatest in the low-income countries in which the Bank will continue to press its policy viewpoint through sector programs if SALs cannot be negotiated.[76] It is no accident, therefore, that structural adjustment lending to poor countries is minimal.

This determination to exercise leverage on the shaping of policies in Third World countries is carried to the extreme in the Berg Report. There, it is insinuated that access to all sources and forms of aid should be made conditional upon acceptance of the type of policy reform it is recommending,[77] raising the spectre of existing aid coordination bodies led by the World Bank becoming donors' cartels maintaining a uniform stand on what is appropriate policy for governments of the Third World. They would, of course, exercise greatest leverage over those most dependent on aid, the least developed countries, and at a time when their need for aid and, therefore, their vulnerability, is at its greatest. Whatever the intentions of the Bank, this possibility raises a serious threat to the national sovereignty of the world's poorest countries.

The Likely Scope of Structural Adjustment Lending

If the Bank's own assessment of the political difficulties many governments would face in implementing its type of structural adjustment is correct, then the demand for its new facility is not likely to be that great. If, on the other hand, that assessment is incorrect or 'donor cartel' pressure becomes more of a reality than it is now, and a significant number of countries do turn to the Bank for assistance, there are strong grounds for believing that the Bank's financial structure would place severe limits on its ability to extend structural adjustment lending.

We have already seen that the IDA is under great financial pressure. IDA funds are 'replenished' periodically by contributions from a small number of industrialized capitalist, OPEC, and higher-income underdeveloped countries. In the sixth replenishment of 1981–83, the United States, the largest donor, originally pledged $3.2 billion out of the total of $12 billion, but congressional opposition meant that this amount was not fully paid over the planned period but instead stretched over into subsequent years.[78] In retaliation for past U.S. foot-dragging, other donors had, in 1980, tied their contributions 'pro rata' to the U.S. contributions so the whole IDA program was jeopardized by the U.S. position. In the event, a number of donor countries waived the 'pro rata' rule and some made additional contributions but IDA lending plans were nevertheless seriously compromised. In 1982 IDA credits were 30 percent below their 1980 level and, in spite of a recovery, were still 13 percent below that level in 1983. IDA 7, at $9 billion is one-quarter less than IDA 6—fully 40 percent less once inflation is allowed for. At the same time, with the admission of China to the Bank, IDA now has to service more people so that in per capita terms IDA 7 represents a 70 percent cut relative to IDA 6. The countries most affected by this cut back would be those in sub-Saharan Africa, as well as India, Bangladesh, Burma, Sri Lanka and Pakistan. While some of these (e.g., India) could compensate by increasing commercial borrowing, this avenue is not open to most poor Third World countries.[79]

The IBRD too, has its financing problems. Most of its activities are financed by borrowing on the major capital markets of the world and, under the terms of its constitution, the Bank maintains a one-to-one ratio between subscribed capital and its borrowing. This is a very conservative capital/debt ratio which many, including the Brandt Commission,[80] feel should be relaxed. Instead, the Bank has chosen to increase its subscribed capital, roughly doubling it to SDR 71.6 billion between 1980 and 1982. Since only about 7.5 and 10 percent of subscribed capital is actually paid in, the balance being callable only in the unlikely event of IBRD bondholders requiring support, the increase in capital serves largely to permit the Bank to borrow more. But the plan of the Bank to double its borrowing in 1982–86 relative to that of the previous five years is felt to be an ambitious one that could well 'crowd out' other official borrowers on very weak bond markets.[81] Already, in 1982, the Bank was compelled, reluctantly, to abandon its policy of fixed interest rate lending, as it found itself borrowing at increasingly higher rates: instead, it introduced a 'pooling' system which adjusts average rates to borrowers every six months. It also had to raise front end fees on both IDA and IBRD loans to relax pressure on its net income.[82] The Bank is also resorting, increasingly to short-term borrowing to finance its loan portfolio.

In reaction to these financial pressures the Bank is attempting to make its own dollars go further by encouraging both graduation and cofinancing. By reducing the proportion of IDA loans in total loans to countries like India and China (i.e., by 'hardening' the blend), the Bank can focus its IDA resources on those countries least able to service debt—especially in sub-Saharan Africa. But graduating countries from the IBRD will be politically very difficult during the current crisis when even those countries which borrowed freely on commercial terms in the late 1970s, such as Brazil, Mexico, Yugoslavia, etc., all of which are large borrowers from the Bank too, are finding it difficult to raise commercial bank credits.[83] If they do not graduate from the Bank, this will put additional pressures on its already strained resources and put a limit on those available for structural adjustment lending.

Structural adjustment loans are not particularly helpful to the Bank in its promotion of cofinancing. While commercial banks' participation with the Bank in project lending, at $2.2 billion in 1982 and $1 billion in 1983, is significant, the provision of general balance of payments support is an altogether different proposition. The evidence to date suggests that SALs do *not* act as a catalyst for commercial bank credits as the Bank hoped they might. Thus, of the 12 countries receiving structural adjustment loan approvals to March 1982, only one country, the Philippines, enjoyed an increase in net credit flows from foreign commercial banks from the date of approval of the loan to June 1982.[84] It seems then that those countries which can borrow from banks, with or without an IMF seal of approval, do so while almost all of those turning to the IBRD have done so partly *because* access, or further access, to bank credits was *not* a possibility.

A final financial constraint on the future growth of structural adjustment loans derives from the fact of their very rapid disbursement. Bank project lending has a notoriously long gestation period. The Bank practice has been to hold a very high proportion (now about 42.5 percent) of its assets in liquid form to enable it to meet future commitments without the need for sudden, costly, forays into the bond market.[85] The greater the proportion of SALs and of 'policy-based' lending generally in its total portfolio, the more rapidly would its commitments be converted into cash flow and the greater would be its overall borrowing requirement at any one time, as it moved to restore its liquidity ratio. Structural adjustment lending has a much more immediate impact, therefore, on both liquidity and borrowing needs.

These constraints will put an upper limit on the amount of Bank resources available for this type of lending in the near future even if the 10 percent ceiling is relaxed, as some argue it should be.[86] They are also likely to constrain the Bank from adjusting lending of this sort in accordance with global need. The financing constraint of the Bank is, however, likely to be less of an impediment to the expanded use of SALs than is the conditionality which accompanies these loans.

The Special Assistance Program

In February 1983 the Bank introduced a Special Assistance Program, a form of structural adjustment lending designed to ease the problems of major debtor countries. The objectives of this $2 billion, two-year program, are to help break key financing bottlenecks in these countries to facilitate disbursement of Bank project funds. There is an emphasis on "high priority operations which support policy change" and help utilize existing capacity "particularly in export-oriented activities." The five components of the program are expanded structural adjustment lending (with, if need be,a relaxation of the 30 percent limit on country lending *and* the 10 percent limit on the Bank's overall lending), loans for strengthening particular sectors, a readiness on the part of the Bank to finance an increased share of project costs (and expecially recurrent costs), enhanced policy dialogue and closer consultation with donors.[87]

The SAP is yet another indication of the primacy of the debt problem in the policies of industrialized countries toward the Third World. It does almost nothing to assist the problems of the poorest Third World countries and, in essence, is an expanded pool of structural adjustment funds available to large debtors.

It must, however, be stated that the World Bank has lobbied extensively to secure an expanded flow of concessional funds to Third World countries as any cursory glance at their recent publications will confirm. On this issue therefore, there is undoubtedly some friction between the Bank and its major 'shareholders'. By mid-1984, the plight of sub-Saharan African countries had become so acute that, apparently, the Bank's point of view was beginning to prevail. It announced that it was preparing a special action plan for poverty stricken sub-Saharan African countries, the details of which would be unveiled at its next Annual Meeting. It remains to be seen what kind of conditionality will be attached to this program and how sensitive it will be to the real structural and political problems African countries face in adjusting to the new global realities.

Concluding Observation

There are several features of structural adjustment lending that need to be applauded. Additional balance of payments support in the form of freely usable, quickly disbursed foreign exchange is, arguably, the most appropriate form of foreign aid at this particular point in time; without it, any attempt at structural adjustment, whatever its nature, will be more difficult and require more immediate sacrifices from the population of the country in question. Secondly, the focus of the Bank on stimulating supply is an important improvement over the more demand-oriented IMF approach to lending. Thirdly, the terms of borrowing are more appropriate to the medium-long-term adjustment process than are IMF loans, and IDA assistance is *incomparably* more appropriate for the least developed countries. Finally, some would argue that the avoidance of quantitative macro indicators to which the flow of assistance is attached in rigid fashion, also represents progress but as we have seen, this is very controversial.

The essential weaknesses of the program are its 'piggybacking' on IMF conditionality and its seemingly rigid and questionable attachment to a specific model of adjustment. This model is highly consistent with that of the IMF in its orientation toward export-led growth, stimulation of the private sector and the use of market forces. It also puts problems of efficiency and growth squarely before those of equity and in this respect marks a retreat from the Bank's basic needs/antipoverty policies.

This form of lending is likely to be tightly constrained both from the demand side, due to the very heavy conditionality requirements in the form of the range and seriousness of the policy changes requested, and from the supply side, in terms of the financing problems of the Bank. Yet the Bank's influence over what is considered to be appropriate structural adjustment is exercised in more ways than simply through its financial commitment to the new facility; through the conditionality of its project and sectoral loans, through its general advice to governments, through its publications and through its participation in aid consortia. It is in this last area that the Bank might seek to exercise leverage over countries not sharing its perspective, as we shall see in the next chapter.

The question naturally arises as to what types of adjustment are appropriate if the World Bank model is not. Some suggested alternative approaches have already been sketched out in Chapter 2. The reservations expressed above about the suitability of the Bank's approach strengthen the case for those types of alternatives, the salient features of which bear repeating at this point. To begin with, there should be no across-the-board commitment to export orientation or sweeping macro measures designed to stimulate this orientation. Instead, there should be a careful product-by-product evaluation of prospects and of the range of policy, financial and physical supports required to realize them. Second, the occasion of crisis should not be used as a rationale for withdrawing from the provision of basic needs and the attack on poverty, but rather as an opportune moment for reinforcing a commitment to them with all that this implies for the structure of industrial and agricultural production. Third, aid donors should support this commitment where aid recipients can demonstrate they are addressing the institutional structures and other constraints that create and reproduce poverty. Fourth, attempts to deal with inefficient import substitution industries should focus on ways of reducing their import dependence and gradually realizing their long-run potential for strengthening the domestic economy, rather than simply exposing them to sudden and wholesale foreign competition. Fifth, budget adjustments should *not* be at the expense of basic needs expenditures and should recognize the close relationship, emphasized in the Bank's own publications, between productivity and basic needs. Sixth, it should be acknowledged that the mix between private and public sector activity should not be the object of leverage by donors from outside, but should be a matter for political decision within each member country. Seventh, the use of market incentives is not always an appropriate means of ensuring efficiency, especially when confronting structural problems, and has its own distributional and political implications. Governments may, therefore, wish to tackle problems of efficiency through other means and, where this is the case, should be encouraged to do so. Finally, technocratic solutions from above and/or outside should be recognized as constituting a particular *approach* to development which may not be shared by all countries. Where there is a desire for alternative, more decentralized participatory, approaches, they should not be opposed by donors.

This by no means exhausts the lessons to be drawn from the perceived weaknesses in the IBRD approach, but it is indicative. In short, the overriding requirement of any assistance for structural adjustment is that it be both flexible and permissive, and that it not be premised on the belief in the existence of a single blueprint for solving the problems of the Third World. The ultimate test of the World Bank's program will, therefore, be the extent to which its *practice* deviates from the "strident and one-sided line"[88] it takes in its position papers. By attaching its conditionality to that of the IMF, the Bank necessarily limits the creativity and sensitivity that can be built into its own programs. In this sense reform of World Bank conditionality and reform of IMF conditionality need to proceed simultaneously.

Notes

[1] In 1982 net lending by The Bank was $5.2 billion compared with $6.0 billion by the IMF. In 1983 these figures were $7.1 billion and $8.7 billion respectively.

Calculated from balance sheets of IBRD and IDA in The World Bank, *Annual Report*, 1983 (Washington, D.C.: IMF, 1983); figures taken from IMF, *Annual Report*, 1983, p. 85.

[2] The World Bank *Group* also includes the International Finance Corporation which will be discussed, in passing, later.

[3] The main sources of information on structural adjustment loans on which this chapter draws very heavily are: E. Peter Wright, "World Bank Lending for Structural Adjustment", *Finance and Development* (September 1980); Pierre M. Landell-Mills, "Structural Adjustment Lending: Early Experience", *Finance and Development* (December 1981); Ernest Stern, "World Bank Financing of Structural Adjustment" in Williamson, *IMF Conditionality* (Washington, D.C.: Institute for International Economics, 1983), pp. 87–107. World Bank, "Review of Structural Adjustment", R81–64, 1981; and World Bank, "Structural Adjustment Lending: Progress Report", R84–150, June 6, 1984.

[4] John Williamson, "The Lending Policies of the IMF" (Institute for International Economics: Policy Analyses in International Economies, No. 1 August 1982). Williamson argues for the IMF and IBRD declaring joint responsibility for SALs so that IBRD expertise on supply issues can be more systematically built into Fund activities. Tony Killick, Graham Bird, Jennifer Sharpley and Mary Sutton recommend that supply-side considerations and policy changes become features of IMF conditionality. See Tony Killick, ed., *The Quest for Economic Stabilisation: The IMF and the Third World* (London: Heinemann Educational Books, 1984), Chapter 8.

[5] World Bank, *Annual Report*, 1983, p. 40.

[6] See Wright, "World Bank Lending", p. 22.

[7] Ibid., p. 21.

[8] World Bank, *IDA in Retrospect—The First Two Decades of the International Development Association* (Washington, D.C.: The World Bank, 1982), pp. 55–56.

[9] Sydney Dell, "A Note on Stabilisation and the World Bank", *World Development*, Vol. 12, No. 2 (February 1984).

[10] See, E. Stern, Speech delivered to International Conference on LDC Financing sponsored by the Federal Reserve Bank of New York, May 6–9, 1984 (Mimeo), p. 5.

[11] World Bank, *IDA in Retrospect*, p. 96.

[12] Stern, "World Bank Financing", p.91

[13] Ibid., pp. 87–91.

[14] World Bank, *Accelerated Development in Sub-Saharan Africa: An Agenda for Action* (Washington, D.C.: The World Bank, 1981), p. 121.

[15] World Bank, *Review of Structural Adjustment Lending*, p. 8.

[16] Ibid., pp. 18–19.

[17] Ibid., p. 11.

[18] This is presumably what the Brandt Commission (1981) has in mind when it speaks of "clear, fair and explicit rules—rules which will protect the interests of all members of the system including the weaker ones." See *North-South: A Programme for Survival*, Report of Independent Commission on International Development Issues (Cambridge, Mass.: MIT Press, 1980), p. 218.

[19] See Robert W. Oliver, *Early Plans for a World Bank*, Princeton Studies in International Finance No. 29 (New Jersey: Princeton University Press, 1971), p. 34.

[20] From the Fund's side there has been: Joseph Gold, "The Relationship Between the International Monetary Fund and the World Bank", *Creighton Law Review*, Vol. 15, No. 2 (1981/82); from the Bank's: see Stern, "World Bank Financing"; Landell-Mills, "Structural Adjustment Lending"; and Wright, "World Bank Lending". For a discussion of earlier relationships between the Fund and the Bank, as well

as for the 'official' history of the Bank in other respects, see E. Mason and R. Asher, *The World Bank Since Bretton Woods*, (Washington, D.C.: The Brookings Institute, 1973).

[21] Gold, "The IMF and the World Bank", p. 513.

[22] *The Globe and Mail* (Toronto), September 27, 1982.

[23] G. K. Helleiner, Commentary in *Economic Stabilisation in Developing Countries*, ed. William R. Cline and Sidney Weintraub (Washington, D.C.: The Brookings Institute, 1981), pp. 371–372.

[24] Gold, "The IMF and the World Bank", p. 313–514.

[25] World Bank, *Review of Structural Adjustment Lending*, p. 15.

[26] Ibid., p. 14.

[27] Ibid.

[28] Stern, "World Bank Financing", p. 102. Stanley Please has argued recently that this specialization should be given formal recognition in the designation of one or other of the two agencies as lead institution for each borrowing country—the World Bank for countries with essentially supply problems—the IMF for those with demand management problems. See his *The Hobbled Giant-Essays on the World Bank* (Boulder: Westview Press, 1984), Chapter 6. The weakness in this proposal is that as long as the World Bank sees an IMF program as a *prerequisite* for a SAL, it will never be able to take the lead; current arrangements *do* have a logic when looked at from this point of view .

[29] Derived from World Bank, *Annual Report*, 1982.

[30] Of the 16 countries with SALs up to June 1983 only one, Bolivia, had not first received an IMF facility. By January 1983, however, even that country was reported to be seeking IMF assistance. See *The Globe and Mail* (Toronto), January 24, 1983.

[31] The situation was complicated by the fact that Tanzania did not, at first, publicly embrace some of the key recommendations of the experts, e.g., on exchange rate changes, but the Bank persisted in its position even after it had been given indications that Tanzania *would* accept them.

[32] World Bank, *Annual Report*, 1982, p. 40.

[33] See Teresa Hayter, *Aid as Imperialism* (Middlesex: Penguin Books, 1971), especially the Appendix.

[34] Ibid., p. 78.

[35] See, for instance, World Bank, *IDA in Retrospect*, p. 56; and World Bank, *Accelerated Development in Sub-Saharan Africa: An Agenda for Action*, the Berg Report (Washington, D.C.: World Bank, 1981), p. 127.

[36] Hayter, *Aid as Imperialism*, p. 51.

[37] See R. H. Green, "Incentives, Policies, Participation and Response: Reflections on World Bank Policies and Priorities in Agriculture", and Martin Godfrey, "Export Orientation and Structural Adjustment in Sub-Saharan Africa", both in *IDS Bulletin*, Sussex, Vol. 14, No. 1 (January 1983). See also John Loxley, "The Berg Report and the Model of Accumulation in Sub-Saharan Africa" in Jonathon Barker, *The Politics of Agriculture in Tropical Africa* (London: Sage, 1984).

[38] See Godfrey, "Export Orientation and Structural Adjustment".

[39] For an extended critique of this view, see Green, "Incentives, Policies, Participation and Response", and Philip Daniel, "Accelerated Development in Sub-Saharan Africa: an Agenda for Structural Adjustment Lending?"; and Griffith-Jones, "A Chilean Perspective", both in the same issue of the *IDS Bulletin* (January 1983).

[40] See Cheryl Payer, *The World Bank: A Critical Analysis* (New York: Monthly Review Press, 1982), Chapter 5. On the general point of the Bank lacking a collective

memory or the willingness to criticize itself, see Loxley, "The Berg Report", and Charles Harvey, in a review of the Berg Report in *African Contemporary Record*, forthcoming.

[41] See Green, "The Berg Report".

[42] See Michaela Von Freyhold, *Ujamaa Villages in Tanzania: Analysis of a Social Experiment* (New York: Monthly Review Press, 1979), Chapter 6.

[43] Green, in World Bank, *Accelerated Development in Sub-Saharan Africa*, p. 37.

[44] Godfrey, "Export Orientation and Structural Adjustment".

[45] International Bank for Reconstruction and Development, Articles of Agreement. Article 1.

[46] Ibid.

[47] Payer, *The World Bank*, p. 19.

[48] See R. T. Naylor, "Reaganism and the Future of the International Payments System", *Third World Quarterly* (October 1982). This is an excellent exposition of the impact of the Reagan administration on the policies and practices of the IMF and the World Bank.

[49] Department of the Treasury, *United States Participation in the Multilateral Development Banks in the 1980s* (Washington, D.C.: Government Printing Office, 1982), Chapter 2, p. 18.

[50] See Walden Bello, David Kinley, and Elaine Elinson, *Development Debacle: The World Bank in the Philippines* (San Francisco: Institute for Food and Development Policy and Philippine Solidarity Network, 1982). This book, based on IBRD documents, is a searing indictment of the Bank's role in assisting the perpetuation of oppression in the Philippines.

[51] A. W. Clausen, "A Concluding Perspective" in *The Future Role of the World Bank* (Washington, D.C.: The Brookings Institute, 1982), p. 68.

[52] These figures are for countries with a population of over one million and are to be found in IMF, *The World Economic Outlook* (Washington, D.C.: IMF, 1982).

[53] See Clausen, "A Concluding Perspective", and also his *Address to the Board of Governors*, Toronto, Canada, September 6th, 1982. The IFC is an affiliate of the World Bank which lends directly to private industry. It is also empowered to purchase equity, unlike the World Bank. The term 'graduation' applies strictly speaking, to countries ceasing to be eligible for World Bank loans. We use it here in its broader sense to mean a gradual 'maturation' of countries from complete dependence on IDA assistance at one extreme to ineligiblity to borrow from the Bank at the other.

[54] Manfred Bienefeld, "Efficiency, Expertise: NICs and the Accelerated Development Report" in *IDS Bulletin* (Jan. 1983).

[55] World Bank, *Annual Report*, 1982, pp. 40–41.

[56] See for example, Mahbub ul Haq, "Employment in the 1970s: A New Perspective", *International Development Review*, No. 4 (1974).

[57] See Robert L. Ayres, *Banking on the Poor: The World Bank and World Poverty* (Cambridge Mass.: The MIT Press, 1983), pp. 74–75. Aast Van de Laar, in his *The World Bank and the Poor* (The Hague: Martinus Niijhoff, 1980), argues that the new focus of the Bank simply followed a shift in U.S. external assistance policy.

[58] Robert S. McNamara, "Developing Countries and the World Bank in the 1980s" in *The Future Role of the World Bank*, p. 11.

[59] World Bank, *Focus on Poverty: A Report by a Task Force of the World Bank* (Washington, D.C.: World Bank, 1982), p. 3. For a full description of the Bank approach to basic needs lending, see its *The World Bank and the World's Poorest*

(Washington, D.C.: World Bank, June 1980) and *Poverty and Basic Needs* (Washington, D.C.: World Bank, September 1980).

[60] World Bank, *Focus on Poverty*, p. 7.

[61] Ibid.

[62] Ibid., p. 11.

[63] Bettina S. Hurni, *The Lending Policy of the World Bank in the 1970s: Analysis and Evaluation* (Boulder: Westview Press, 1980), p. 31.

[64] Ayres, *Banking on the Poor*, Chapter 4.

[65] Ibid., p. 89.

[66] Ibid., p. 90.

[67] World Bank, *Focus on Poverty*, p. 7.

[68] Ibid., p. 14.

[69] Payer, *The World Bank*, p. 20.

[70] Ibid.

[71] World Bank, *Focus on Poverty*, p. 8.

[72] Bello, et al., *Development Debacle.*

[73] The World Bank, *Sub-Saharan Africa: Progress Report on Development Prospects and Programs* (Washington, D.C.: World Bank, 1983).

[74] World Bank, "Structural Adjustment Lending, Progress Report", 1984, pp. 17–19.

[75] World Bank, *Review of Structural Adjustment Lending*, p. 16.

[76] Ibid., p. 17.

[77] World Bank, *Accelerated Development in Sub-Saharan Africa*, Introduction and Chapter 9.

[78] World Bank, *Annual Report*, 1982, pp. 15–16.

[79] World Bank, *World Development Report* (Washington, D.C.: World Bank, 1984), pp. 3.28–3.29.

[80] *North-South: A Programme for Survival.* The Report of the Independent Commission on International Development Issues under the Chairmanship of Willy Brandt, recommended a gearing ratio of at least 2:1. See page 249.

[81] See "A Survey of the World Bank", *The Economist* (September 4th, 1982), p. 25.

[82] World Bank, *Annual Report*, 1982, p. 52; and "A Survey of the World Bank", p. 25.

[83] World Bank, *Annual Report*, 1983, pp. 38–39.

[84] See Bank for International Settlements statistics on bank deposits and credits, 1979–82.

[85] Eugene J. Rotberg, *The Work Bank: A Financial Appraisal* (Washington, D.C.: The World Bank, January 1981). This is an excellent booklet in terms of explaining the structure of, and the rationale behind, the Bank's finances. See also *The World Bank*, an information booklet published by the Bank, June 1981, for a complete description of Bank and IDA activities and finances.

[86] See *North-South; A Programme for-Survival*, p. 291.

[87] World Bank, *Annual Report*, 1983, pp. 39–40.

[88] This term is used by Harvey to describe the Berg Report's position on the role of the private sector relative to that of the state; it could be applied equally to its position on export-oriented growth strategies and the use of market incentives. See Harvey, in *African Contemporary Record.*

6

AID AND THE ECONOMIC CRISIS

Introduction

While private capital flows were the most important source of financing of current account deficits of developing countries over the last decade, flows of official development assistance (ODA) played a substantial role and were of vital importance to the poorer countries. As the global recession deepened, aid donors, as a group, reacted by cutting back on the growth of flows of aid and by adopting a more self-interest approach to the terms of aid, at least with regard to 'tying'. On the other hand, the needs of the developing countries for aid became even greater, thus the gap between needs and availabilities widened. At the same time, the problems being faced by developing countries gave rise to pressures to alter the composition of aid flows away from project financing toward general import support. While some donors have attempted to accommodate these pressures there is a growing tendency for them to do so only in exchange for a greater say in the economic policies of recipient countries.

This chapter examines recent trends in the volume and terms of ODA flows and looks in general terms at the pros and cons of import support and the type of conditionality to which it appears to be giving rise.

Trends in Aid Flows

Flows of ODA grew at 12.6 percent between 1970 and 1982 but since non-concessional finance grew much more rapidly (at 14.7 percent p.a.), the relative importance of ODA flows in the total external financing of Third World countries declined from 42 percent to 37 percent during that time (Table 6.1).

Just over a half of all ODA takes the form of bilateral flows from countries which are members of the Development Assistance Committee (DAC) of the OECD—consisting of the wealthier industrialized capitalist countries. This represents a significant proportionate decline since the earlier seventies when DAC bilateral assistance accounted for about 70 percent of all ODA. This fall is explained largely by an increase in the flow of multilateral aid, most of it contributed by DAC members through the World Bank (IDA), the Commission of the European Economic Communities, the United Nations or various regional development banks. Thus while DAC bilateral assistance grew by 10.4 percent p.a. in current price terms between 1970 and 1982, multilateral aid grew at 17.5 percent p.a. In addition, bilateral

Table 6.1

Total Net Resource Receipts of Developing Countries from all Sources, 1970–1982 ($ billion at current prices)

	1970	1971	1972	1973	1974	1975	1976	1977	1978	1979	1980	1981	1982
1. **Official Development Assistance**	8.23	9.14	9.84	12.68	16.50	20.95	20.35	20.98	28.10	31.93	37.33	36.63	34.24
Bilateral	7.16	7.84	8.46	10.72	13.68	17.11	16.49	16.15	22.09	25.69	29.54	28.70	26.79
DAC Countries	5.66	6.31	6.61	7.08	8.23	9.79	9.50	10.08	13.12	16.33	18.11	18.28	18.53
OPEC Countries	0.39	0.44	0.66	2.03	4.15	5.68	5.17	4.28	6.90	6.96	8.73	7.61	5.51
CMEA and Other Donors	1.11	1.09	1.19	1.61	1.30	1.64	1.81	1.79	2.07	2.40	2.70	2.81	2.75
Multilateral Agencies	1.07	1.30	1.38	1.96	2.82	3.84	3.87	4.83	6.01	6.24	7.79	7.93	7.45
2. **Grants by Private Voluntary Agencies**	0.86	0.91	1.04	1.37	1.22	1.34	1.35	1.49	1.65	1.95	2.31	2.02	[illegible]
3. **Non-concessional Flows**	10.95	11.83	13.30	19.86	19.81	34.31	34.89	44.56	57.91	57.72	56.41	69.27	[illegible]
Total Receipts (1+2+3)	**20.04**	**21.88**	**24.18**	**33.91**	**37.53**	**56.00**	**56.59**	**67.03**	**87.66**	**91.60**	**96.05**	**107**[illegible]	[illegible]

Source: Organization for Economic Cooperation and Development, DAC, *Development Cooperation Review* (Paris: OECD, 1983).

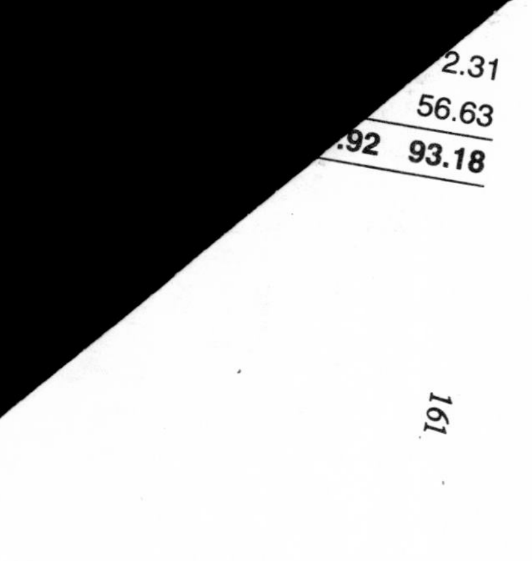

very significantly over this period rtant than all multilateral flows put during the 1974–75 recession, accounted ODA in these years.

and 1982 the total of ODA received current terms by $2.75 billion or by the outcome largely of a fall in OPEC was the war between Iraq and Iran by almost $0.9 billion, but all OPEC their current account surpluses as a trade and a reduction in oil demands, es to cut back their aid contributions. o-thirds of all OPEC aid, reduced its this time.

In real ter... oth inflation and exchange rate movements (principally the appreciation ... e dollar), flows of ODA receipts stagnated in 1981, and fell by 4.5 percent in 1982. The fall in OPEC bilateral aid was offset by a real increase in DAC bilateral and in multilateral assistance in 1981, but in 1982 the real value of multilateral assistance also fell (Table 6.2). The rate of growth of aid in real terms has been quite low since 1975, being no higher than 1.3 percent p.a. (bilateral 0.7 percent p.a., multilateral 4 percent p.a.), though growth patterns have not been smooth.

Figures for ODA receipts are, however, somewhat inadequate as indicators of aid trends because of the time lags involved between flows of aid by donors and their receipt by developing countries, especially when those flows are mediated by multilateral agencies. Flows of resources from DAC countries might, therefore, be a more reliable guide to aid developments and these are presented in Table 6.3. This reveals that ODA fell by $1.6 billion in 1981 after having risen sharply the previous year. The fall was distributed between bilateral assistance and contributions to the IDA and regional development banks and, as Table 6.4 shows, affected 12 out of the 17 DAC donor countries. The bulk of the decline was, however, accounted for by the United States whose assistance fell by 26 percent in real terms in 1981, reflecting the abrupt change in the policies of the Reagan administration toward regional development banks, as discussed in Chapter 5. This, in turn, led to some disruption in the multilateral contributions of other DAC members, given the pro-rata arrangements in force governing IDA replenishments. Some of the 1981 decline, however, simply reflects abnormal 'bunching' of contributions to multilateral organizations in 1980. In 1982 the ground lost in the previous year was recovered largely as a result of expanded contributions to multilateral institutions although this again is thought to represent an unusual 'bunching' which will not last. Indeed, there has been a pronounced slowing down in *real* growth rates of multilateral contributions from 13.0 percent p.a. between 1970 and 1975/76, to 5.6 percent p.a. between 1975/76 and 1981/82 to only 2.0 percent p.a. between 1978 and 1981/82. This should be compared with the decline

Table 6.2

Total Net Resource Receipts of Developing Countries from all Sources, 1970–1982 ($ billion at 1981 constant prices)

	1970	1971	1972	1973	1974	1975	1976	1977	1978	1979	1980	1981	1982
1. Official Development Assistance	21.30	22.18	21.48	24.72	29.10	32.03	30.19	28.82	33.53	33.79	36.21	36.62	34.97
Bilateral	18.45	19.03	18.47	20.90	24.13	26.16	24.45	22.18	26.36	27.19	28.65	28.70	27.37
DAC Countries	14.58	15.31	14.43	13.80	14.51	14.97	14.09	13.85	15.66	17.28	17.56	18.28	18.93
OPEC Countries	1.0	1.07	1.44	3.96	7.32	8.69	7.67	5.88	8.23	7.36	8.47	7.61	5.63
CMEA and Other Donors	2.86	2.65	2.60	3.14	2.29	2.51	2.69	2.46	2.47	2.54	2.62	2.81	2.81
Multilateral Agencies	2.86	3.16	3.01	3.82	4.97	5.87	5.74	6.63	7.17	6.60	7.56	7.93	(7.61)
2. Grants by Private Voluntary Agencies	2.22	2.21	2.27	2.67	2.15	2.05	2.00	2.04	1.97	2.06	2.24	2.02	2.36
3. Non-Concessional Flows	28.22	28.71	29.04	38.71	34.94	52.46	51.77	61.21	69.11	61.08	54.71	69.27	(57.84)
Total Receipts (1+2+3)	**51.75**	**53.11**	**52.79**	**66.10**	**66.19**	**86.54**	**83.96**	**92.07**	**104.61**	**96.93**	**93.16**	**107.92**	**95.18**

Source: Organization for Economic Cooperation and Development, DAC, *Development Cooperation Review* (Paris: OECD, 1983).

Table 6.3

The Net Flow of Financial Resources from DAC Countries to Developing Countries and Multilateral Agencies

	$m						Percentages					
	1970	1975	1979	1980	1981	1982	1970	1975	1979	1980	1981	1982
Official Development Assistance	6,949	13,846	22,819	27,264	25,634	27,853	44	31	30	36	29	33
Bilateral Grants and Grant-Like Flows	3,321	6,268	11,703	14,123	13,185	13,412	21	14	15	19	15	16
of which: Technical Cooperation	1,524	2,922	4,685	5,477	5,246	5,390	10	7	6	7	6	6
Bilateral Loans on Concessional Terms	2,351	3,539	4,628	3,985	5,102	5,122	15	8	6	5	6	6
Contributions to Multilateral Institutions	1,277	4,039	6,488	9,156	7,346	9,319	8	9	9	12	8	11
of which:												
UN	371	1,197	1,699	2,170	2,227	2,264	2	3	2	3	2	3
EEC	158	673	1,216	1,575	1,561	1,470	1	2	2	2	2	2
IDA	582	1,316	1,996	3,101	2,433	2,766	4	3	3	4	3	3
Regional Development Banks	101	418	918	1,717	753	1,494	1	1	1	2	1	2
Other Official Flows	1,122	3,912	2,894	5,272	6,609	7,433	7	9	4	7	7	9
Bilateral	845	3,833	3,138	5,378	6,470	7,458	5	9	4	7	7	9
Multilateral	276	79	– 244	– 106	139	– 26	2	x	x	x	x	x
Private Flows	7,018	25,706	48,098	40,661	55,489	46,076	44	57	63	54	62	55
Grants by Private Voluntary Agencies	860	1,346	1,997	2,386	2,005	2,307	5	3	3	3	2	3
Total Net Flows	15,948	44,810	75,808	75,583	89,737	83,669	100	100	100	100	100	100

Source: Organization for Economic Cooperation and Development, DAC, *Development Cooperation Review* (Paris: OECD, 1983).

Table 6.4

Net Official Development Assistance from DAC Countries to Developing Countries and Multilateral Agencies
($ million and percent of GNP)

Countries	Average 1971–73		1976		1979		1980		1981		1982	
	$m	As % of GNP	$m	As % of GNP	$m	As % of GNP	$m	As % of GNP	$m	As % of GNP	$m	As % of GNP
Australia	266	0.54	377	0.41	629	0.53	667	0.48	649	0.41	882	0.57
Austria	23	0.11	50	0.12	131	0.19	178	0.23	313	0.48	354	0.53
Belgium	191	0.52	340	0.51	643	0.57	595	0.50	575	0.59	500	0.60
Canada	457	0.42	887	0.46	1,056	0.48	1,075	0.43	1,189	0.43	1,197	0.42
Denmark	100	0.46	214	0.56	461	0.77	481	0.74	403	0.73	415	0.77
Finland	21	1.42	51	0.17	90	0.22	110	0.22	135	0.28	145	0.30
France	1,286	0.64	2,146	0.62	3,449	0.60	4,162	0.64	4,177	0.73	4,028	0.75
Germany	881	0.32	1,593	0.36	3,393	0.45	3,567	0.44	3,181	0.47	3,163	0.48
Italy	159	0.13	226	0.13	273[a]	0.08	683	0.17	666	0.19	817	0.24
Japan	711	0.23	1,105	0.20	2,685	0.27	3,353	0.32	3,171	0.28	3,023	0.29
Netherlands	282	0.59	728	0.83	1,472	0.98	1,630	1.03	1,510	1.08	1,474	1.08
New Zealand	21	0.23	53	0.41	68	0.33	72	0.33	68	0.29	65	0.28
Norway	64	0.40	218	0.70	429[a]	0.93	486	0.85	467	0.85	559	0.99
Sweden	211	0.50	608	0.82	988	0.97	962	0.79	916	0.83	987	1.02
Switzerland	53	0.16	112	0.19	213	0.21	253	0.24	237	0.24	252	0.25
United Kingdom	648	0.41	885	0.39	2,157	0.52	1,852	0.35	2,195	0.44	1,793	0.37
United States	3,242	0.28	4,360	0.26	4,684	0.20	7,138	0.27	5,783	0.20	8,202	0.27
Total DAC Countries	**8,616**	**0.33**	**13,953**	**0.33**	**22,820**	**0.35**	**27,264**	**0.38**	**25,635**	**0.35**	**27,853**	**0.38**

[a]Excludes administrative costs

Source: Organization for Economic Cooperation and Development, DAC, *Development Cooperation Review* (Paris: OECD, 1982 and 1983) for 1982, Table II.A.2., p. 199; for 1983, Table B.6, p. 190.

in the annual real growth rates of overall ODA, over the same periods, from 6.2 percent, to 2.5 percent and 1.7 percent.

Recent trends in aid flows are not therefore easy to disentangle but the picture which emerges is one of a slowing down in flows rather than of any decline. As a percentage of GNP, the record of DAC countries in 1981/82 was no better than it was in 1979/80 (Table 6.4) but, equally, and perhaps remarkably given the recession, it was no worse. But since 1981 the 'political environment' for aid does seem to have deteriorated and there is a generally acknowledged 'uncertainty' surrounding the medium-term future of aid flows.[1] Before the onset of global recession these flows were not expected to grow at more than the average of the last decade.[2] Since then the estimates have been revised downwards. In its projections for the performance of Third World countries to 1995 the World Bank assumes a growth rate in real official transfers of 2.0 percent p.a. on a 'low case' scenario and of 3.4 percent p.a. on a 'high case' scenario.[3] As we have seen in Chapter 2, the IMF projects no increase in the real growth of aid flows to 1990 in its base case. This pessimism is more than a reaction to the position of the U.S. government on funding multilateral institutions; it is a recognition that several major donors are grappling with large and growing fiscal deficits, management of which will effectively restrain aid growth in the foreseeable future.[4]

Aid and the Least Developed Countries

The assault on multilateral aid and the uncertainty surrounding the medium-term flows of aid are of particular significance to the least developed countries which are most highly dependent upon aid. Aid flows accounted for almost three-quarters of the external receipts of low-income countries in 1980, and for 82 percent of the receipts of the least developed countries (LLDCs) (Table 6.5).

In 1979, the latest year for which such figures are available, ODA accounted for between 30 and 37 percent of total imports of low-income countries, for between a quarter and a half of all investment and for between 4.3 and 7.6 percent of GNP (Table 6.6). For the LLDCs, the importance of ODA is even more striking being the equivalent of 50 percent of imports, 81 percent of all investment and 9.7 percent GNP. Furthermore, when large aid recipients (India, Indonesia, Indo-China and Egypt) are excluded, the relative importance of aid in terms of each of these three measurements rose dramatically between 1974/75 and 1979 due, especially, to the increasing dependence of sub-Saharan Africa on aid. This trend must have continued to 1983 because while official transfers to Africa (excluding South Africa) rose by 13.7 percent between 1979 and 1983, GDP rose by only 6.2 percent and imports by 0.7 percent.[5]

Since the poorest countries are also the most dependent on multi-lateral aid (Table 6.5), they are, as shown in Chapter 5, particularly vulnerable to the recent shifts in U.S. aid policy. This is especially so since anticipated

Table 6.5

Net External Financial Receipts of Developing Countries by Income Groups, 1980 (net disbursements)

	All LDCs		LICs		of which: LLDCs		MICs		NICs		OPEC	
	$b	% of Total	$b	% of Total	$b	% of Total	$b	% of Total	$b	% of Total	$b	% of Total
ODA	36.36	38.0	17.11	74.0	6.44	82.1	12.66	45.9	0.50	1.9	0.52	10.0
DAC Bilateral	18.02	18.8	8.54	37.0	3.22	41.1	6.64	24.1	0.40	1.5	0.27	5.2
OPEC Bilateral	8.26	8.6	1.65	7.1	0.82	10.5	4.04	14.6	0.02	0.1	0.04	0.8
CMEA Countries	2.14	2.2	(1.27)	5.5	(0.32)	4.1	(0.44)	1.6	0.02	0.1	0.14	2.7
Other Countries, Bilateral	0.20	0.2	(0.15)	0.6	(0.05)	0.6	(0.05)	0.2	—	—	—	—
Multilateral Agencies	7.74	8.1	5.50	23.8	2.03	25.9	1.49	5.4	0.06	0.2	0.07	1.4
of which: OPEC Financed	0.29	0.3	—	—	—	—	—	—	—	—	—	—
Non-Concessional Flows	59.31	62.0	6.0	26.0	1.40	17.9	14.92	54.1	26.34	98.1	4.66	90.0
Total Receipts	**95.67**	**100.0**	**23.11**	**100.0**	**7.84**	**100.0**	**27.58**	**100.0**	**26.84**	**100.0**	**5.18**	**100.0**

Source: Organization for Economic Cooperation and Development, DAC, *Development Cooperation Review* (Paris: OECD, 1982); Ibid., 1983, pp. 176–177, for definitions of country groupings which are different from those used by the IMF.

Table 6.6

ODA Receipts of Low-Income Countries as Percent of GNP, Imports and Investment, 1974/75 and 1979.

	ODA as % of:					
	GNP		Imports		Investment	
	1974/75	1979	1974/75	1979	1974/75	1979
Asian Low-Income Countries	3.3	2.8	32	24	18	14
of which:						
Bangladesh	7.8	14.6	64	63	119	136
Burma	1.7	6.9	27	105	18	38
India	1.8	1.4	27	18	9	7
Indochina[a]	17.1	7.9	103	67	161	128
Indonesia	2.5	1.8	16	12	13	8
Nepal	2.8	8.3	26	59	36	89
Pakistan	7.8	4.1	41	21	53	28
Sri Lanka	4.4	11.4	17	26	28	70
Other	4.8	3.5	26	29	40	13
Sub-Saharan Africa	5.8	7.8	22	40	31	54
of which:						
Ethiopia	4.8	4.9	44	34	47	66
Ghana	1.9	1.8	10	18	15	24
Kenya	4.2	6.5	12	23	18	24
Mozambique	0.6	12.3	3	49	—	—
Senegal	8.5	11.7	25	38	42	61
Somalia	37.0	53.8	82	112	115	209
Sudan	5.4	10.2	24	56	30	68
Tanzania	9.6	13.6	30	57	44	73
Upper Volta	16.4	19.6	63	68	60	98
Zaire	6.8	5.9	20	72	21	47
Other	5.9	7.7	23	34	31	55
North Africa and Middle East	15.1	7.9	51	32	78	39
of which:						
Egypt	16.8	7.6	55	37	78	39
Yemen, Arab Rep.	7.3	9.5	64	22	—	—
Other	15.0	8.4	13	19	—	—
Total Low-Income Countries	**4.6**	**4.3**	**31**	**30**	**24**	**23**
Memo:						
Total low-income countries[b]	6.1	7.6	28	37	39	52
Least-developed countries	7.8	9.7	43	50	60	81

[a]Comprises Kampuchea Laos and Viet Nam

[b]Exclude India, Indonesia, Indochina and Egypt

Note: Low-income countries are those with per capita incomes of less than $600 in 1980.

Source: Organization for Economic Cooperation and Development, DAC, *Development Cooperation Review* (Paris: OECD, 1982).

cut backs in aid are likely to follow closely on the heels of a period of import contraction for the two poorest groups of Third World countries; indeed, import volumes in 1983 were on average below those of 1980 for 'other net oil importers' and 'low-income countries.'[6] The generally adverse political environment for aid and U.S. intransigence over IDA replenishments come, therefore, at the very time that low-income countries are facing acute foreign exchange constraints.

Terms and Composition of Aid and the Crisis

Even more important than putting pressure on total aid flows, the current economic crisis has had the effect of making donor countries more sensitive than usual about the trade generating benefits of aid. In the context of record levels of unemployment since the 1930s and of intensifying commercial rivalry between major industrialized capitalist economies, this emphasis is only to be expected. In Europe and parts of Scandinavia, its most overt manifestation is in the rising proportion of ODA taking the form of concessional export credits. These credits are also being 'mixed' with standard credits from state agencies or private sources to increase the competitiveness of corporations in bidding for sales contracts in developing countries. The growth of pure concessional credits and of 'mixed credits' has been important in the aid flows of several DAC members over the past three years, and is likely to continue into the foreseeable future.[7]

The share of concessional export credits in ODA is perhaps largest in Austrian aid, accounting for 63 percent of the total in 1981 compared with only 50 percent in 1980. But this was only the extreme case. West Germany, Sweden, the Netherlands, Denmark and France have all expanded the flows of mixed credits in their aid totals quite significantly since 1979 and recently Canada announced its intention to do so.[8] In the case of France such credits accounted for 16 percent of all ODA in 1981. They were much less important for other donors, 6.4 percent for Sweden, 2.6 percent for the Netherlands and 2 percent for Denmark, but seem to be growing quite rapidly.[9]

Two major consequences flow from the expansion of these types of credits. The first is that they serve to reduce the grant element in ODA. In the case of Austria, this fell from 70 percent in 1980 to 55 percent in 1981 on account of these credits. Because Austria is a small donor, contributing less than 1 percent of total ODA flows, this had no significant impact on developing countries as a whole. But those donors reportedly using mixed credits more extensively account for 30 percent of all aid and hence this trend could have considerable significance if it continues. In the case of France it helps explain the relatively low grant element in total ODA *and* the fall in the grant element between 1979 and 1982. In the case of the Netherlands, Sweden and Denmark, the sums involved are too small at this stage to have much of an impact on grant performance (Table 6.7).

The second tendency of these credits is that they raise the proportion of aid which is, in effect, tied since they are extended only to suppliers

Table 6.7

Quality of DAC Assistance in Terms of Grants and Tied Aid, 1979, 1981 and 1982 (%)

	Grant Element			**Tied Aid** (includes multilateral aid)		
	1979	**1981**	**1982**	**1979**	**1981**	**1982**
Australia	100.0	100.0	100.0	25.7	35.0	28.3
Austria	86.1	55.1	61.1	45.0	77.1	76.7
Belgium	98.1	97.7	98.3	50.0	46.1	45.8
Canada	97.2	97.3	98.8	53.2	58.3	64.8
Denmark	96.7	95.6	95.7	22.4	21.4	20.1
Finland	96.6	95.6	95.9	6.8	13.0	11.8
France	93.5	89.6	90.1	45.5	42.5	45.4
Germany	84.6	85.9	88.7	15.9	19.1	21.8
Italy	99.6	91.4	90.6	3.9	8.5	17.1
Japan	77.8	75.5	74.3	32.4	30.9	20.7
Netherlands	92.1	95.2	93.9	4.0	16.4	12.9
New Zealand	100.0	100.0	100.0	2.5	48.2	46.9
Norway	100.0	100.0	99.2	15.7	19.0	20.9
Sweden	100.0	99.9	99.8	17.2	13.8	13.3
Switzerland	95.8	97.0	97.3	32.5	37.6	na
United Kingdom	95.7	96.8	98.5	42.4	49.6	42.1
United States	91.7	94.0	93.8	50.7	49.1	31.5
Total DAC	**90.8**	**90.0**	**90.6**	**34.6**	**37.1**	**na**

Source: Organization for Economic Cooperation and Development, DAC, *Development Cooperation Review* (Paris: OECD, 1981 and 1982).

resident in the donor country. It is, therefore, no accident that countries like Austria and France have higher than average proportions of their aid tied or that, in the case of Austria, the proportion tied rose dramatically between 1979 and 1981 (Table 6.7). For most countries, however, there is no simple relationship between the overall performance of aid in terms of tying and the trend in concessionary or mixed credits because the latter are such a small proporation of total aid. It is to be noted, however, that 10 out of 17 DAC donors have during the recent recession increased the proportion of aid which is tied.

Concern over the growing popularity among donors of these 'associated credits', led DAC to draw up a document of 'Guiding Principles' to govern their use.[10] The aim of the principles, which were adopted in June 1983, is to attempt to ensure that the use of these credits does not undermine priority development objectives nor diminish the competition for aid procurements. Among other principles, DAC members have agreed that the grant element of such arrangements should be no less than 20 percent and that it should be higher for poorer Third World countries than for others. The global economic crisis has put pressure on donors to enter into this new form of cofinancing in order both to make aid go further and to generate more exports and jobs from aid funds. The objective of the Guidelines, as DAC emphasizes, is to attempt to reconcile these pressures with the requirements of recipient countries for genuine and efficient foreign assistance.[11]

The movement to concessional export credits and to mixed or associated credits is but part of a broader effort by donors to raise the proportion of goods procured in their own countries, whatever their declared commitment to the untying of their aid might happen to be.[12] To this end, for instance, aid agencies have been under pressure to inform themselves more thoroughly of the capability of national firms to contribute to aid procurement needs.[13] From the point of view of recipient countries this need not, in itself, be a negative development, if contracts are tendered and firms in donor countries win them because of superior efficiency. There is, however, always the danger of administering procurements to favour national suppliers regardless of efficiency and this is difficult to detect. In addition, it appears that the design and selection of aid projects is being increasingly influenced by the supply capabilities of industries in donor countries, prompting DAC to comment that "[s]uch practices could easily distort recipients development priorities and lead to programming decisions inconsistent with development objectives."[14] In future, therefore, it may become more difficult in practice to differentiate between aid which is formally tied and untied aid which is *de facto* tied, with potential negative consequences for aid recipients.

It is difficult to know to what extent this move toward informal tying represents a break with past practice or merely an extension of it. Thus, while West Germany declared only 19.1 percent of its aid tied in 1981, about 60 percent of aid procurements were furnished by German firms. Likewise, Swedish suppliers accounted for almost a half of total procurements under bilateral aid even though 'tying' was confined to only 10.5 percent of the total.[15] In order to ascertain the proportion of aid which is genuinely untied one would need to know the degree to which procurements in donor countries were competitive with goods available elsewhere. In the absence of comprehensive data on procurements themselves, leave alone any analysis concerning competitiveness of procurements, caution is called for in the use of data on the proportion of aid which is formally regarded as 'untied'.

Yet not all of the pressures for increased tying emanate from the donor countries. The deteriorating economic situation in many Third World countries has altered the aid relationship in a variety of ways, some of which serve to increase the *demand* for tied aid by the recipients themselves and others which propel donors toward tying as a means of actually increasing the effectiveness of their aid. At the root of both of these developments is the increasing difficulty of administering aid in a situation of general economic crisis.

The major symptoms of crisis as outlined in Chapter 1, viz. the acute shortage of foreign exchange, growing rates of inflation, overvalued exchange rates, goods shortages and mounting fiscal deficits, enormously complicate the task of aid administration. They severely impede project implementation by rendering it difficult for donors to acquire inputs of goods, services (especially transport) and local cost funding. This raises the gap between aid commitments and aid disbursement and delays project completion. At the same time, procurement difficulties find expression in rapidly rising prices for all purchases of goods which *are* available locally. The upshot of this is that in the absence of exchange rate adjustment, the real value of aid funds available for local costs, which are in any case usually quite limited, falls dramatically. Under these circumstances the completion of new aid projects becomes more problematic, and the maintenance and repair of existing facilities becomes steadily more difficult. As excess capacity and unemployment rise in sectors dependent on imported inputs, both donors and recipients begin to see the need to reorder aid priorities as a matter of some urgency.[16]

In adapting to this type of crisis situation, which is encountered in many, especially least developed, countries, some donors have expanded general import support and local cost (budgetary) support and have reduced the rate at which new project aid is extended.[17] This double-edged adjustment is an eminently sensible one as it helps to break supply bottlenecks while simultaneously reducing the demands that project aid makes on local supplies, foreign exchange and budgetary funds. When aid takes the form of general import support it also generates local counterpart funds which help ease the budgetary crisis. Likewise, local cost funding may also bring with it freely usable foreign exchange which helps ease balance of payments pressures. For these reasons, import and budgetary support are extremely attractive to recipient countries.

From the donor's point of view, this type of program assistance makes sense not only because of the goodwill it generates among recipient countries, but also because it facilitates disbursement of aid funds both directly and, indirectly, by enabling new and past projects to proceed more smoothly. Where donors do not have the flexibility to switch funds from project to 'emergency program' financing in this way, the result is often a sharp deterioration in the disbursements to commitment ratio or a generalized overrunning of project cost budgets as aid administrators are forced to bid on the local market for scarce commodities.

As far as import support is concerned, however, procurement is generally tied to the donor country. This tends to reduce the flexibility of the aid of those countries with an otherwise liberal position on tying (e.g., the Netherlands and Scandinavian countries); but, because of the emergency nature of this type of assistance, this is not perceived as a major problem by recipient countries which, in fact, press very hard for such aid. Even more highly valued by recipients is budgetary support if it comes in the form of foreign exchange. It assists budgetary balance but, unlike import support is tied neither to specific procurement sources *nor* to specific imported commodities.

Precise data on trends in this kind of non-project assistance are not readily available, but there is evidence that it has increased substantially since 1979. Thus, while overall DAC bilateral commitments fell by 9 percent in 1981 relative to 1979/80, and while overall non-project aid declined even more, by 10 percent, the category 'other general non-project aid' rose by almost $1.5 billion or by 78 percent (Table 6.8). This category covers general purpose contributions, balance of payments stabilization loans and budget support. Unfortunately, there is no breakdown available of which countries received this assistance in 1981, but in 1979, it appears that low-income countries received about half the total and the least developed about 15 percent. For a number of poorer countries this type of assistance formed a significant proportion of bilateral aid. At the same time, a number of middle-income countries were also substantial beneficiaries (Table 6.9). It is likely that its rapid expansion since 1979 has benefited the low-income countries more than proportionately, but this cannot be ascertained from available published data.

Import and budget support are not, however, unambiguously beneficial or costless. In addition to the association of the former with increased tying, both are often accompanied by attempts by donors to impose policy conditionality on recipients. The roots of this tendency are not usually conspiratorial but rather stem from the difficulties donors face in 'selling' program aid, of whatever type, politically in their home country. Not being able to identify aid flows with specific project accomplishments can be a political liability, regardless of any benefits program aid might bestow on recipients in terms of the maintenance and rehabilitation of the existing capital stock and government services; this is especially the case when the general political climate for aid in donor countries is not propitious. Budgetary support is particularly difficult for donors to 'sell' to their electorates. First of all, the potential demand for this kind of aid is virtually limitless. Secondly, there is a danger of the recurrent budgets of recipients becoming structurally dependent on foreign assistance (for most poor Third World countries the dependence of the capital budget on aid is, as suggested earlier, an established fact). Thirdly, there is the likelihood of this type of aid being seen to be directly supporting an unproductive state bureaucracy in many recipient countries (support through project aid being less obtrusive but no less real!).[18] In addition, it would be politically unacceptable in donor countries if both budgetary support *and* import support were to be seen as allowing recipients to avoid or delay making necessary changes in domestic policy to deal with their economic difficulties. Thus, when program aid is seen as an emergency substitute for project aid there are pressures on donors to ensure that it is purely temporary in nature and that "it is instrumental in encouraging rather than delaying needed adjustment policies."[19]

In practice, bilateral donors, like commercial banks, prefer to ride on the coat-tails of conditionality imposed by the IMF and/or the World Bank since these institutions are in a much better position to monitor and enforce compliance.[20] Unlike commercial banks, however, donors *are* able to adopt

Table 6.8

DAC Bilateral Assistance for Longer-Term (commitment basis) Development and Emergencies

	$b		% of Total		% of Non-Project Aid	
	Average 1979 and 1980	1981	Average 1979 and 1980	1981	Average 1979 and 1980	1981
Total Bilateral	24.9	22.7	100.0	100.0		
Project Aid and Technical Cooperation	13.7	12.6	55.0	55.5		
Non-Project Aid (NPA)	11.2	10.1	45.0	44.5	100.0	100.0
of which:						
Emergency Financing	1.58	1.13	6.4	5.0	14.1	11.2
Emergency Food Aid	0.02	0.05	0.1	0.2	0.2	0.5
Disaster Relief	0.51	0.40	2.1	1.8	4.5	4.0
Debt Relief	1.05	0.68	4.2	3.0	9.4	6.7
Financing with some Emergency Content	5.35	5.60	21.5	24.7	47.7	55.5
Food Aid	3.45	2.22	13.9	9.8	30.7	22.0
Other General NPA	1.90	3.38	7.6	14.9	17.0	33.5
Sector Aid	3.70	2.73	14.9	12.0	33.2	27.0
Other and Unspecified	0.56	0.64	2.2	2.8	5.0	6.3

Source: Organization for Economic Cooperation and Development, DAC, *Development Cooperation Review* (Paris: OECD, 1982).

Table 6.9

Selected Countries that Received Large Absolute Amounts of "Other General Non-Project Aid", 1979

	Other General NPA – $m	% Bilateral Aid
Low-Income		
Bangladesh	157.3	20.7
India	165.9	13.0
Pakistan	74.4	15.7
Sudan	34.6	12.5
Tanzania	65.9	9.0
Zambia	74.5	32.1
Middle-Income		
Egypt	310.2	18.3
Papua New Guinea	249.3	83.2
Peru	30.3	11.8
Thailand	30.2	5.9
Turkey	339.7	51.0

Source: Derived from Organization for Economic Cooperation and Development, DAC, *Review of Development Cooperation* (Paris: OECD, 1982).

an 'interventionist' stance if an IMF program is not in place. They have representatives resident in recipient countries and generally have close contact with host governments through an established framework of aid consultation and review. Moreover, the project and sectoral aid activities of donors are, as we have seen, influenced very directly by the general economic situation and the economic policies being pursued, in recipient countries. This permits donors to develop an informed view of local problems that foreign commercial banks, operating as they often do, at arms length, generally lack. Project and sector aid also provides donors with other levers of intervention in the policy affairs of recipient countries.

Yet, when conditionality is exercised by bilateral donors, it has quite different qualitative connotations from that exercised by multilateral institutions. It exposes donors to accusations of interference in the political affairs of another sovereign state and lays recipient governments open to the charge of dancing to the tune of a foreign piper. For these reasons, donor conditionality is usually not as overt or as explicit as IMF conditionality and takes quite a different form. The pressures tend to be more subtle focusing on desired policy changes rather than on quantitative performance criteria. In this respect, this type of conditionality is closer to that of the World Bank than that of the IMF, but it differs from both in that it is normally exercised informally rather than through written agreements. Donors generally prefer that conditionality be imposed by the IMF or the IBRD because this shields them from accusations of political interference and because the leverage of these multilateral institutions is often much greater than that of a single donor. It might be thought that bilateral donors would have broader horizons than the IMF and be more sensitive to the distributional and political implications of stabilization programs; that they might, indeed, use the fact that the Fund depends on them to support its programs in the poorest countries (in much the same way that it depends on the banks in the middle-income countries) to exercise a degree of leverage over the Fund itself. Alas, there is no evidence of this. On the contrary, there have been indications of donors coming together to develop a uniform approach to conditionality along orthodox lines where other programs are not in place, a development encouraged by DAC but which must be regarded with some awe by recipient governments.[21] In the case of one country with which the author is familiar, the World Bank itself has attempted to orchestrate a concerted effort by donors to pressure a recipient government into accepting policy changes being proposed by the IMF which the government felt were inappropriate.[22] Bilateral donors have been forced to take a position in the dispute even where they were reluctant to do so,[23] and several of them have applied pressure on the government, through all the various forms of their assistance, to implement some of the policies in dispute. Given that the country in question, Tanzania, is so heavily dependent upon bilateral and World Bank aid, these pressures to adjust policy are much greater than any that could be applied by the IMF. Other least developed countries are equally vulnerable. The danger of donor cartels emerging to exercise collective leverage is one reason why not all recipient countries see it as advantageous to have the World Bank coordinate donor/recipient consultative meetings. Even so, the World Bank has organized, or is organizing, consultative groups in over 40 Third World countries which, together, receive over a third of all DAC, ODA. It is worth noting that in 10 of these, (including Tanzania) accounting for 14.3 percent of DAC aid, the consultative group was in 1983 either non-active or cancelled.[24]

The growth in import support has also been accompanied by donors becoming much more actively involved in the detailed allocation of imports to both sectors and enterprises in recipient countries.[25] At the same time, the general conditions of crisis have forced donors to engage directly in project management activities simply to prevent their programs from grinding to a halt. In these areas, therefore, donors are by force of circumstances undertaking executive or managerial functions that they would prefer to see handled by nationals of the recipient country.[26] These forms of day-to-day interventionism by donors are bound to increase if the crisis persists and they pose a real dilemma for more enlightened donors. The dilemma arises not only because donors have to account to their home political constituencies for the way in which funds are used, but also because aid has a momentum of its own which is only loosely related to the needs of recipients. There are numerous bureaucratic pressures operating on donors to keep up the flow of disbursements even if the cost is one of a paternalistically high level of direct intervention in project implementation and resource allocation. That governments of recipient countries acquiesce in this interventionism is indicative of their dependence on aid flows and their added vulnerability in times of crisis. While one can agree that "if qualification for programme assistance requires detailed involvement and influence on the part of the donor in the entire development strategy and macro policy of the recipient, it may be preferable to do without it," recipient countries may see themselves as having little room for manoeuvre in the midst of crisis.[27]

What remains largely unexplored is the relationship between current economic difficulties being experienced by Third World countries and their past heavy reliance on aid financing. There is a growing awareness that the design of project aid has often made inadequate provision for the recurrent cost requirements and the on-going foreign exchange needs of projects.[28] Until the recent crisis, project aid seems also to have reinforced policy biases against the maintenance of, or growth in, the level of export earnings of many poorer countries.[29] In addition, lack of aid coordination in recipient countries appears to have weakened efforts to realize the potential of Third World countries to generate more of their foreign exchange requirements through 'own-earnings'. The recent emphasis on improving the effectiveness of aid through better coordination and improved management is, from this point of view, a welcome development, provided it does not lead to greater donor intervention in Third World policy formulation.[30] What seems to be required, therefore, is a strengthening of the capabilities of recipient governments in each of these areas and more awareness at the design stage of projects of their on-going implications for recurrent local and foreign exchange costs.

Improved quality of aid might be the key to permitting poorer Third World countries to begin to *reduce* their overall dependence on aid in the medium/long-term. In the short-run, the overwhelming need is to switch resources out of new projects and into rehabilitation and maintenance of capital and services deemed to be productive and efficient. The economic crisis gives Third World countries an ideal opportunity *not* to rehabilitate projects that should never have been implemented in the first place. Part of the rehabilitation thrust should be focused on projects that can generate foreign exchange and/or budget revenue and, in this way, help to alleviate the need for import or budgetary support in future. Project aid which is allowed to proceed should also be closely scrutinized for its potential short-run contribution to internal and external balance.[31]

The danger is that short-term expediency may gradually be transformed into longer-run strategic commitments. The possibility of conflict developing between the need to expand exports in order to rehabilitate the economy, on the one hand, and the need for longer-term national economic integration and the direct meeting of basic needs, on the other, is a live one. It is true that without rehabilitation, which must surely entail some expansion in export capacity, strategies of national economic integration would themselves be impossible; but it is equally true that, to become a longer-term reality, policies of national economic integration and the meeting of basic needs must find concrete expression in the short-term. There must, therefore,

...ate balance in the use of current resources between projects that ...oreign exchange earnings and those that have as their prime focus, ...ting of basic needs and/or the building up of linkages within the ...l economy. There can be no simple prescription for this, but it ...d be possible to earmark some project funds to the latter and to improve the formulation design and implementation of the projects concerned so as to minimize their net foreign exchange usage.

The problem with allowing the donors to take the initiative to improve coordination is not, therefore, that improved coordination is not needed; on the contrary, it is essential if aid funds are to be used effectively and sparingly. The issue is rather that of the proper focus of responsibility. Since aid flows are of critical importance to the economies of many Third World countries, failure to coordinate aid policies and practices is tantamount to an abdication by recipient governments of responsibility for major areas of economic policy. Aid coordination is too vital a concern to be delegated to donors. If, as might sometimes be the case, recipients lack the capacity to coordinate aid, this weakness should be addressed as a matter of urgency—possibly with donor assistance; local capacity will not be improved by donors stepping directly into the breach.

Recipient governments might be less anxious to call or participate in consultative meetings if they feel that such gatherings may be used by donors to collectively impose their views of appropriate economic policy on recipients. This undoubtedly explains why some of the World Bank consultative groups are no longer functioning.[32]

The current global crisis is therefore, putting pressures on donor countries to reduce the flow of aid and to alter its composition and terms. The increased emphases on import and budgetary support and on improved aid coordination and management are appropriate responses to the difficulties being faced by many Third World countries. They may, however, increase the leverage of donors over the economic policies of recipient countries, reinforcing orthodox view of what constitutes appropriate adjustment policies. The least developed countries which are heavily dependent on aid cannot, therefore, expect to draw on bilateral assistance as a means of avoiding IMF or IMF-type conditionality and are particularly susceptible at this time to external influences on the formulation of domestic economic policy.

Notes

1 The OECD Development Assistance Committee (DAC), *Development Cooperation Review* (Paris: OECD, 1982), Chapters V and VI, deals at length with the generally adverse economic climate for aid.

2 World Bank, *World Development Report* (New York: Oxford University Press, 1982), p. 36.

3 Ibid., 1984, p. 36.

4 Fiscal deficits of the seven largest industrial capitalist economies rose from 3.1% of GNP in 1979 to 5.6% in 1983. See IMF, *World Economic Outlook* (Washington, D.C.: IMF, 1984), p. 174.

[5] IMF, *World Economic Survey*, 1984, pp. 170 and 191.

[6] Ibid., pp. 183–184.

[7] See DAC, *Development Cooperation Review*, Chapter XIII and 1983 Chapter V for a country-by-country assessment of trends in donor aid policy in recent years.

[8] See *The Globe and Mail* (Toronto), April 9, 1984.

[9] DAC, *Development Cooperation Review*, 1982, Chapter XIII.

[10] These guidelines are published in DAC, *Development Cooperation Review*, 1983, pp. 169–170.

[11] Ibid., p. 72.

[12] It should be noted, however, that even when operating within strict *overall* guidelines for the tying of aid, donors can occasionally show great flexibility with regard to untying aid to individual recipients. See for example, Philip E. English, *Canadian Assistance to Haiti* (Ottawa: North-South Institute, 1984), pp. 144–148.

[13] DAC, *Development Cooperation Review*, p. 71.

[14] Ibid.

[15] Ibid., and 1982, p. 15 for additional information on Sweden.

[16] See, John Loxley, "Discussions with Aid Donors, Aid and the Economic Crisis in Tanzania" (Dar es Salaam: Tanzania Advisory Group, Working Paper No. 3, December 1981, Mimeo.) for a discussion of these problems in Tanzania.

[17] Canada is one such donor. See Roger Young, *Canadian Development Assistance to Tanzania* (Ottawa: North-South Institute, 1983), pp. 96–97.

[18] DAC, *Development Cooperation Review*, 1983, op. cit., p. 70.

[19] Ibid., 1982, p. 96.

[20] Ibid.

[21] Ibid., p. 99 and 1983, Chapter IX.

[22] See Loxley, "Discussions with Aid Donors", p. 6.

[23] This is confirmed in G. Edgren, "The Issue of Conditionality in Aid", *Canadian Journal of Development Studies*, Vol. III, No. 2 (1982).

[24] DAC, *Development Cooperation Review*, 1983, p. 125.

[25] That import support can imply heavy administrative demands on donors for this reason is emphasized in DAC, *Development Corporation Review*, 1982, p. 97.

[26] Loxley, "Discussions with Aid Donors", p. 3.

[27] G. K. Helleiner, "Aid and Dependence: Issues for Recipients" in his *International Economic Disorder: Essays in North-South Relations* (Toronto: University of Toronto Press, 1981), p. 231.

[28] DAC, *Development Cooperation Review*, 1983, pp. 67–70.

[29] Ibid., Chapter XI.

[30] Ibid., Chapter IX and see also World Bank, *World Development Report*, 1984, the main theme of which is 'management.'

[31] For a more detailed discussion of similar proposals see R. H. Green, "African Economies in the mid-1980's" in Jerker Carlsson, *Recession in Africa* (Uppsala: Scandinavian Institute of African Studies, 1983), pp. 173–203.

[32] This is certainly so in the case of Tanzania.

7

FUTURE DIRECTIONS

The rapidity with which the international financial system has been undergoing transformation over the past decade should serve to caution against facile attempts to predict how it might evolve in the coming years. Prediction is not the object of this chapter. Rather, the intent is to examine the very divergent contemporary views on how the system might or should evolve and to seek to explain the thinking that underlies these viewpoints. The starting point will be a consideration of the alternative perspectives on the debt crisis and the policy prescriptions to which they give rise. The arguments of the 'liquidity school' which dominate official policy will be contrasted with those of the 'solvency school' which call for a more interventionist stance on the part of the international financial institutions. The possibility of large debtors cooperating to improve their bargaining power with creditors will then be considered. This will be followed by discussion of what one might hope to achieve through reform of the international monetary and financial system. An emerging liberal/fabian consensus on reform will be the focus of attention here. After outlining the contents of this reform package and the various critiques that have been levelled against it from both ends of the political spectrum, consideration will be given to various political strategies that might be pursued by the Third World to improve the terms on which they participate in the world economy.

The International Debt Problem

Two major bodies of opinion on how the international debt crisis might be resolved are discernible in the literature, reflecting quite different perceptions of the nature of that crisis. The first sees it as a liquidity problem which is by and large being managed efficiently by initiatives already taken; the second views it as a more intractable solvency crisis which will pass only after wider-reaching structural reforms have been implemented. The lines between these two broad approaches are not drawn cleanly; each contains a great diversity of opinion and offers a multiplicity of proposals some of which overlap between groups. Nevertheless, they are identifiable as contrasting approaches and can be treated as such.[1]

Liquidity School Proposals

The 'liquidity' position is held by the IMF, the World Bank, the DAC of the OECD, the U.S. government and generally speaking, by the banks themselves. It denies the existence of a generalized debt crisis, maintaining that Third World debts are basically sound and repayment capacity adequate provided that suitable 'structural adjustment' measures are taken. Debt problems are regarded as being country-specific and essentially short-term in nature. Most will be eased as the world economy improves and hence, any intervention at this stage should be 'ad hoc' on a case-by-case basis. Subject to there being no major world depression, the existing institutional framework should be adequate to deal with existing and foreseeable problems, though marginal reforms may be in order.

This position has been put most coherently by A. Basora, Director of the U.S. State Department's Office of Development Finance, in the form of a five-point strategy representing official U.S. thinking on the matter.[2] He argues that resolving the debt problems requires (i) the restoration of world growth and the freeing up of international trade; (ii) adjustments by deficit countries to reduce borrowing to sustainable levels and to end inflation; (iii) availability of balance of payments finance to enable structural adjustment; (iv) international cooperation at the official level to provide emergency short-term assistance; and (v) continued commercial bank lending to countries undertaking suitable adjustment measures. For the State Department, 'suitable' measures are identical with those adopted by the IMF and the World Bank.

Underlying this approach is the feeling that the debt crisis came to a head in 1982 and was managed efficiently by an unparalleled degree of cooperation between states, multilateral institutions and commercial banks. An international financial collapse on the scale of the 1930s was, thereby, averted. This, it is maintained, demonstrates the strength and flexibility of existing international institutions. With the U.S. economy seemingly in the process of strong recovery, the worst is considered past and more generalized solutions, therefore, uncalled for. Projections made by the Institute for International Economics seem to support this interpretation. If OECD countries can sustain a minimum 3 percent p.a. growth rate between 1984 and 1986, the debt burden of most major debtors will be manageable; their current account deficits will fall in absolute dollar terms as well as in proportion to export earnings and the ratio of their net debt to total exports will also decline. The relative debt burdens of countries accounting for three-quarters of total debt outstanding will improve.[3] The IMF projections of Chapter 3 are consistent with these.

Some proponents of the liquidity view see the debt problem as being one which is 'internal' to banks and one which banks should be allowed to solve without greater government intervention.[4] They argue that the market will discipline those banks which have made mistakes, that the international banks "are capable of finding and implementing solutions" to the debt crisis and "strong enough to manage their own internal problems and provide leadership in redressing balance sheets, reassessing risk, redistributing risk, restoring confidence and renewing growth." This will entail continued close cooperation between banks, governments, multilateral agencies and debtors, but will not require "bailing out" the banks, talk of which is considered "just political or editorial claptrap."

Because this perspective on the debt situation is held by the most influential governments and institutions in the industrialized capitalist world, it is one that will most certainly prevail. 'Ad hoc' initiatives on specific country debt problems and marginal reforms at most to the international financial system, will continue to be the order of the day for as long as this approach appears tenable. For the transnational banks this will necessitate a willingness to roll over short-term debts and to reschedule maturing longer-term debt for many years to come. It will also entail maintenance of the recently developed relationship of mutual dependence between banks and the IMF.

The 'Solvency School' Proposals

The 'liquidity school' approach can be characterized as a 'reactive' one: initiatives and reforms being taken only after the need for them is clearly established. It is premised on a belief that a world depression is unlikely, that past 'fire fighting' remedies will provide an on-going solution to the debt problem if orderly world recovery takes place and, more specifically, that IMF structural adjustment programs and accompanying austerity measures will prove to be sustainable and effective. Critics question one or more of these premises and advocate instead, a more interventionist approach, often calling for contingency planning to prevent problems arising as an alternative to simply reacting to problems after they have arisen. On the whole they also propose generalized long-term solutions as opposed to 'ad hoc', country-specific measures.

Many such critics hold that the debt crisis is one of solvency rather than liquidity, pointing to the unprecedented debt-servicing burdens to support their argument.

They generally acknowledge the efficiency of emergency measures taken to date but feel that these are only makeshift, and do not deal with the fundamental reality of the situation facing most larger debtors, which is their utter inability to service their debts in the foreseeable future. At best, these measures merely postpone the day of reckoning by deferring for some years payment of part of the principal as it falls due. Even on optimistic forecasts of world recovery and interest rate declines, major debtors would still experience debt-servicing ratios (excluding short-term debt) of over 40 percent p.a. by 1986,[5] while the ratio of debt to exports for 21 major borrowers would still be in excess of 120 percent by 1990.[6] These forecasts assume interest rate levels for 1984/85 of between 8 and 9 percent p.a., or 30 to 40 percent below levels prevailing in mid-1984. We have also seen that IMF projections point to increasing burdens of debt servicing to 1987 and quite high, but declining, levels thereafter—and they too were based on interest rate assumptions which are no longer valid. On current prescriptions, debt-rescheduling exercises and the quest for short-term debt roll-over will be annual occurrences in the years ahead—with all the uncertainty that this entails. Servicing these debt payments which *are* made from the proceeds of foreign exchange earnings, IMF facilities or further bank loans, will depend crucially on the ability of major debtors to adhere to IMF programs. Yet, we have seen that major debtors appear to be meeting current account targets only by draconian cuts in imports, and these and the large reductions in real budget deficits have resulted in severe cut backs in investment and the level of activity and increased doubts about future growth prospects. The huge rates of inflation combined with acute austerity measures and record unemployment levels are generating widespread discontent among the urban population of debtor countries. In consequence, while some skeptics believe that the current debt problems are not capable of "mathematical solution",[7] many more are with justification, questioning the political feasibility of current policy responses.

It is argued, therefore, that the fragility of the debt situation is such that there is a high probability of default or repudiation occurring. If this were to happen, the acknowledged weaknesses of the international banking system could generate financial chaos. Thus, the essentially unregulated nature of the Euromarket, the volatility of funds, the extensive mismatching of maturities and the prevalance of inter-bank positions which convert "the risks faced by anyone on its operations into risks faced by all other banks,"[8] could transmit shock waves from a default or repudiation throughout the whole international banking system. The absence of any clear lender of last resort under existing arrangements means that the scope and nature of state intervention in such an eventuality would be determined only *after* the onset of a banking crisis. While the 'liquidity' school argues, correctly, that the vagueness surrounding lender-of-last-resort facilities is a "calculated reticence" which serves to discourage default or repudiation, it is also true that this lack of clarity might, itself, help generate instability in a context in which loans are declared, formally, to be non-repayable.[9]

To deal with these perceived inadequacies in current arrangements a number of writers have proposed the introduction of an international banking 'safety net'. This could take the form of an international deposit insurance scheme, of a global lender of last resort, or a mutual aid mechanism organized by the banks themselves. The difficulty with these proposals is that most of them presuppose uniformity in the national regulation of banking practices and, as we have seen, this is simply not the case. They are, therefore, not feasible at this time since "neither commercial nor central banks can be expected to enter into open-ended (or even limited) commitments vis-a-vis institutions subject to widely differing 'regulatory standards.'"[10]

Other writers seek solutions in measures which would avoid or reduce the need for emergency resort to a safety net of any kind. One increasingly popular proposal, of which these are numerous variants, is that of recycling bank debt. The idea would be for some agency (the IMF,[11] the IBRD[12] or a new body[13] have all been suggested) to take over outstanding bank loans in exchange for the issue of long-term notes. This would remove the uncertainty and potential instability generated by annual rescheduling exercises, reduce the danger of default or repudiation, and provide for the orderly, long-run drawing down of debt. In return for the strengthening of their debt portfolios, banks would have to agree to the discounting of their debts and/or to receiving reduced interest income. This would have an immediate adverse effect on their profit and loss positions. Proponents argue, however, that this would be more realistic bookkeeping than current practice in which front-end fees, wide interest margins over LIBOR, and lax reserve requirements exaggerate the earnings quality of rescheduled debt. The banks, of course, do not share this view and would oppose any such move to reduce their earnings. They have a more optimistic perspective on their risk exposure and on the long-run quality of their assets, perhaps because they believe that Western states will not allow a banking collapse in the wake of default or repudiation by a large debtor. There is, however, a question of the extent to which the banks are putting short-run returns to stock holders before global stability. While current rescheduling terms are highly profitable for banks, they are extremely onerous for debtors. Increased fees and spreads tended to offset much of the decline in nominal interest rates in 1982/83 and have compounded the increases since that time. Such revenue strategies have strengthened the conviction of 'recyclists' that the debt problem is too serious to be left in the hands of the banks.

The IMF and the World Bank disagree. They do not appear to be disturbed by bank earnings on reschedulings and, in spite of a philosophical commitment to supporting private enterprise, have no desire to be cast in the role of debt collector on behalf of the banks. They already face criticism from such diverse sources as the U.S. Congress and some left-wing analysts that their balance of payments assistance programs serve mainly to bail out banks; as we saw this was the main objection in Congress to raising the U.S. quota in the IMF. The adoption of a recycling role would give much greater weight to such criticism. But neither the wish to avoid public censure, nor the reluctance to become debt collectors adequately explains the unwillingness of the international institutions to move in this direction. Essentially, they do not believe that the current debt situation is so unstable as to warrant the recycling solution. What is more, they fear the *moral hazard* attached to such proposals (i.e., that any initiative in the direction of recycling might itself precipitate default or repudiation).

Zombanakis has attempted to avoid moral hazard in his proposal for an IMF guarantee scheme.[14] Rather than taking over bank debt, the IMF would enter into long-term agreements with debtors—a 13-year period is used as an example—over which time debts would be rescheduled and the economy adjusted in accordance with IMF programming. The Fund would guarantee loan repayments in years 11 to 13 for all countries adhering to its conditionality in the event that programs did not work and repayment was not possible. The guarantee fund would be financed by standby letters of credit from Group of Ten countries, thereby ensuring collective responsibility for what would be a new lender-of-last-resort facility tacked on to the existing international financial system. The attractions claimed for this proposal, apart from avoidance of moral hazard, are recognition of much lengthier periods needed for structural adjustment to be effective, provision for long-term debt rescheduling and the requirement for nominal changes to existing international institutions. Its main shortcoming is that it makes no provision for dealing with either those countries which fail to adhere to IMF programs or those which do adhere but which nevertheless still experience chronic balance of payments problems in the years prior to the guarantee becoming effective. Perhaps Zombanakis feels that central banks would act as lenders of last resort in this eventuality; this, at least, was the intention of a related proposal of his that central banks facilitate the recasting of Eurodollar loans into domestic currency loans to reduce pressure on the Eurodollar market. There is, however, little indication that central Banks wish to be more explicit at this time about any possible lender-of-last-resort responsibilities they might feel obliged to undertake. Furthermore, recasting the Euro-money market in this way can hardly be described as a minimal change implying "no interruption of the present *modus operandi* of the financial system":[15] it would replace inter-bank lending in dollars by transactions between domestic banks and central banks in local currencies. If carried to the extreme, the inter-bank market as we know it would cease to exist, inter-bank borrowing and lending being confined to domestic currency operations only.

Zombanakis' guarantee scheme shares one feature in common with current debt-rescheduling exercises and with many of the proposals for debt recycling, which is that it envisages no reduction in the repayment of principal owed by debtors. Debt obligations remain unchanged as indeed do interest obligations (the agency retaining the spread between current interest charges to borrowers and reduced interest payment to banks on account of risk reduction). What changes is the period of time over which repayment is due. While this, of course, reduces the present value of repayments there are many who would argue that it does not go far enough to alleviate the problems faced by debtors, nor does it sufficiently penalize the banks for past imprudence. In effect, they maintain that debtors are bearing an unfair burden at this time in adjusting to the debt crisis and would continue to do so under most such proposals.

To meet this objection, one could build a debt-discounting element into recycling proposals, which would entail introducing an explicit political dimension into debt valuation. Others seek to avoid the controversy this process is likely to generate by proposing that bank debt be marketed.[16] In the 1930s international debts took the form of bonds, the market value of which declined during the debt crisis. As a result, lenders shared the burden of default through reduced asset values, while debtors were able to buy back bonds at a fraction of their face value once economic recovery started. By creating a secondary market in international bad debts, some hope to achieve a resolution of the current debt problem that, likewise, apportions the burden of adjustment among both debtors and creditors.

What remains unclear in these proposals is the impact such discounting would have on bank profits and share valuations. Even a small discount is likely to significantly reduce bank capital which, in turn, would lead to a compression of lending since, normally, banks must maintain a fixed relationship between capital and loans outstanding. The secondary effects of these proposals could therefore be quite destablizing in themselves.[17]

The persistence of high real rates of interest has also prompted a spate of proposals for putting a cap or a ceiling on rates or for capitalizing interest payments when rates exceed an agreed upon ceiling.[18] Once again, though, the likely impact of these measures on bank earnings and share valuations is unclear.

Possible Debtor Reactions to the Crisis

Many advocates of debt recycling and debt relief see their proposals as prescriptive initiatives to deprive debtors of what Kissinger has termed their "capacity for blackmail."[19] So far the response of debtors to their predicament has been quite restrained but there are indications of gradually building resentment of, and resistance to, current approaches to managing the debt crisis. Individual countries have, on a number of occasions, forced the pace and terms of debt rescheduling. Poland, Brazil, Romania, Mexico, and Argentina have each separately taken initiatives of this kind. Recent increases in interest rates have, however, generated more aggressive negotiating positions. Ecuador and Bolivia have suspended payments of certain types of debt while Venezuela has proposed that its debt be rescheduled at fixed interest rates.[20] Some countries are already finding it difficult to meet payments on rescheduled debt (e.g., Costa Rica)[21], while others have been granted complete moratoria on payment of principal for as long as a year (e.g., the Philippines).[22]

In addition to these individual initiatives there are, however, growing pressures for debtors to take collective action in renegotiating debt. Celso Furtado has been at the forefront in urging the formation of a debtor cartel which would negotiate a uniform and comprehensive rescheduling of debt including a period of grace in which principal repayments would be suspended and interest payment partially refinanced.[23] This would require the active participation in negotiations of the central banks and governments of the industrialized capitalist countries since transnational banks would need their assistance to cushion the impact of this type of debt relief. The cartel would also seek support for non-recessionary adjustment policies as alternatives to IMF austerity measures, which Furtado considers have been discredited by the Fund's own studies. More ambitiously, he urges major debtors to use their collective strength in pressing for an entirely new international monetary and financial system in which Third World interests would be taken into account.

Latin American states have to date not followed Furtado's advice, but both the Commission for Latin America (ECLA) and the secretariat of the Latin American Economic System (SELA) have recommended tentative steps in this direction in the form of the establishment of machinery for the exchange of information on terms of debt refinancing and on international financial markets generally.[24] This body would also offer advice on debts to governments. If accepted, this recommendation would lead to debtors creating an institution which would perform for them the same kind of functions that the Institute of International Finance is expected to perform for transnational banks. Once established, such an institution could well evolve into the type of cartel proposed by Furtado; the likelihood of this will be directly proportionate to the political problems faced by debtor governments in implementing prevailing adjustment programs and in meeting unrecycled debt obligations.

The major Latin American debtors have also begun meeting together to discuss their common problems, suggesting the possibility of cooperative action being taken to deal with their debt difficulties. The first such meeting prompted a sharp warning from the World Bank against debtors taking any coordinated steps to impose unilateral debt moratoria.[25] As it transpired, the meeting produced a consensus that world economic recovery and flexibility on the part of the IMF were the keys to orderly debt repayment. A subsequent agreement between 28 Latin American and Caribbean leaders—the Quito Agreement—called, however, for more realistic debt negotiations.[26]

Eleven Latin American countries have more recently put forward a series of concrete proposals to help alleviate their debt difficulties. The so-called Cartagena consensus calls for debt repayments to be limited to "a reasonable percentage of export earnings compatible with maintaining growth", for interest rates and margins to be reduced, and for commissions to be eliminated. International institutions are requested to be more flexible in their conditionality, to permit adjustment with growth to make allowances for unforeseen increases in interest rates. The debtors also call for expanding funding of these institutions, and greater access to the markets of industrialized countries.[27] Their intent is to emphasize the political nature of the debt problem and the responsibility of creditor countries to assist in finding workable solutions. While explicitly rejecting the notion of a debtor's cartel, the option of a more drastic collective response is still open to these countries should recovery not be sustained and/or should current IMF stabilization measures prove to be unacceptable politically.

Ironically, in 1984 major debtors themselves were instrumental in preventing an Argentinian default. Mexico, Brazil, Venezuela and Colombia loaned Argentina $300 million in a $500 million package designed to enable that country to meet overdue interest payments. This seems to represent the polar opposite of collective debtor action to ease their debt payment obligations. It should be noted, however, that as a *quid pro quo* for the loans from these major debtors, commercial banks contributed $100 million at unusually low interest rates, prompting the observation that this experience might later serve as a model for other collective initiatives by debtors with the principal objective not of rescuing the banks, but of securing a better deal from them.[28]

The ultimate expression of debtor strength would, of course, be the outright repudiation of debt, a possibility that cannot be ruled out. New governments, ushered into power as a protest against austere structural adjustment programs designed to secure debt repayment, might find popular support for repudiation. Moreover, economic arguments against such a move are less persuasive now than in earlier years. It has already been shown (Chapter 3) that the net flow of foreign funds less interest payments is now negative, hence the loss of access to bank finance no longer acts as a deterrent for many debtors. There would, no doubt, be other forms of retaliation which might be costly: trade and aid might be curtailed; debtors' assets abroad might be seized and such foreign transactions that survived would generally be moved onto a cash basis, which would cause difficulties given the depleted foreign reserve holdings of most debtors. Yet even these possible reactions are less of a threat to debtors now than they were some years ago. The strategic interdependence of the economies of debtor and creditor countries (Mexico and the U.S. being the most extreme example), the relatively depressed state of world trade and the heightening of competitive, often protectionist, rivalries among major creditor countries, all reduce the likelihood and possible effectiveness of comprehensive economic sanctions against countries repudiating debt.[29] The results of a simulation exercise show that if the initial dislocation could be survived, several large debtors would experience improved GNP growth rates in the medium-term if they repudiate their debt.[30] That debtors have not moved in this direction is indicative of the commitment of their governments firstly, to the 'status quo' in terms of international political and economic relations—a commitment not unrelated to the uncertain costs associated with repudiation, and secondly, to solutions to the debt problem which place extreme burdens on certain sections of their society and especially on the working class. Political protest against those solutions and further pressure on debtors from rising interest rates could conceivably lead to a re-examination of international relations and, consequently, to a reconsideration of attitudes toward prevailing arrangements for servicing foreign debt. Outright repudiation is still an extreme measure and debtors would, perhaps, opt first for the imposition of a less threatening debt moratorium. If this were to happen, one could expect a more interventionist approach by governments of the industrialized capitalist countries with serious consideration being given to some variant or other of proposals being advocated by the 'insolvency' school. The indications at this time are, however, that it would take a much more immediate threat of banking collapse than currently exists to prompt movement in this direction.

The key to the stability or otherwise of the world financial system at this time would appear to lie, therefore, in the nature of the IMF and World Bank adjustment programs in debtor countries. If these programs fail, the foundation for continued cooperation by individual commercial banks will be undermined, prompting attempts at withdrawal by individual banks. In such a situation, the herd instinct which typifies banking behaviour (and which, incidentally, might be exacerbated by the activities of the newly formed Institute of International Finance) might lead to a complete collapse of existing 'fire fighting operations', and force debtor countries to consider, more seriously, the options of debt moratoria or repudiation. Given the shortcomings of IMF/IBRD adjustment programs outlined above, in terms of their appropriateness, social cost and likely efficacy in a depressed world economic environment, the possibility of the debt crisis coming to a head in this manner will be a live one for many years to come.

Reform of the International Institutions

The Liberal/Fabian Consensus of Reform

The emergence of the debt problem as a serious threat to global stability and the widespread crisis conditions in the Third World at this time, seem to many observers to provide a compelling case for the urgency of reform of the international monetary system. The mutuality of interests between the industrialized countries of 'the North' (capitalist and socialist alike) and the developing countries of 'the South' in solving the global crisis, is the rationale for a liberal or, as some would argue, fabian consensus which is emerging on the shape that international reform should take. This consensus is, as yet, in embryonic form. Within the literature it describes are many different shades of political and technical opinion and numerous competing proposals at the level of detail. For this reason, some might argue that 'consensus' is too strong a term, overstating and oversimplifying the degree of agreement among those said to subscribe to it. Yet a general approach to reform proposals *is* discernible, one that supersedes the many nuances and idiosyncracies contained in its constituent individual reform statements. The most polished statements of this position are to be found in the first and second Brandt Commission reports and the Commonwealth Secretariat's *Towards a New Bretton Woods*, but similar stands were taken in the Arusha Initiative and in earlier formulations of proposals for a New International Economic Order.[31] This emerging consensus recommends far-reaching changes in the membership and power structure of international institutions. It also advocates significantly altering the flow, timing and terms of financial resources for the benefit of Third World countries. Not surprisingly, therefore, it enjoys a broad measure of support among the developing countries.

As a long-range goal the consensus calls for a new international monetary system which would be universal and democratic in character, to be established through the medium of a special United Nations Conference on International Monetary Reform. In essence, this would entail active participation by those socialist countries which are currently not members of the IMF/IBRD group and a reduction in the influence of the industrialized capitalist world in general and of the U.S.A. in particular. Greater reliance on the special drawing right would help replace national currencies as reserve assets and means of exchange and, in the process, erode further the influence of major capitalist nations in the international monetary system. International monetary policy would provide for foreign reserves to expand over the long-term at a rate sufficient to encourage the steady growth of world trade. These longer-term additions to reserve assets through issues of SDRs would be linked to the automatic transfer of resources to developing countries.

In the short-run a series of emergency measures are recommended to deal with the financial problems, debt or otherwise, facing developing countries. These encompass an immediate issue of SDRs allocated not as in the past, according to quota, but as in the longer-term 'link' proposals, according to need based on some measure of country income levels. A further expansion in the flow of unconditional resources to the world's poorest countries would be achieved through enlarged IMF quotas, and reform of the compensatory finance facility. A doubling of quotas over the 1982 level and adjustment in subsequent years in line with the growth of world trade have been proposed. This would raise the amounts that could be borrowed in both the lower and the upper tranches and would also permit increased borrowings under the CFF as it now operates. The consensus argues, however, that borrowing from the CFF should, ideally, be geared to balance of payments shortfalls and not to IMF quotas. The CFF should be made more flexible by being extended to cover payments shortfalls due to deterioration in the income terms of trade as a whole (in effect, being broadened to cover increases in import prices), and by tying repayment to improvements in balance of payments or to "ability to repay." Some portion of the issues of SDRs might be used to finance this greatly expanded role for the CFF.

To complement these changes in the Fund's operations and to address, in particular, the needs of the LDCs, IDA resources would be increased considerably and the World Bank would expand its capital base and increase its gearing ratio to permit greater borrowing per unit of its capital. The World Bank group as a whole would be permitted to channel a much greater proportion of its expanded lending, up to 30 percent is suggested, into program lending or import support.

Increased capital flows from multilateral agencies would be accompanied by a greater aid effort by bilateral donors who are urged to raise their ODA, defined in terms of grants, to the 0.7 percent GNP level adopted by the UN in 1970. They are also called upon to increase their aid to the LDCs to reach the target of 0.15 percent GNP adopted at the 1981 UN Conference on the Least Developed Countries. Within these totals, they are urged to shift away from project aid toward more balance of payments support in the short-term.

Additional flows of official assistance from all sources are seen as a complement to, and not a substitute for, increased private flows. The whole consensus package is viewed by its proponents as a stimulus to flows of private capital in the form of both bank credit and direct foreign investment. In addition, the provision of institutionalized guarantees and insurance arrangements for private investors is considered to be an important component of the package itself.

A salient recommendation of the consensus view is that the IMF should begin to play an explicitly anticyclical role in the world economy. The CFF and SDR initiatives would have this objective and might be supplemented by the activation of special credit facilities along the same lines as the oil facilities if the situation so warrants. Additionally, the Fund would be called upon to aggressively exercise its mandate of surveillance over exchange rates with a view to achieving greater exchange rate stability and a more symmetrical adjustment to world payments imbalances. Implicit in this recommendation is a requirement that the Fund be more active in the formulation of the economic policies of the industrialized capitalist nations as but one element in a movement toward greater harmonization of these policies than has been the case to date. The proposals call for cooperation between these nations to go well beyond monetary policies and embrace fiscal as well as trade policies, with special emphasis on the dismantling of protective barriers and other impediments to international trade. The argument is, therefore, that narrow national interests can and should be put aside in favour of the common good internationally and that the IMF will play a key role in engineering this process.

The consensus also calls for modification in the *terms* on which the Fund extends assistance to Third World countries. On the narrowly financial side it advances proposals for the least developed countries to borrow from the IMF on concessional terms through interest subsidies. These would be financed from the proceeds of further IMF gold sales, from repayments flowing into the Trust Fund or from resource transfers from more developed members. This last possibility would entail either direct contributions from the industrialized members or an interest differential charged on loans to wealthier Third World countries. It is argued that interest rate subsidization will become increasingly attractive to borrowers as the IMF draws more heavily on funds borrowed at market rates of interest. From the point of view of the Fund and country donors, the attraction of interest subsidies lies in being at once both oriented toward the most needy *and* tied to conditional resources.

The precise nature of conditionality is the second and more important aspect of terms of assistance addressed by the consensus. Significant departures from current practice are recommended so that conditionality would be more supply-oriented and tailored directly, and flexibly to the needs of specific countries. The emphasis would be on 'expansionary stabilization' or adjustment with growth. This would entail less reliance on a small number of demand-oriented macro performance criteria and more emphasis on the growth of investment, output and net foreign earnings with provision being made for amendments to targets in the light of unforeseen developments in the world economy outside the control of the borrower. Across-the-board restrictions on the amount which may be borrowed from the Fund would be replaced by an approach which varies the amount of borrowing in accordance with the availability of funds to borrowers from commercial or other official sources. The pace of adjustment would be geared to the circumstances of individual countries but with a general tendency to allow longer periods of time for structural adjustments to be effected than is current IMF practice. To facilitate this, the consensus argues that the Fund should make greater use of the three-year extended facility as opposed to conventional one-year standbys. Such multi-year programming is considered more suitable to a supply side emphasis in adjustment and would also permit the avoidance of shock treatment where demand restraint is thought to be required. The problems the Fund encountered in the past with the CFF would in part be avoided by it cooperating closely with IBRD staff who have more familiarity with supply side programs. In many respects IBRD structural adjustment programs appear to be the model underlying the consensus approach to the reform of IMF conditionality, and it is envisaged that the two institutions would, in future, work together, side by side, in the design and implementation of adjustment programs. Both bodies would, however, be required to depart significantly from current approaches to adjustment by specifying the distributional implications of their adjustment programs and by taking into consideration the policies and objectives of borrowers in this area. It is not suggested, however, that income distribution targets be written into performance criteria.

It is apparent that the consensus position is not arguing against the *principle* of conditionality but rather in favour of modifying current practice. Indeed, while certain of the above proposals build much more automaticity into the system than currently exists (e.g., the CFF reforms) and provide for considerable increases in the flow of non-conditional resources (e.g., SDRs, private capital flows, etc.) which would tend to reduce the policy formulation and watchdog roles of the IMF and the IBRD, yet other proposals go to the opposite extreme. Some variants of the real economy or supply-oriented approach to conditionality would result in the IMF becoming intimately involved in a much wider range of policy decisions, often at quite micro levels, than even the World Bank seeks in its structural adjustment lending.[32] These proposals have, not surprisingly, generated skepticism about their political acceptability as well as their practicality among those close to the Fund.[33] At the other extreme, some feel that performance criteria should be minimal, measurable, but meaningful. They advocate confining them, therefore, to one or more key variables such as the balance of payments, the savings rate or the real exchange rate, usually with contingency provisions.[34]

The Response of the IMF and the U.S. Administration

For its part the IMF does not believe that such wide-ranging reform is required because it disagrees with much of the diagnosis of the problem underlying the consensus position. Nevertheless, it does subscribe to some of the individual proposals outlined above. Thus, while the fund has not seen new allocations of SDRs as a priority issue and has never advocated 'linking' SDR allocations to aid needs, its management does, on the other hand, envisage the emergence of the SDR as the principal reserve instrument in the international monetary system.[35] And while it does not believe that it should be the source of concessional aid to the least developed countries, it accepts the need for substantial increases in the flow of such assistance. The Fund also does not appear to aspire to becoming an activist international central bank, performing the interventionist role envisaged for it by the various strands of the consensus position. It does not, therefore, advocate that it should participate more actively in foreign exchange markets, take over from commercial banks the allocation of international surpluses, discount the debt of those banks or direct the adjustment process in countries not borrowing from it (e.g., surplus countries). Instead, it interprets its mandate and the need for its services more modestly (realistically?) by seeking to secure a more harmonious international payments system through 'moral suasion', special studies and 'ad hoc' initiatives. To this end, in recent years it has become an outspoken advocate of essentially monetarist policies in the industrialized capitalist countries, calling for continued monetary restraints, a reduction in government deficits over the medium-run and a concerted effort to reduce structural rigidities and imbalances—foremost amongst which is a plea for policies that shift income distribution from labour to capital. The Fund is also calling for greater harmonization of economic policies among these countries, the reduction of protectionism and the subsidization of industries, and the abolition of restrictive work rules and of disincentives to savings.[36] These initiatives are essentially oral ones and are not supported by sanctions of any kind against countries not cooperating.

Fund activism has been more substantial in the area of bank debt, albeit in an ad hoc, non-systematic manner. The close working relationship the Fund now maintains with transnational banks has been pivotal in preventing a complete collapse of lending to major debtors, and in maintaining bank solvency thus far. This new management role is seen to be well within the Fund's mandate of regulating the world payments system. Its rationale lies, ultimately, in the Fund's ability to develop and enforce adjustment programs, and will survive only as long as banks and/or debtor countries see their interests being served by the application of Fund conditionality.

These more modest interventions and perceptions of the Fund's role are shaped, of course, by the views of the major world powers which control the institution and especially by those of the U.S. administration. As noted, the economic policies of the Reagan administration have had the effect of boosting the value of the dollar and, temporarily at least, reversing the trend away from its use as the principal international reserve asset. These policies have been distinctly monetarist. It would hardly be consistent for the Reagan administration to promote, at the same time, allocations of SDRs and other, essentially Keynesian, policies on an international level—especially ones which would be perceived as shifting economic decision taking on a global level away from itself and toward a more participatory world body.

The U.S. administration would also see many aspects of the consensus position as undermining conditionality and allowing Third World countries to deal with the current crisis without having to endure the harsh domestic adjustments that it, itself, has visited on the U.S. economy and especially on U.S. workers. In this, both the IMF and the IBRD management would wholeheartedly concur. As we have seen, their view of the appropriate blend of adjustment and financing is one which emphasizes the former with the latter being considered as a complement to adjustment programs, not a substitute for them. In the consensus view, additional flows of finance would act as a buffer against most transitory or cyclical external shocks and adjustment policies would address what are considered to be 'structural' deficits in the balance of payments. Notwithstanding the practical difficulties of differentiating in this way between different sources of external imbalance, conditionality would obviously be considerably reduced in scope. In reducing reliance on macro performance criteria in favour of policy commitments or more detailed real performance targets, there is also a suggestion that even when it is applied, conditionality should be more flexible and less austere, which equally disturbs supporters of current IMF practices. It should be recalled that even the IBRD, which provides the model for the more interventionist strand of the consensus position, does not believe that its approach to conditionality should be exercised outside the framework of IMF orthodoxy.

There is one further, seemingly intractable, obstacle to the IMF altering the nature of its conditionality in the direction proposed by the consensus view. This is that it does not accept that it is excessively demand focused or that it ignores supply side stimulation. Further, it believes that it is, already, sensitive to the domestic political and social objectives of its members and to their differing capacities for rapid adjustment. Neither does it accept that it tightened up conditionality in 1981; instead it argues that the deteriorating world situation called for a renewed focus on adjustment efforts, earlier recycling policies being considered inappropriate to the task.[37]

Underlying the reluctance of both the Fund and the powers that control it to consider more fundamental institutional reform is their essentially 'liquidity' view of the current debt crisis. The debt aspect of the global financial crisis is the one that most directly concerns the industrialized capitalist countries since it is the one that is most threatening to their own stability. The crisis facing the least developed countries has minimal economic consequences for the countries of the industrialized world and at best poses only a moral challenge to them. This being so, the situation is seen to call for only those reform measures considered expedient for the management of an essentially short-run, liquidity, problem. An expansion of Fund conditional resources to a quite modest absolute level combined with 'ad hoc', country by country, tripartite negotiations and a slight tightening of bank regulations is considered adequate to deal with this problem. Only when debtors have demonstrated a commitment to adjustment and severe austerity has the U.S. been prepared to support consensus-type requests for lower interest margins and longer-term debt rescheduling.[38]

Left Critiques of the Consensus Position and Their Limitations

The nature of the system's response to crisis since 1981 underscores a fundamental flaw in the logic of the consensus approach—which is its assumption that reforms of the type it advocates are, self-evidently, in the mutual interests of both 'the North' and 'the South'. Left critics argue that dividing the world in this simplistic geographical fashion serves only to obscure the intense nationalistic rivalries between the industrialized capitalist economies of the north, rivalries which impose severe constraints on what is possible in terms of collective initiatives. The specific interests of individual nations vary greatly being conditioned by such diverse factors as their unequal size and resource endowment, their labour force militancy and productivity, their inflation and unemployment levels. Even where policy measures might bring benefits to 'the North' as a whole, the distribution of those benefits might be most unequal between nations because of their different attributes and conditions. Thus the consensus position on international monetary reform would seriously undermine what remains of U.S. hegemony in this area, while a blanket dismantling of protectionist measures would affect some 'Northern' economies more seriously than others. Only when collective benefits clearly outweigh the sum of individual country costs or, more accurately, when collective benefits coincide with the specific interests of the major powers of 'the North', will the appeal to common interests act as a sufficient stimulus to action on world reform. This qualification assumes even greater weight when it is considered that the term 'North' is not confined to these capitalist nations but also includes the Soviet Union and the countries of Eastern Europe.

What is more, beneath the level of the nation state in 'the North' is a great diversity of both class and other group interests, which the consensus position plays down. These generate political forces which shape the domestic and foreign policies of individual governments. Acceptance of consensus-type reforms requires the balance of support of these class and group political forces which, given the complexity of their interests, cannot be assumed on 'a priori' grounds. Thus, any reforms which reduce the risk to which international bankers are exposed might be opposed by other fractions of national capital not enjoying these safeguards or by workers who, ultimately, pay the taxes which finance these 'safety nets.' Likewise, the beneficiaries of protection in 'the North', the owners of capital, the workers and the local or regional governments affected would oppose its removal, while consumer groups who seek lower prices and, banks and TNCs who might have capital at stake in 'Southern' source countries, together with importers, all of whom seek higher profits, might be strong advocates of liberalization. Proposals to expand foreign aid raise equally vexacious issues of competing class and group interests in 'the North'.

The response of 'the South' to the consensus proposals suggests that common interests have a greater validity there. Even so, the diversity of nations and interests within 'the South' should not be overlooked. The term includes countries which are vastly different with regard to their social systems, the degree of economic and political independence, and the extent and manner of their integration with the world economy. These differences have not been sufficient to undermine the united stance of the Third World on global reform but they have undoubtedly complicated, if not inhibited, action to back up that call. Certainly, they would need to be given due consideration in formulating political strategy in pursuit of action.

Likewise, their domestic social structures will help determine the extent to which nations of 'the South' actively press for global reform. In particular, nations ruled by groups which owe their wealth, power and influence to close ties with foreign capital and states are unlikely to press hard for reforms not favoured by those foreign interests.

The failure of the consensus approach to recognize that national and class or group interests would often act as a powerful counterweight to 'common interests,' explains, according to Frances Stewart,[39] not only the lack of progress in implementing reform but also the discernible deterioration of the situation, in recent years, in such areas as concessional aid and protectionism. It is not that the interdependence of which the consensus approach speaks is not real; it most certainly is. It has been demonstrated, for example, that if the rate of increase of new commercial bank lending to Third World countries were to fall from the 20 percent level of 1981 to zero, the real GDP growth rate of these countries would be 3 percent p.a. lower than it otherwise would be—but growth rates in OECD countries would also be lower, by as much as 1 percent p.a.[40] Left critics have sometimes failed to appreciate the strength of this interdependence.[41] The point is, however, that 'the North' is less persuaded by such arguments than by the perceived threat (to continue with the example) to bank capital and to their economies generally that a further large expansion of bank debt seems to imply. Lacking a persuasive material base in mutuality of interests, one which allows for competing interests among nations, classes and groups, the consensus approach is reduced to appeals to morality which, by and large, go unheeded in 'the North' and especially so during times of recession and economic insecurity.[42] It is for this reason that Brandt II and the Commonweath Study *Towards a New Bretton Woods* have had, as yet, no visible impact on the policies of the industrialized capitalist countries despite being well received by countries of 'the South'.

Marxist analysts take this critique further. They argue that 'common interests' globally are clearly subordinate to the specific international interests of the capitalist class in the industrialized countries. They characterize the global situation as one of 'imperialism' in which capital of different national origins competes for profits on an international level supported in a number of ways and if need be, even with military force, by their respective nation states. U.S. imperialism is regarded as being still the dominant power in the world economy though its influence has been waning in the face of increasing competition from West Germany and Japan, and the steady expansion of the non-capitalist world since 1945 accompanied, most recently, by the defeat of the U.S. in Indo-China.

In this view of the world, the international institutions exist to facilitate the operations of imperialism, and do so either in a conspiratorial manner or in a systemic manner depending on the particular 'school' of Marxism involved. The conspiratorial approach, drawing much of its inspiration from the dependency theorists, sees the IMF as a conscious agent of U.S. imperialism which deliberately baits underdeveloped countries into a 'debt trap' so as to force upon them "a philosophy of economic development which invariably favours the capitalist class and imposes the burden of austerity on the working classes and the poor."[43] Governments which borrow from the Fund (and Bank) are regarded as being "always more or less collaborators and co-conspirators against the best interests of their own people."[44] At the same time the World Bank is considered to be "perhaps the most important instrument of the developed capitalist countries for prying state control of its Third World member countries out of the hands of nationalists and socialists who would regulate international capital's inroads, and turning their power to the service of international capital."[45]

The more 'systemic' Marxists argue a slightly different case, seeing the international institutions existing to enforce a body of rules on imperialist rivals and on the ruling classes of the developing countries so as to permit the 'law of value' or 'the logic of capital' to arbitrate conflicts between them. Mandel has argued that this view "is at once more sober and more ominous than the conspiracy theory. For it implies that whatever the composition of the body, and whatever the inclinations of the governments represented in it, there is no way to escape its 'diktats' in the long run, unless the logic of capital is broken, along with the capitalist mode of production, and all the international institutions that sustain it."[46]

Both strands of Marxist thinking see no merit in reform proposals of the consensus type. They maintain that by attempting to reduce the instabilities and inequities of capitalism such reforms seek to pre-empt more revolutionary social transformation; thus, the underlying objective of reform is the maintenance of the capitalist system rather than its replacement. Suggesting that the international institutions are no more socially useful than the Mafia,[47] they see reform as being utterly futile, implying instead that the abolition of these bodies would be more appropriate.

In general, Marxian approaches serve as a useful antidote to the more benign mainstream view of the international institutions, prompting a more cautious attitude toward the whole question of what reforms might accomplish. Nevertheless, in the above versions, policy prescriptions are less than satisfactory because while containing a central core of truth, the analysis is overly deterministic and hence, overly simplistic. To begin with, the powers which control these institutions do not always share the same interests at this level—rivalry and competition being a defining characteristic of imperialism. Nor do the interests of these powers, either individually or collectively, remain unchanged over time. This being so, it cannot be assumed 'a priori' that these institutions are or always will be mere instruments of U.S. foreign policy, that the U.S. policy toward them is unchanging or that they are always and forever incapable of initiatives which, from the point of view of the Third World members, are progressive. The decision to advance IMF credits to the Bishop government of Grenada against U.S. objections is a case in point. The steps taken in the 1970s to issue SDRs, to advance unconditional credits and to provide interest subsidies to the poorer countries are other examples. One can, of course, argue that these initiatives were a form of 'defensive modernization' designed only to strengthen the grip of capitalism on the Third World;[48] but this too seems overly simplistic. Grenada was brought back into the capitalist fold not by IMF credits but by armed invasion, while IMF credits could not prevent revolutionary movements from taking power in Cuba, Kampuchea, Vietnam or Nicaragua.

A more plausible view would be that, as embryonic surrogates for a world government, these international institutions perform a variety of functions which are often contradictory. While the principal function is clearly that of assisting world (capitalist) accumulation, they cannot ignore altogether the need to ameliorate some of the distributional problems between nations that the current international division of labour creates. Thus, like nation states they are also called upon to play a *legitimation* function.[49] Whereas individual states provide unemployment relief, family allowances and a variety of other services and transfers to the poorer sections of society, the international institutions provide, in similar fashion, some concessional facilities to poorer countries albeit within, as far as possible, the general framework of their preferred model of accumulation. Some of the consensus proposals are quite consistent with this function though, as the common interests argument implies, most are consistent with the accumulation function as well.

At the same time, like nation states, these institutions are subject to competing class and group pressures the nature of which varies with the political complexion of the dominant member governments, through which these pressures are channelled, and the general state of the world economy. At the moment, pressures for monetarist policies dominate with a much greater emphasis on accumulation than legitimation, reflecting the orientation of the U.S. and British governments, in particular. Nevertheless, within this general thrust of policy it must be acknowledged that no single member government can always impose its will on individual loan decisions—not even the U.S.A.—if its interests do not coincide with those of other dominant members. Thus while, for the most part, the major powers generally agree on which loans to approve, occasionally differences can arise, as in the recent cases of Grenada or El Salvador. As U.S. hegemony weakens one can expect these differences to increase in number and frequency with the result that more eclectic considerations might determine the outcome of individual loan requests. If this were to happen, there might be less pressure on individual developing countries to conform to preconceived strategies or forms of economic organization.

The Marxist positions we have referred to do not sufficiently acknowledge both the complex and often contradictory functions of these institutions, nor the diverse and often competing interests of their dominant members. As such, they exaggerate the extent to which these bodies monolithically project the interests of the U.S. and underestimate their *potential* capability to pursue policies which will permit individual countries to gain some breathing space in dealing with instability in non-orthodox ways—a potential which, admittedly, has been all too insufficiently realized to date.

These particular versions of Marxism also deal very inadequately with the fact that a number of socialist countries in both 'the North' and 'the South' are members of the IMF. In addition, there are other Third World countries pursuing economic strategies which are either socially progressive, nationalistic or both, strategies which come under pressure when they are forced to resort to the international institutions for stabilization assistance. For them, the above proposals offer no useful policy guidance whatsoever, denying their real need for additional foreign exchange resources, needs that cannot be met elsewhere. To sidestep this issue by reducing the governments involved to the level of co-conspirators against the best interests of their people, as Payer does, or by describing the countries as "so-called socialist countries" as Mandel does, is to trivialize the genuine political and social differences within the Third World and the difficulties some governments face in attempting to pursue alternative models of development to that preferred by the international institutions themselves.

The shallowness of the analysis of this issue is nowhere more apparent than in Cheryl Payer's recent work on the World Bank which otherwise contains a thoughtful, well-documented critique of the role of the Bank and the nature of its project lending. Payer identifies a number of socialist and recipient countries as 'good countries.' These are defined in terms of their willingness "to challenge the prerogatives of capital in the interests of improving the lives of their poor citizens."[50] She also speaks of some aid agencies as 'good' agencies being those "genuinely concerned about development for people and to promote genuine self reliance as a means of national independence." She then proceeds to argue that these 'good' countries are either denied Bank aid because of U.S. opposition or else the aid they receive is intended to subvert their revolutions (the Bank not being a 'good' donor) and is, therefore, undesirable anyway.

This crude categorization of both donors and recipients in what one writer has described as a "cowboy and indian" view of the world,[51] grossly oversimplifies the politics of aid. It suggests that aid recipients categorized as 'good' are not aware of the potential dangers of dealing with the IBRD, or with any other aid donor for that matter, and that they are powerless in the selection, design and implementation of aid projects. Moreover, it reduces all aid motivations to 'good' or 'bad' without recognizing the complex and often contradictory nature and effects of aid, from whatever source. Above all, it fails to deal with the political reality that socialist progressive and nationalistic Third World members of the international institutions by and large support the call for a consensus-type reform of the international monetary system, and that even non-member Third World socialist countries such as Cuba add their voice to this call. The very strength of the consensus position politically is indeed its broad appeal to Third World countries notwithstanding their different social systems or specific interests. The international monetary and trade system imposes similar major constraints on the development efforts of all such countries, whether they are pursuing capitalist or socialist models of accumulation and while, as Thomas suggests, those in the latter camp might be expected to campaign more militantly for international reform because the economic restructuring they attempt is generally more far reaching, they still find common cause with countries seeking less ambitious, more 'fractured and pragmatic' economic adjustments.[52] Third World socialists place great importance on this unified policy stance in the international diplomatic arena and decry the tendency of industrialized countries to highlight, unduly, the divergence of conditions and interests within the Third World which they interpret as being designed to undermine Third World unity.[53]

What the 'conspiracy' and some of the more classical 'systemic' Marxists lack, therefore, is a theory of international relations either for countries in transition to socialism *or* for less radical but still progressive and/or nationalistic governments, whose notions of development may conflict with those of the international institutions on which they depend for financial assistance. This lacuna is particularly critical for governments which, in the process of pursuing their chosen model of development, have no desire to become economic or political satellites of either one big power or another, whether capitalist *or* socialist. For these governments, reform of multilateral institutions is a particularly attractive, if elusive, goal.

To most Third World countries the reforms suggested by the consensus position are logical and meaningful and, if realizable, would help alleviate many of the difficulties they face in participating in the world economy at this time. They also have a strong anti-imperialism dimension even if the proponents avoid the use of this terminology. Opening up the institutions to broader membership would inevitably lead to a redefinition of conditionality in such a way as to legitimate alternative models of accumulation to that based, excessively, on export orientation; models which might also be more equitable. Increasing the flow of unconditional funds on concessional terms would certainly permit a more equitable sharing of the world burden of adjustment and allow some breathing space for governments attempting more radical structural transformation of their economies along autocentred or convergent lines. Third World socialist countries would, therefore, stand to benefit just as much as, if not more than, other Third World countries from implementation of the consensus reforms.

In supporting the case for international reform it is recognized that any benefits that might accrue from reform would be accessible to all Third World nations regardless of how equitable or democratic are their economic and political systems. To avoid strengthening regimes which are brutally repressive and which systematically preserve inequalities through the use of state military power, some propose that basic human rights criteria be built into loan decisions. They propose a basic minimum definition of human rights violations which covers arbitrary deprivation of life, arbitrary arrest, detention or exile, torture, denial of the right to travel and apartheid. This, it is argued would exclude a number of repressive regimes such as South Africa, El Salvador and Guatamala from the benefits of reforms.[54] These definitions of human rights violations are consistent with the "Universal Declaration of Human Rights" and with decisions of the United Nations and would apply to sustained violations rather than random events. Given prevailing international vested interests it is, however, doubtful that countries could ever agree on such an approach, let alone implement it and it may be there is little that can be achieved *at the international level* to encourage equitable economic and political *national* models of development. The consensus approach would at least explicitly *permit* alternatives that are, at the moment, systematically discouraged by the international institutions. Ultimately, of course, it is at the national level that the issue of strategy is determined politically, but international institutions can reinforce or hinder national efforts—hence the appeal of reforms that are permissive.

The Politics of Reform

One can, of course, accept the *desirability* of the consensus package (or, at least, many of its elements) and at the same time consider it unattainable in practice. The vision of a world system in which national economic policies are harmonized is one which clearly denies the fundamentally competitive nature of capitalism and is unlikely ever to be realized. Yet other proposals can, legitimately, be labelled Utopian,[55] in the sense that politically they are utterly unattainable *at this time*. The appeal to common interests which is so often their accompanying justification has, to date, carried less weight than the threat they are perceived to pose to specific national and subnational (imperialist and class) interests of individual major powers and especially the U.S.A. The question that arises, therefore, is that if implementation of the consensus package is regarded as a desirable goal to strive for, in what circumstances might significant elements of it conceivably become reality and, in the meantime, what should be the strategy of Third World countries in their struggle for reforming the international monetary and financial system?

One of the more controversial strategy proposals for the Third World is that of Samir Amin. He argues that the most effective way to bring 'the North' to the bargaining table to construct a new international order would be for the South to recognize its diversity and build on it through South-South cooperation after "de-linking" from the current international division of labour.[56] Whatever their resource base, level of development or social system, developing countries would withdraw from the existing world system to build national and collective self-reliance, the latter being based on a charter of cooperation which would expand South-South trade and payments, technological ties and surplus retention. After building and consolidating their economic power in this way, they could then force the developed countries "to carry out the internal readjustments which are necessary for a truly new international order."[57]

This suggestion has the merit of recognizing that economic power is what is at issue in debates about reform. The emphasis on greater self-reliance within, and cooperation between, Third World countries is also to be applauded. As a package, however, these component parts do not hold together convincingly. There might have been more internal consistency in an earlier variant of this proposal in which Amin envisaged revolutionary socialist regimes de-linking from world capitalism, building self-reliance and, in the process, linking up with like-minded countries in their region;[58] so at least in that variant, there was an assumption that the domestic interest groups and classes which benefit from the integration of the Third World in the prevailing international order had been replaced through social upheaval. In the current proposal it is assumed that Third World governments of whatever social or political hue would find it self-evidently beneficial to 'de-link', yet this is obviously not so, their interests being tied closely to the 'status quo', and in his earlier work Amin himself accepts these political and social realities.[59] In addition, in the light of recent world developments, it cannot be assumed that major world powers would sit idly by and allow the de-linking of countries they consider of strategic importance to take place.

Both variants are, however, equally suspect in glossing over the practical difficulties governments would face in de-linking in this way and hence they grossly exaggerate the speed with which and the extent to which, self-reliant strategies could be pursued without plunging Third World nations into even greater economic chaos than they are currently experiencing. Third World countries as a group do not have the capacity to absorb their own primary exports nor to supply the capital goods that such a program might warrant. However desirable the goals of self-reliance and South-South linkages might be, and we consider them to be most desirable, they could only be realized over an extended period of time. In the interval, Third World governments pursuing these goals would have to contend to a greater or lesser extent with the shortcomings of the international system, would have a vested interest in its reform, and would need to consider more immediate (and more plausible) political avenues in striving for reform. This argument would apply equally to governments pursuing convergence strategies which, while seeking to meet the basic needs of their people through greater use of domestic resources and the building up of domestic linkages, would do so in a non-autarkic manner, shifting the basis on which they participate in the international system, rather than withdrawing from it.[60]

An alternative proposal envisages neither multilateral action 'a la Brandt', nor Third World de-linking 'a la Amin', but rather a focus on particular issues where one or more developing countries are thought to be able to exercise considerable leverage over the policies of 'Northern' countries.[61] The obvious case is the one of international bank debt examined above, in which individual debtors possess considerable potential power to influence the policies of creditor governments, the banks *and* the multilateral agencies. The scope for collective action in this area, to negotiate easier repayment terms, is enormous and will remain so for the duration of the debt crisis which, even on the most optimistic scenarios, will last beyond this decade. Similar collective action might be considered by the least developed countries on the repayment of multilateral debt, but this possibility is rarely considered in the literature.

This approach could also be applied, selectively, in other areas. 'Southern' countries could seek to apply leverage to the policies of 'Northern' countries through control of the sale of strategic commodities, by threats to deny them markets, by shifting foreign reserve holdings, altering tax arrangements, etc.[62] There are numerous possiblities each characterized by a specific issue over which effective leverage could be applied by one or more Third World countries. This contrasts with the consensus approach which presents a list of general demands and appeals to mutual interests, not power, for their implementation. It is, however, envisaged that this more selective approach could be pursued within the framework of the *objectives* of the consensus approach.

'Issue linkage' of this form may imply putting pressure on selective 'Northern' countries to force concessions. At a time of increasing rivalry and competition between capitalist nations this approach could be particularly fruitful. It is, however, unlikely to yield across-the-board reforms of the type demanded by the consensus view and, as already discussed in relation to a debtor's cartel, would need to be based on an accurate view of collective interest and on a realistic assessment of the costs of any possible economic retaliation.

Though selective in its orientation, this strategy could still yield significant benefits to Third World countries if applied successfully, the oil cartel being, of course, its source of inspiration. Other approaches based on selectivity may yield more marginal benefits. Thus, there is the argument that not all the proposals of the consensus view face the same degree of opposition from the industrialized world and hence developing countries should select a number of proposals which pose minimal threats to 'Northern' interests but which might yield marginal benefits to 'the South'. In this, 'non-utopian' category would be placed reform of the CFF, interest rate subsidization, more balance of payments support by the IBRD, IDA and bilateral donors, etc. This marginalist, incremental approach is recognized as having a limited capability to meet the needs of the developing countries but its proponents feel it would be more productive than current approaches and would not pre-empt other types of initiative.[63]

One could also view greater South-South cooperation as an initiative which, at least in the foreseeable future, poses little threat to 'Northern' interests and one which is likely to yield at best only marginal benefits. Yet the longer-term potential of such cooperation to contribute to profound structural reorientation of the world economy clearly marks out this type of initiative as being qualitatively different from attempts to wring minor reform concessions out of 'Northern' countries. Proposals to establish a Third World currency, whether within or outside the framework of a Third World bank,[64] and efforts to create an all-African monetary authority[65] cannot hope to result in the mobilization of but paltry sums for the immediate common use of the countries involved. But, if implemented, they would have importance as purely Third World initiatives which would not only ease payments problems of member countries but which would also strengthen commercial linkages between them. Above all, they would go some way toward strengthening Third World political unity at a time when the U.S. in particular seems anxious to undermine it by denying the existence of common interests *between* Third World countries.[66]

Thus, while a case can be made for all Third World countries to subscribe to the consensus call for international monetary and financial reform, the reality is that collectively they lack sufficient political power to force the acceptance of these reforms by the industrialized countries of 'the North'. Not even the Soviet Union which recognizes and approves of the general anti-imperialist thrust of the consensus proposals can be counted on to support the Third World wholeheartedly in this call. It objects to being classified with capitalist countries as part of the North and, to the consternation of Third World representatives, refuses to commit itself to the bilateral aid targets proposed arguing that there are no grounds for asking the U.S.S.R. "to share the responsibility and material costs of eliminating the consequences of colonialism, neo-colonialism and the trade and monetary crisis of the capitalist economy."[67] It also feels that the reforms deal only with distributional issues and fail to stress the necessity for transforming relations of production throughout the world; as such, while being generally anti-imperialist, they are at the same time, not specifically anti-capitalist.[68] The upshot of this is that the Soviet Union, and other centrally planned European economies, are ambivalent toward the reform proposals, examining each individually and refraining from throwing their political weight behind the Third World in international bodies in which they jointly participate. This ambivalence finds concrete expression in the remarkably poor performance of CMEA countries since 1970 (see Chapter 6, Table 6.2).

It would appear, therefore, that the blanket consensus approach to international reform is not a credible political option at this time and that more selective thrusts, whether on the basis of the less contentious components of the consensus package or as part of possibly more ambitious 'issue-oriented' bargaining, are the most that might be feasible. This situation could change very quickly, however, if the recent recovery in world growth and trade is aborted and/or if current measures for dealing with the debt crisis prove to be inadequate. As we saw in Chapter 1, the economic policies of the U.S. government are rife with contradiction and, as such, may soon prove unsustainable. Should this be so and the result is a further collapse of world trade as experienced in 1982, the consequences for developing countries could be catastrophic. The emergency programs of the large debtor countries would become worthless while the plight of the least developed countries would approach desperation. In this situation, the call for a United Nations Conference on a New Bretton Woods Arrangement might be found to be attractive to the major world powers if they are to salvage the world trade and payments system.[69] At that point, as the threats to common interests unambiguously outweigh those to specific interests, solvency proposals and 'consensus' solutions might cease to appear to be unnecessary or utopian, and a Third World united by its common misery might well be able to negotiate significant concessions from 'the North'.

Even if world recovery is sustained for a while, the larger debtors may not be able to cope with the political implications of the adjustment programs called for by their IMF and IBRD 'aid' packages. The threat of one or more major defaults or repudiations might also serve to put solvency and consensus reform issues on the international political agenda. Moreover, the problems of the least developed countries are widely acknowledged, even by the international institutions themselves, to be so acute that they will not be solved by a modest recovery in world trade alone. Before long, their crisis conditions may necessitate a significant change in current policies of the IMF and IBRD group if only for the crassest of legitimation reasons and again, at that time, 'consensus' proposals may assume a political relevance they do not now enjoy. The tragedy will be that on any one of these scenarios, the human suffering required to create a political climate receptive to even the modestly progressive reform package of the consensus, may be enormous. Such is the peculiar logic of the prevailing international economic order based, as it is, on inequalities of income, wealth and power both within and between nations.

Notes

[1] For a review of these two schools of thought from a liquidity school perspective see William R. Cline, *International Debt and the Stability of the World Economy* (Washington D.C.: Institute for International Economics, Policy Analyses in International Economics No. 4, September 1983).

[2] Reported in *The Globe and Mail* (Toronto), March 10th, 1983.

[3] Cline, *International Debt*, Chapter 3.

[4] See, for instance, the address by Robert Hutting, Vice Chairman of the Royal Bank of Canada to the Financial Analysts' Federation, Toronto as reported in the *The Globe and Mail* (Toronto), May 17, 1983. All quotations in this paragraph are taken from this source.

[5] Cline, *International Debt.*

[6] Morgan Guaranty Trust Company of New York, *World Financial Markets* (June 1983), p. 9.

[7] *The Economist* (April 30, 1983), p. 21.

[8] Edward J. Frydl, "The Debate over Regulating the Eurocurrency Markets", *Federal Reserve Bank of New York Quarterly Review* (Winter 1979–80), p. 17.

[9] For an elaboration of these points see John Loxley, "Regulation and Restructuring: Responses to the International Financial Crisis", *Journal of Contemporary Crises* (1984).

[10] Richard Dale, "Safeguarding the Banking System", *The Banker* (August 1982), p. 55.

[11] Brian Reading, "Wanted, A Loser of Last Resort", *Investors Chronicle* (October 1st, 1982).

[12] Samuel Alberto Yohai, "How the World Bank Might Recycle Assets", *Euromoney* (January 1983).

[13] Peter B. Kenen, "A Bailout Plan for the Banks", *New York Times* (March 6, 1983).

[14] Minos Zombanakis, "The International Debt Threat—A Way to Avoid a Crash", *The Economist* (April 30, 1983).

[15] Ibid., p. 14.

[16] See Cline, *International Debt*, p. 116.

[17] Ibid., see Chapter 7 for an evaluation of these proposals and a discussion of their possible secondary effects on bank credit.

[18] See Albert Fishlow, "The Debt Crisis: Round Two Ahead?" in *Adjustment Crisis in the Third World*, eds. Richard E. Feinberg and Valeriana Kallab (Washington, D.C.: Overseas Development Council, 1984), pp. 53–57.

[19] Henry A. Kissinger, "Saving the World Economy", *Newsweek* (January 24, 1983), p. 49.

[20] *The Globe and Mail* (Toronto), July 3, 1984.

[21] Ibid., June 25, 1984.

[22] Ibid., June 1, 1984.

[23] Celso Furtado, "How the Debtors can Forge a New International Deal", *South* (December 1982).

[24] See the joint report of Latin American Economic System (SELA) and Economic Commission for Latin America (ECLA), "Basis for a Latin American Response to the International Economic Crisis", Quito, 16 May 1983, (Mimeo).

[25] *Financial Times* (London), August 19, 1983.

[26] *The Globe and Mail* (Toronto), January 14, 1984.

[27] *IMF Survey*, July 2nd, 1984.

[28] This rescue package and its potential dangers are discussed in *The Globe and Mail* (Toronto), April 3, 1984.

[29] See Ajit Singh, "How the Bankers' Darling Fell on Hard Times", *South* (November 1982).

[30] Thomas Enders and Richard Mattione, "Latin America: The Crisis of Debt and Growth" (Washington, D.C.: The Brookings Institution, March 1984), reported in *Latin America Weekly Report*, February 24, 1984.

[31] See *North-South: A Programme for Survival*, The Report of the Independent Commission on International Development Issues under the chairmanship of Willy Brandt (London: Pan, 1980).

Common Crisis: North-South Cooperation for World Recovery, The Brandt Commission 1983 (London: Pan, 1983).

Commonwealth Secretariat, *Towards a New Bretton Woods: Challenges for the World Financial and Trading System* (London: Commonwealth Secretariat, 1983).

"The Arusha Initiative: A Call for a United Nations Conference on International Money and Finance", *Development Dialogue*, No. 2 (1980). "Declaration on the Establishment of a New International Economic Order", Resolution No. 3201 (S-vi) of the Sixth Special Session of the United Nations.

[32] See T. Killick, G. Bird, J. Sharpley, and M. Sutton, "Towards a Real Economy Approach to Payments Adjustment", draft chapter in two volume study by the ODI

on the IMF and the Third World, ed. T. Killick (ODI: Heinemann Education books, forthcoming).

[33] Bahram Nowzad, "The Extent of IMF Involvement in Economic Policy Making", *Amex Bank Review*, Special Paper No. 7 (September 1983).

[34] See John Williamson, "The Lending Policies of the International Monetary Fund", *Essays in International Finance*, No. 146 (New Jersey: Princeton University, December 1981); and Ariel Buira, "IMF Financial Programs and Conditionality", *Journal of Development Economics*, Vol. 12 (1983), for a discussion of some of these alternatives.

[35] See, for instance, J. de Larosiere, "Towards a Solution of International Economic Problems", *Finance and Development* (September 1979). For a carefully argued case for a large allocation of SDRs at the present time, though one that does not argue for a 'link', see John Williamson, *A New SDR Allocation?* (Washington, D.C.: Institute for International Economics, March 1984).

[36] See IMF, *Annual Report*, 1983, pp. 11–16.

[37] These positions can be gleaned from successive IMF Annual Reports and Statements of the Managing Director. See, for instance, J. de Larosiere, *The Role of the International Monetary Fund in Today's World Economy* (Washington, D.C.: IMF, 1982).

[38] E.g., the U.S. has looked favourably on Mexico's adjustment efforts and influenced banks to reduce margins on loans to that country. For a general statement of this position, see *IMF Survey* (June 18, 1984).

[39] Frances Stewart, "Brandt II: The Mirage of Collective Action in a Self-Serving World", *Third World Quarterly*, Vol. 5, No. 3 (July 1983).

[40] Morgan Guaranty Trust Co. of New York, *World Financial Markets* (October 1982), p. 6.

[41] For instance, Riccardo Parboni in *The Dollar and its Rivals* (London: Verso, 1981), p. 115 maintains that "if very severe deflationary policies are adopted by (developing) countries, the reverberations on the rest of the world are scant."

[42] See, for instance, the first report of the Brandt Commission, p. 77.

[43] Cheryl Payer is perhaps the best known representative of this school of thought. See her *The Debt Trap* (New York: Monthly Review Press, 1974). This particular quotation is from her "The Bretton Woods Twins", *Counterspy* (Sept.–Nov. 1982), p. 37.

[44] Payer, "The Bretton Woods Twins".

[45] Cheryl Payer, *The World Bank: A Critical Analysis* (New York: Monthly Review Press, 1982), p. 20.

[46] Ernest Mandel, *The Second Slump* (London: New Left Books, 1978), p. 191.

[47] Payer, *The Word Bank*, p. 357.

[48] For a disussion of the politics of defensive modernization with regard to the World Bank, see Robert L. Ayres, *Banking on the Poor: The World Bank and World Poverty* (Cambridge, Mass.: MIT Press, 1983).

[49] See James O'Connor, *The Fiscal Crisis of the State* (New York: St. Martin's Press, 1973).

[50] Payer, *The World Bank*, pp. 359–362.

[51] R. T. Naylor, "Which World's Bank?", 1983 (Mimeo).

[52] C. Y. Thomas, "From Colony to State Capitalism: Alternative Paths of Development in the Caribbean" (University of Guyana, June 1981, mimeo).

[53] See, for instance, Samir Amin, "N.I.E.O.: How to Put Third World Surpluses to Effective Use", *Third World Quarterly*, p. 70.

[54] This list is taken from a "Proposal to Establish Basic Human Rights Criteria as a Co-determinant of Canada's Voting Decisions in the International Monetary Fund (IMF)" by The Taskforce on the Churches and Corporate Responsibility, Toronto Canada, June 1983 (mimeo).

[55] Riccardo Parboni, *The Dollar and Its Rivals* (London: Verso, 1981), p. 112.

[56] Amin, "N.I.E.O.".

[57] Ibid., p. 69.

[58] Samir Amin, "Accumulation and Development: A Theoretical Model", *Review of African Political Economy*, No. 1 (1974).

[59] Ibid.

[60] See C. Y. Thomas, *Dependence and Transformation: The Economics of the Transition to Socialism* (New York: Monthly Review Press, 1974).

[61] For an elaboration of this approach, see Stewart, "Brandt II"; L. N. Rangarajan, "Commodity Conflict Revisited: from Nairobi to Belgrade", *Third World Quarterly* (July 1983); and Andres Federman, "Opinion", in *South* (April 1981 and June 1982).

[62] Stewart, "Brandt II".

[63] For a book devoted entirely to the search for such selective measures, see G. K. Helleiner, ed., *A World Divided* (Cambridge: Cambridge University Press, 1976).

[64] See Dragoslav Avramovic, "Putting up the Money", *South* (July 1983), for a discussion of the possible functions and structure of a South Bank.

[65] This proposal was accepted by the Association of African Central Bankers at the 1983 annual meeting. See *Daily News* (Tanzania), August 11–14, 1983.

[66] R. T. Naylor, "Reaganism and the Future of the International Payments System", *Third World Quarterly* (October 1982).

[67] This excerpt from the Soviet Statement to UNCTAD 4 is reproduced in C. W. Lawson, "Socialist Relations with the Third World: A Case Study of the New International Economic Order", *Economics of Planning*, Vol. 16, No. 3 (1980), which also reviews the response of socialist countries to the demands for a NIEO.

[68] "Restructuring International Economic Relations and the Peoples' Anti-Imperialist Front", *World Marxist Review* (May 1979), pp. 33 and 35.

[69] Such a crisis might, of course, give rise to negotiation on a more limited scale (e.g., a Western Summit, a meeting of the group of Five or a special meeting of the Bank for International Settlements) but the severity of the crisis and its far reaching global implications would suggest considerable diplomatic pressures might build up for more representative crisis management.

SUMMARY AND CONCLUSION

The most recent global crisis has generated high levels of unemployment, reduced living standards, and stimulated an air of insecurity in industrialized nations which is unprecedented since the end of World War II. In the Third World its impact has been even more profound. Two major groups of Third World countries have been most adversely affected; the major debtor countries and the least developed or poorest countries. Because the stability of the major debtors is linked closely with the stability of the world's banking system, their problems are the ones which have received most attention. An elaborate series of emergency measures have been taken to shore up their repayment capabilities to prevent an outright repudiation or default on their debt. The International Monetary Fund has increased its resources and assumed a new role in securing the continued, and almost involuntary, involvement of foreign banks in emergency packages designed to prevent bank debts from being declared non-performing assets. So successful have these efforts been over the short run that the debt crisis has been labelled by the major world powers, the international institutions and the banks, as being a 'liquidity crisis' only. In this way, more far-reaching institutional proposals for dealing with the problem, which imply a 'solvency' crisis, have been rejected. The emergency packages rely heavily on IMF austerity programs which have been criticized in recent years for being inequitable, ineffective and too harsh. In addition, it is argued that such programs impose an export-oriented strategy of development on borrowers. This type of strategy has, in the past, often owed its success to the severe repression of workers. In addition, in the context of depressed world economic conditions and the adoption of the strategy by numerous IMF and IBRD clients simultaneously, there are doubts that it can generate the kind of growth success experienced by some of the major borrowers in the 1970s. If these shortcomings lead to the failure of IMF emergency packages there is a general acknowledgement that the debt crisis would certainly *become* a crisis of solvency if it is not one already, with serious implications for the stability of Western banks and economies.

Much less attention has, unfortunately, been paid to the problems of the least developed countries, problems which are, if anything, more acute and less easily dealt with. They pre-date the debt crisis by many years and involve severe import growth compression due to weak export markets, deteriorating terms of trade and lack of access to commercial credits. No special financial facilities have been put at their disposal and the emphasis of the international agencies and bilateral donors has been that these economies must 'adjust' to the crisis rather than 'finance' their way through it. Concessional IMF facilities which were made available in the preceding decade are no longer accessible. Under pressure from governments pursuing conservative 'monetarist' policies, and especially from the Reagan and Thatcher governments, both the IMF and the World Bank have taken much more unaccommodating policy stances toward the world's poorest countries and have restrained financial assistance at the very time of its greatest need. The new balance of payments support offered by the World Bank provides a useful type of finance but on very demanding conditions which serve only to reinforce those of the IMF. Similar types of conditional finance are being made available by bilateral donors implying that the Third World, and especially its poorest members, are facing a greater degree of policy leverage than ever before from *all* their sources of foreign finance and are in a situation in which their capacity to resist, if they wished to do so, is especially weak. The result is that they too are under pressure to introduce export- and market-oriented models of development and to do so in an austere, possibly inequitable manner which is dangerous to their political stability. Alternative development models which share the burden of adjustment more equitably, which more directly meet the basic needs of people and which aim for greater self-reliance and a more selective participation in the world economy are at odds with those being championed by the international institutions and, increasingly, by bilateral donors.

In the current world political climate proposals to make the management of the world monetary and financial system more universal and more democratic have little hope of implementation. Moreoever, proposals to substantially increase the flow of unconditional financial resources on easier terms to Third World countries find little support among the major capitalist powers which currently dominate that system. As an agenda for world reform this liberal/fabian consensus package has merit in that it serves to unite the Third World politically and to serve as an anti-imperalist platform. Its weakness lies in its underlying assumption that appeals to common interests between 'the North' and 'the South' will be sufficient to achieve results. In reality the diversity of interests at both the international level (imperialism, socialism and capitalism) and at the intra-national level (class and group) serve to offset common interests both in and between 'the North' and 'the South'. Nevertheless, many of the consensus proposals would help deal with generally acknowledged shortcomings in the prevailing system and, if implemented, would ease adjustments being made in Third World countries. They would at the same time, permit the pursuit of alternative development strategies to those currently being advocated by the international agencies. For these reasons a case can be made for supporting the call for reform along the lines of the consensus proposals; counter arguments by some schools of Marxism were found to be simplistic and unpersuasive. The question remains, however, of how Third World countries can mobilize sufficient political power to make reform a live option.

Appeals to common interests will need to be replaced by more selective 'issue oriented' bargaining in areas where Third World countries might be able to exercise leverage on one or more 'northern' states. Acceleration of South-South economic ties is also to be encouraged and, possibly, concerted Third World efforts to realize selected reforms that are less threatening to the major world capitalist powers.

In the last analysis, rapid progress in implementing proposals for a more rational and equitable world monetary and financial system is only likely to be made if the existing arrangements are threatened with imminent collapse. Such a situation is conceivable if the current global recovery is not sustained and/or if the widespread application of IMF-type conditionality fails to maintain the debt-servicing capabilities of major debtors at planned levels. In either or both of these eventualities a united Third World might be able to wrest significent concessions from 'the North', because only then are common interests likely to dominate the agendas of international financial institutions and their member states.

POSTSCRIPT: THE CRISIS CONTINUES

Recent developments in the global economy have served to confirm that the international debt crisis is far from being under control. Indeed, it has become apparent in the past two years that the *extent* of the debt problem goes well beyond what it appeared to be at the height of the 1982–83 crisis. In particular, it is now evident that the debt burden of many African countries is so huge as to be almost unmanageable. In part this problem has arisen because of the severity of the recession in Africa in the early 1980s coming, as it did, on top of a decade of low export growth rates, and because of the failure of international institutions to meet this recession with enlarged concessional capital flows. In some African countries it reflects also the recent need to use large amounts of scarce foreign exchange resources to pay for food imports. In others the debt-servicing burden is the legacy of past unproductive investments and/or of previous emergency balance of payments loans. In a handful of middle-income African countries the debt is predominantly bank debt, but in most others it takes the form primarily of official debt and of suppliers' credits and unpaid import arrears. The latter two categories of debt are extremely expensive, and tardiness in repayment usually gives rise to the imposition of import surcharges which only add to the problem. At the same time it is very difficult to alter repayment schedules for official multilateral debts. Indeed, several African countries now find themselves paying back more in interest and principal on outstanding IMF loans than they are receiving in new credits.

Solving the African debt problem will be no easy task. Few countries can hope to expand their export earnings rapidly or depress imports any further than they have to date. Few have much scope for imposing further domestic austerity, whether this be self-imposed or required as the price of additional IMF assistance. In many cases the damage already done by the dismantling of social programs by governments struggling to balance their books is significant and may be difficult to reverse. Children of low-income groups in particular seem to be paying a very heavy price as austerity reduces their access to food, clothing, schooling and health care.

Thus, while not as devastating as the food crisis, the African debt crisis may well prove to be as intractable. The Organization of African Unity (OAU) has called for a political solution to this problem, involving the take-over of private foreign bank debt by the central banks of industrialized capitalist countries and the forgiveness, conversion to grants, or rescheduling of bilateral debts. In doing so the OAU overrode the calls by more militant African governments, such as Tanzania, for the formation of a debtors' cartel and a collective reneging on loans. While recognizing the role played by domestic policy deficiencies in the emergence of the debt crisis, the OAU quite clearly puts prime responsibility on general global disorder as the source of the crisis.

The major official response to Africa's problems has come from the World Bank which does not share the OAU's view on the importance of global disorder in the origin of those problems. The World Bank has introduced a $1 billion Joint Program of Action (JPA) for Sub-Saharan Africa. It is hoped that this will mobilize additional bilateral funds to assist African countries wishing to pursue acceptable adjustment programs to deal with their economic problems. There is a strong suggestion that the policy measures deemed 'acceptable' will be similar to those advocated by the Berg Report, a critical analysis of which is to be found in Chapter 5. These measures are premised on the belief that inappropriate domestic policies are the basic cause of the African crisis. There is also a suggestion that, as with structural adjustment loans, the World Bank may demand that an IMF program be in place before JPA assistance is forthcoming, although this is not clear. The danger, therefore, is that this emergency program will provide too little financing and be too demanding in terms of the extent and nature of adjustments required. The African debt crisis, like the African food crisis, requires much bolder and much grander international initiatives than this, but these are unlikely to be forthcoming in the current international political climate. As it is, at U.S. insistence, the JPA has already been halved from the original level proposed. The outlook for these least developed countries is, therefore, unquestionably bleaker now than it appeared two years ago when the first draft of the main text was completed.

The second major development in this area is that, while a collapse of the international banking system has been avoided and no major debtor has defaulted on or repudiated its debts, some of the key assumptions underlying the current strategy of global debt crisis management are looking extremely questionable. The belief has been that if debtors met IMF conditionality there would continue to be an inflow of capital from private banks to ease adjustment. Recently, flows of bank credit to Third World countries have actually declined and even countries not experiencing debt-servicing problems have had difficulty borrowing. Mexico's adjustment program has been considered by the IMF to be one of the most successful to date, yet the indications are that commercial banks will not provide the funding required by that country to cover its external financing needs, which could reach $4 billion p.a. in the next few years. Argentina is facing similar difficulties. This can only mean further import contraction with serious domestic repercussions (coming, as it would, on the heels of several years of cutbacks in imports), or else further adjustments in debt-servicing plans.

These reduced capital inflows weaken not only the ability of debtors to meet their debt-servicing commitments, but also their *incentive* to do so. Brazil, for instance, is now paying $10 billion more each year in interest and principal than it receives in new bank loans or overseas direct investment. The loss of access to foreign capital no longer acts, therefore, as a disincentive to debt repudiation or default.

What is more, while almost all the improvements to their balance of payments on current accounts between 1981 and 1984 took the form of import contraction, the major debtors did enjoy a respectable growth in their exports in 1984/85. An improvement in Third World export earnings is clearly crucial to current and medium-term debt crisis containment scenarios. Yet, there are now obvious signs of a slowdown in economic growth in the U.S.A., to the point where the 3 percent p.a. real growth rate that most observers agree is the minimum required if current debt-servicing programs are not to be disrupted, may not be met in the immediate future. At the same time the U.S. Congress is dealing with over 300 bills seeking to protect U.S. industries from overseas competition and many of these bills are aimed at Third World exports. This combination of circumstances can only mean that the international banking system is perhaps even more precariously balanced now than it was when the debt crisis surfaced three years ago.

Yet, even before these developments reduced the ability of the Third World to service its debt, it is apparent that the debt burden is becoming unmanageable, notwithstanding debt reschedulings, and that middle-income developing countries are suffering from debt payment fatigue. After early successes in cutting back domestic demand and restraining imports, all major debtors are finding it extremely difficult politically to enforce protracted domestic austerity. Thus, both Brazil and Mexico have clashed with the IMF in recent months and have been threatened with interruption of their funding as a result of disagreements over their levels of government spending and their rates of inflation. Deterioration in the balance of payments due to renewed global recession or enhanced protectionism can only heighten the problems of domestic economic management in debtor countries.

These problems have not yet become serious enough to prompt debtors to take collective action, but debtors continue to meet together and their calls for global action on the debt problem are becoming more militant. Cuba has argued for the cancellation of all South American debt on the assumption that it is unpayable on economic, political and moral grounds. This move would be one element in a new international economic order initiative to be financed in part by reduced military spending by both East and West. Other debtors in the region have rejected Cuba's solution and, it is to be noted, Cuba itself continues to meet its debt-servicing commitments.

The more moderate position of the Cartagena Group is that the rate of debt servicing should be commensurate with ability to pay. Earlier this year Peru caused great consternation in international banking circles by unilaterally applying this principle, restricting its debt servicing to a maximum of 10 percent of its export earnings. Because this type of move endorses a commitment to debt repayment, yet at the same time tailors payments to the means available, it has an appeal to reasonableness which might well lead to its adoption on a much wider scale. If this were to happen—and the slowdown of world trade growth and the flow of bank credit can only enhance the prospects of it happening—then the initiative in debt crisis management would shift from the banks and states of the industralized capitalist world to the states of the Third World. Western banks would be forced to adjust their bad debt provisions whether they wished to or not. They would face an immediate escalation in the proportion of their loans considered 'non-performing'. The results of even this 'reformist' alternative to outright repudiation or default would, therefore, still be quite traumatic for the international banking system.

What all this means is that earlier optimism about the debt crisis being under control was premature. The extent of the crisis is much greater than it appeared to be, and both the global capitalist environment and the domestic economic realities of debtor countries seem to indicate that current approaches to managing the crisis are grossly inadequate and overly burdensome on large sections of Third World society. Further international instability and Third World economic and political turmoil seem inevitable. In some cases, this may lead to a recasting of social and political relationships in Third World countries in a way which permits a participatory and equitable model of development to be followed. It may also give rise to political movements that wish to restructure relationships of economic dependency which still continue to impede autonomous growth in Third World countries.

But it is by no means inevitable that progressive and creative political movements and economic policies will be the outgrowth of Third World crises of austerity; this may indeed be the exception rather than the rule. Furthermore, even when this outcome may occur, the adverse global environment will place severe constraints on the pace, degree and nature of possible economic restructuring that progressive governments can undertake. For these reasons, it is felt that the conclusions of Chapter 7 still stand; that there is point in Third World countries seeking to work together for reform of the international system. The struggle for a new international economic order must not be seen as an alternative to the struggle for a more just, prosperous and secure domestic order; rather, the one must complement and reinforce the other. The area of international debt management is the one area in which militant Third World action might wrest reform concessions from the world capitalist powers; it is also the one area in which the interests of international capital and those of the workers and peasants of Third World are so patently at odds that an eventual militant and collective Third World response is highly likely. Such a response would be a rational and long overdue reaction to an inequitable world system which sacrifices the welfare of the world's poorest to safeguard and further the interests of international capital and its custodians in both the industrialized capitalist countries and in the Third World itself.

SELECTED BIBLIOGRAPHY

Amin, Samir. "Accumulation and Development: A Theoretical Model." *Review of African Political Economy*. No. 1 (1974).

Aronson, J. D. *Money and Power: Banks and the World Monetary System*. London: Sage, 1977.

Avramovic, Dragoslav. "The Debt Problem of Developing Countries at the End of 1982." Mimeographed. Geneva: Graduate Institute of International Studies, December 1982.

Ayres, Robert L. *Banking on the Poor: The World Bank and World Poverty*. Cambridge, Mass.: MIT Press, 1983.

Bacha, E. F. and C. F. Diaz Alejandro. "International Financial Intermediation: A Long and Topical View". *Princeton Essays in International Finance*. No. 147. New Jersey: Princeton University, May 1982.

Bank for International Settlements. *Maturity Distribution for International Bank Lending* (various years).

Bautist, Romeo M. "Exchange Rate Variations and Export Competition in Less Developed Countries Under Generalised Floating." *Journal of Development Studies*. Vol. 18, no. 3 (1982).

Bello, Walden, et al. *Development Debacle: The World Bank in the Philippines*. San Francisco: Institute for Food and Development Policy and Philippine Solidarity Network, 1982.

Beveridge, W. A. and M. R. Kelly. "Fiscal Content of Financial Programs Supported by Standby Arrangements in the Upper Credit Tranches, 1969–78." *IMF Staff Papers*. Vol. 27, no. 2 (June 1980).

Bhagwat, A. and Y. Onitsuka. "Export/Import Responses to Devaluation Experience in the Non-Industrial Countries in the 1960s." *IMF Staff Papers* (July 1974).

Bienefield, Manfred. "Efficiency, Expertise, NICs and the Accelerated Development Report." *Institute of Development Studies (IDS) Bulletin*. Vol. 14, no. 1 (January 1983).

Belassa, Bela. "Structural Adjustment Policies in Developing Economies." *World Development*. Vol. 10, no. 1 (1982).

Belassa, B., et al. *The Balance of Payments Effects of External Shocks and of Policy Responses to These Shocks in Non-Opec Countries*. Paris: OECD Development Centre, 1981.

Bolin, W. H. and J. del Canto. "LDC Debt: Beyond Crisis Management." *Foreign Affairs* (Summer 1983).

Brett, E. A. *International Money and Capitalist Crisis: The Anatomy of Global Disintegration*. London: Heinemann, 1983.

Buira, Ariel. "IMF Financial Programs and Conditionality." *Journal of Development Economics*. Vol. 12 (1983).

Chernomas, Bob. "Keynesian, Monetarist and Post-Keynesian Policy—A Marxist Analysis." *Studies in Political Economy*. No. 10 (Winter 1983).

Clausen, A. W. "Let's Not Panic About Third World Debts." *Harvard Business Review* (November/December 1983).

Cline, W. R. "Can the East Asian Model of Development be Generalised?" *World Development*. Vol. 10, no. 2 (1982).

———. "Economic Stabilisation in Developing Countries: Theory and Stylized Facts." In *IMF Conditionality*, ed. John Williamson. Washington, D.C.: Institute for International Economics, 1983.

———. *International Debt and the Stability of the World Economy*. Washington, D.C.: Institute for International Economics, 1983.

Cohen, B. J. *Banks and the Balance of Payments: Private Lending in the International Adjustment Process*. London: Croom Helm, 1981.

Colman, David and Frederick Nixson. *Economics of Change in Less Developed Countries*. Oxford: Phillip Allan, 1979.

Commonwealth Secretariat. *Protectionism: Threat to International Order: The Impact on Developing Countries*. London: Commonwealth Secretariat, 1982.

Commonwealth Study Group. *Towards a New Bretton Woods*. Report by a Commonwealth Study Group. London: Commonwealth Secretariat, 1983.

Connolly, M. and D. Taylor. "Adjustment to Devaluation with Money and Non-Traded Goods." *Journal of International Economics* (June 1976).

Cooper, R. M. "Currency Devaluation in Developing Countries." In *Government and Economic Development*, ed. G. Ranis. New Haven: Yale University Press, 1971.

Crockett, Andrew D. "Stabilisation Policies in Developing Countries: Some Policy Considerations." *IMF Staff Papers*. Vol. 28, no. 1 (March 1981).

Coyne, Deborah M. R. *Monetary and Financial Reform: The North-South Controversy*. Ottawa: The North-South Institute, 1984.

Dell, Sidney. *On Being Grandmotherly: The Evolution of IMF Conditionality*. Princeton Essays in International Finance. No. 144. New Jersey: Princeton University, October 1981.

———. "The International Environment for Adjustment in Developing Countries." *World Development*. Vol. 8, no. 11 (November 1980).

Devlin, Robert. "Transnational Banks, External Debt and Peru: Results of a Recent Study." *CEPAL Review* (August 1981).

deVries, M. G. *The International Monetary Fund, 1966–1971: The System Under Stress*. 2 volumes. Washington, D.C.: IMF, 1976.

Diaz Alejandro, Carlos F. "Open Economy-Closed Polity." Discussion paper 390. Mimeographed. New Haven: Economic Growth Centre, Yale University, December 1981.

Donovan, D. J. "Macroeconomic Performance and Adjustment Under Fund Supported Programs: The Experience of the Seventies." *IMF Staff Papers*. Vol. 29, no. 2 (June 1982).

English, Philip E. *Canadian Development Assistance to Haiti*. Ottawa: North-South Institute, 1984.

Foxley, Alejandro. *Latin American Experiments in Neo-Conservative Economics*. Berkeley: University of California Press, 1983.

———. "Stabilisation Policies and Their Effects on Employment and Income Distribution: A Latin American Perspective." In *Economic Stabilisation in Developing Countries*, eds. William R. Cline and Sidney Weintraub. Washington, D.C.: The Brookings Institution, 1981.

Ffrench-Davis, Ricardo. "The Monetarist Experiment in Chile: A Critical Survey." *World Development*. Vol. 11, no. 11 (1983).

Frydel, E. J. "The Debate Over Regulating the Eurocurrency Market." *Federal Reserve Bank of New York Quarterly Review*. Vol. 4, no. 4 (Winter 1979/80).

______. "The Eurodollar Conundrum." *Federal Reserve Bank of New York Quarterly Review* (Spring 1982).

Giovannini, Alberto. "The Interest Elasticity of Savings in Developing Countries: The Existing Evidence." *World Development*, Vol. 11, no. 7 (1983).

Goldstein, Morris and S. Mohsin. *Effects of Slowdown in Industrial Countries or Growth in Non Oil-Developing Countries*. Washington, D.C.: IMF Occasional Paper No. 12 (August 1982).

______. "African Economies in the Mid–1980s." *Recession in Africa*, ed. Carlson Jerker. Uppsala: Scandinavian Institute of African Studies, 1983.

Green, R. H. "Things Fall Apart: the World Economy in the 1980s." *Third World Quarterly*. Vol. 15, no. 1 (January 1983).

Griffith Jones, Stephany. *The Role of Finance in the Transition to Socialism*. London: Allanheld, Osmun & Co., 1981.

Group of Thirty. *How Bankers See the World Financial Market*. New York: Group of Thirty, 1982.

______. *Risks in International Lending*. New York: Group of Thirty, 1982.

Guitan, Manuel. *Fund Conditionality: Evolution of Principles and Practices*. Washington, D.C.: IMF, 1981.

Hardy, C. "Commercial Bank Lending to Developing Countries: Supply Constraints." *World Development*. No. 7 (1979).

Helleiner, G. K. "Lender of Early Resort: The IMF and The Poorest." *American Economic Association, Papers and Proceedings*. Vol. 73, no. 2 (May 1983).

______. "Outward Orientation, Import Instability and African Economic Growth: An Empirical Investigation." Mimeographed. Toronto: University of Toronto, April 1984.

Helleiner, G.K. and R. Lavergne. "Intra-Firm Trade and Industrial Exports to the United States." *Oxford Bulletin of Economics and Statistics*. Vol. 41 (November 1979).

Heller, Peter S. and Richard C. Porter. "Exports and Growth: An Empirical Re-Investigation." *Journal of Development Economics*. Vol. 5, no. 2 (June 1978).

Hollisi, W. L. and J. N. Rosenau, eds. *World System Structure*. London: Sage, 1981.

Hooke, A. W. *The International Monetary Fund: Its Evolution, Organization and Activities*. Washington, D.C.: IMF, 1982.

Hurni, Bettina S. *The Lending Policy of the World Bank in the 1970s: Analysis and Evaluation*. Colorado: Westview Press, 1980.

Independent Commission on International Development Issues. *North-South: A Programme for Survival*. London: Pan Books, 1980.

International Institute for Labour Studies. *Lagos Plan of Action for the Economic Development of Africa 1980–2000*. Geneva: International Institute for Labour Studies, 1918.

International Monetary Fund (IMF). *Annual Report*, Washington, D.C.: IMF, 1980.

______. *The Monetary Approach to the Balance of Payments*. Washington, D.C.: IMF, 1977.

______. *World Economic Outlook*. Washington, D.C.: IMF, 1980, 1983, 1984 (separate volumes).

Jaspersen, Frederick Z. "Adjustment Experience and Growth Prospects of the Semi-Industrial Economies." *World Bank Staff Working Paper*. No. 477. Washington, D.C.: World Bank, August 1981.

Killick, Tony and Mary Sutton. "Disequilibria, Financing and Adjustment in Developing Countries." *Adjustment and Financing in the Developing World: The Role of the International Monetary Fund*. Washington, D.C.: IMF, 1982.

Kindleberger, C. P. *Manias, Panics and Crashes: A History of Financial Crises*. New York: Basic Books, 1977.

Knight, Peter B. "Economic Reform in Socialist Countries." *World Bank Staff Working Paper*. No. 579. Washington, D.C.: World Bank, 1983.

Krueger, Anne O. *Foreign Trade Regimes and Economic Development: Liberalisation Attempts and Consequences*. Cambridge, Mass.: Ballinger, 1978.

Lanyi, Anthony and Saracoglu Riisdii. "The Importance of Interest Rates in Developing Countries." *Finance and Development*. Vol. 20, no. 2 (June 1983).

Lipson, Charles. "The International Organisation of Third World Debt." *International Organisation*. Vol. 35, no. 4 (Autumn 1981).

Loxley, John. *The IMF and the Poorest Countries*. Ottawa: The North-South Institute, 1984.

———. "Saving the World Economy." *Monthly Review* (September 1984).

Magdoff, Harry. "The U.S. Dollar, Petrodollars and U.S. Imperialism." *Monthly Review* (January 1979).

Mandel, Ernest. *The Second Slump*. London: New Left Books, 1979.

Mason, E. and R. Asher. *The World Bank Since Bretton Woods*. Washington, D.C.: The Brookings Institution, 1973.

McKinnon, Ronald L. *An International Standard for Monetary Stabilisation*. Washington, D.C.: Institute for International Economics, 1984.

———. "The Eurocurrency Market." *Princeton Essays in International Finance*. No. 25. New Jersey: Princeton University, December 1977.

Mendelsohn, M. S. *Commercial Banks and the Restructuring of Cross-Border Debts*. New York: Group of Thirty, 1983. Summarized in *IMF Survey* (July 25, 1983).

Michaely, Michael. "Exports and Growth: An Empirical Investigation." *Journal of Development Economics*. Vol. 4, no. 1 (March 1979).

Morse, Elliott R. "Institutional Destruction Resulting from Donor and Project Proliferation in Sub-Saharan African Countries." *World Development Report*. Vol. 12, no. 4 (1984).

Nelson, Joan M. "The Politics of Stabilisation." In *Adjustment Crisis in the Third World*, eds. Richard E. Feinberg and Valerina Kallab. Washington, D.C.: Overseas Development Council, 1984.

Newhaus, Pablo. "Floating Interest Rates and Developing Country Debt." *Finance and Development* (December 1982).

Nowzad, B. "The IMF and its Critics." *Princeton Essays in International Finance*. No. 146. New Jersey: Princeton University, December 1981.

Organisation for Economic Co-operation and Development (OECD). *OECD Paris Financial Statistics Monthly*. Paris: OECD, 1973–1982.

———. *Development Cooperation Review*. Paris: OECD, 1983.

Payer, Cheryl. *The Debt Trap—The International Monetary Fund and the Third World*. New York: Monthly Review Press, 1974.

———. "Tanzania and the World Bank." *Third World Quarterly*. Vol. 5, no. 4 (October 1983).

Parboni, Riccardo. *The Dollar and Its Rivals*. London: Verso, 1981.

Phillips, Ron. "The Role of the International Monetary Fund in the Post-Bretton Woods Era." *Review of Radical Political Economics*. Vol. 15, no. 2 (Summer 1983).

Please, Stanley. *The Hobbled Giant: Essays on the World Bank*. Boulder: Westview Press, 1984.

Porter, Michael G. "International Financial Integration: Long Run Policy Implications." In *Money and Finance in Economic Growth and Development*, ed. Edward S. Shaw. New York: Marcel Dekker, 1976.

Ramos, Joseph. "The Economics of Hyperstagflation—Stabilisation in Post-1973 Chile." *Journal of Development Economics*. Vol. 7 (1980).

Reichmann, T. M. and R. T. Stillson. "Experience with Programs of Balance of Payments Adjustment: Stand-by Arrangements in the Higher Tranches, 1962–63." *IMF Staff Papers*. Vol. 25, no. 2 (June 1978).

Seers, Dudley. "The Tendency to Financial Irresponsibility of Socialist Governments and its Political Consequences." *IDS Sussex Discussion Paper 161* (June 1981).

Sen, A. K. *Poverty and Famines: An Essay on Entitlement and Deprivation*. Oxford: Clarendon Press, 1981.

Sheahan, John. "Market Oriented Economic Policies and Political Repression in Latin America." *Economic Development and Cultural Change*. Vol. 28, no. 2 (January 1980).

Streeten, Paul. "A cool Look at Outward-Looking Strategies for Development." *The World Economy*, Vol. 5, no. 2 (September 1982).

Stewart, Frances. "Brandt II: The Mirage and Collective Action in a Self-Serving World." *Third World Quarterly*. Vol. 5, no. 3 (July 1983).

Taylor, Lance. *Structuralist Macroeconomics: Applicable Models for the Third World*. New York: Basic Books, 1983.

Timothy, N. "The African Crisis: Alternative Development Strategies for the Continent." *Alternatives*. Vol. 9, no. 1 (Summer 1983).

Thomas, C. Y. *Dependence and Transformation: The Economics of the Transition to Socialism*. New York: Monthly Review Press, 1974.

Thorp, Rosemary and Lawrence Whitehead, eds. *Inflation and Stabilisation in Latin America*. London: Nelson, 1980.

Van Wijnbergen, S. "Stagflationary Effects of Monetary Stabilisation Policies: A Quantitative Analysis of South Korea." *Journal of Development Economics*. Vol. 10, no. 2 (April 1982).

United Nations. Centre on Transnational Corportions (UNCTC). *Transnational Banks, Operations, Strategies and Their Effects in Developing Countries*. New York: UNCTC, 1981.

______. Conference on Trade and Development (UNCTAD). *Trade and Development Report 1981*. New York: United Nations, 1981.

Williamson, John. *A New SDR Allocation?* Washington, D.C.: Institute for International Economics, March 1984.

World Bank. *Accelerated Development in Sub-Saharan Africa: An Agenda for Action*. Washington, D.C.: World Bank, 1981.

World Bank. "Adjustment Policies and Problems in Developed Countries." *World Bank Staff Working Paper*. No. 349. Washington, D.C.: World Bank, 1979.

______. *Annual Report 1983*.

______. *IDA in Retrospect: The First Two Decades of the International Development Association*. Washington, D.C.: World Bank, 1982.

______. *World Development Report*, 1982, 1983, 1984 (separate volumes).

Young, Roger. *Canadian Development Assistance to Tanzania*. Ottawa: The North-South Institute, 1983.

INDEX